"A superb survey of Byzantium's many cultural bequests . . . In this deft synthesis of scholarship, classicist Wells shows how the Byzantines exerted a profound influence on all neighboring civilizations. . . . Contains a useful glossary of historical figures, detailed maps and a timeline."
—*Publishers Weekly* (starred review)

"This history is a needed reminder of the debt that three of our major civilizations owe to Byzantium. Highly recommended."
—*Library Journal* (starred review)

"Comprehensive examination . . . Eye-opening in its vast cache of references."
—*Kirkus Reviews*

"A marvelous read for anyone interested in the history of civilization . . . Colin Wells has put together a masterpiece entailing the journey of knowledge through the medium of Byzantium."
—UNRV.com (Roman history website)

"Wells brings vividly to life this history of a long-lost era and its opulent heritage."
—*Booklist*

"Colin Wells's smart and accessible new history . . . *Sailing from Byzantium* offers the reader a fascinating lesson in the strange transience, and even stranger endurance, of empires. . . . Mr. Wells offers capsule summaries of important intellectual developments, while keeping vivid personalities—kings, monks, philosophers, travelers—to the fore. The reader comes away, accordingly, with a broad outline of a complex subject, and a whole bushel of interesting anecdotes."

—*New York Sun*

"In this work of extraordinary learning . . . readers will find themselves guided on a fascinating journey through a story that has never before been presented in such an accessible and thought-provoking fashion."

—Thomas R. Martin,
Jeremiah O'Connor Professor of Classics
at the College of the Holy Cross

SAILING

FROM

BYZANTIUM

HOW A LOST EMPIRE
SHAPED THE WORLD

Colin Wells

DELTA TRADE PAPERBACKS

SAILING FROM BYZANTIUM
A Delta Book

PUBLISHING HISTORY
Delacorte hardcover edition published August 2006
Delta trade paperback edition / August 2007

Published by
Bantam Dell
A Division of Random House, Inc.
New York, New York

Maps by David Lindroth
Cover design by Marietta Anastassatos
Cover photograph © Cameraphoto Arte/Art Resource, NY

Book design by Glen Edelstein

Library of Congress Catalog Card Number: 2006042665

Delta is a registered trademark of Random House, Inc.,
and the colophon is a trademark of Random House, Inc.

ISBN 978-0-553-38273-0

Published simultaneously in Canada

www.bantamdell.com

146119709

For Gran and Grandma Petey
And for my parents
With love and gratitude

Contents

Major Characters

Byzantium

Humanists

Theodore Metochites (1270–1332). Statesman, scholar, patron of the arts. Founded Last Byzantine Renaissance; rebuilt Church of the Chora.

Barlaam of Calabria (c. 1290–1348). First opponent of Hesychasm; taught Greek to Petrarch.

Demetrius Cydones (c. 1324–c. 1398). Byzantine statesman; translated Thomas Aquinas into Greek.

Manuel Chrysoloras (c. 1350–1415). Diplomat and educator; first successful teacher of ancient Greek in the West.

George Gemistos Pletho (c. 1360–1452). Philosopher and scholar; stimulated interest in Plato among Italian humanists.

John Bessarion (c. 1399–1472). Expatriate scholar, translator, patron of Byzantine and Italian humanists in Italy; helped draft the decree of union between Orthodox and Catholic churches (1439), then became a Catholic cardinal.

John Argyropoulos (1415–87). Teacher and philosopher; completed the shift in interest toward Plato that Pletho had initiated among the Italians.

Monks

Gregory Palamas (c. 1296–1359). Mystical theologian and saint; main proponent of Hesychast movement in Orthodox monasticism.

Cyril (c. 826–69) and Methodius (c. 815–85). Orthodox missionary brothers and apostles to the Slavs; inventors and promoters of Old Church Slavonic, the Byzantine-inspired written language of Slavic Orthodoxy.

Emperors

Justinian (c. 482–565; ruled from 527). Carried out Reconquest of Italy; built Hagia Sophia.

Heraclius (c. 575–641; ruled from 610). Saved Byzantium from Persians, then lost wealthiest provinces to the Muslim Arabs at the onset of Byzantium's Dark Age.

Constantine VII Porphyrogenitus (905–59; ruled from 945). Emperor of the Macedonian dynasty and author of *On the Administration of the Empire,* an important historical source for his period.

Basil II (958–1025; ruled from 976). Emperor of the Macedonian dynasty; brought Byzantium to the height of its revived power in First Byzantine Renaissance.

Alexius I Comnenus (c. 1057–1118; ruled from 1081). Founder of Comnenan dynasty, which, after the collapse of the late eleventh century, temporarily revived Byzantine fortunes in the era of the Crusades.

John VI Cantacuzenos (c. 1295–1383; ruled 1347–54). Statesman, regent, emperor, theologian, historian, and finally monk; patron of humanists but also a committed Hesychast; formulated unity policy toward Russia.

Manuel II Paleologos (1350–1425; ruled from 1391). Grandson of John VI Cantacuzenos; friend and patron to many Byzantine humanists during Last Byzantine Renaissance.

Patriarchs of Constantinople

Photius (c. 810–c. 895; patriarch 858–67 and 877–86). Humanist scholar who brought the First Byzantine Renaissance to fruition; initiated the mission of Cyril and Methodius to the Slavs.

Nicholas Mysticus (852–925; patriarch 901–7 and 912–25). Regent for the young Constantine VII Porphyrogenitus during the wars against Byzantium of Symeon of Bulgaria.

Philotheos Kokkinos (c. 1300–c. 1378; patriarch 1353–54 and 1364–76). Hesychast monk who helped carry out unity policy toward Russia.

THE WEST

Theoderic (c. 454–526). King of the Goths (from 471); educated in Constantinople and installed by Byzantines to rule in Italy.

Boethius (c. 480–c. 524). Late Roman philosopher and scholar; attempted to translate Aristotle into Latin.

Cassiodorus (c. 487–c. 580). Late Roman scholar and administrator, then monk.

Liudprand of Cremona (c. 920–c. 972). Lombard noble and diplomat who visited Constantinople twice in the service of Western monarchs.

Enrico Dandolo (c. 1107–1205). Venetian doge (from 1192) who orchestrated the sack and occupation of Constantinople by Western soldiers in the Fourth Crusade (1204–61).

Petrarch (1304–74). Italian poet who founded Renaissance humanism in Italy and tried to learn Greek.

Coluccio Salutati (1331–1406). Humanist chancellor of Florence who arranged for Manuel Chrysoloras to teach Greek there.

Leonardo Bruni (1370–1444). Rhetorician and historian; a student of Chrysoloras and the main proponent of civic humanism.

Poggio Bracciolini (1380–1449). Renowned Latinist who joined the Florentine circle of Chrysoloras as a young man.

Niccolò Niccoli (1364–1437). Elusive classicist who studied with Chrysoloras in Florence; wrote little but exerted a strong influence on artists and other humanists.

Guarino da Verona (1374–1460). Pioneer Italian educator who was Chrysoloras' closest follower.

Tommaso Parentucelli (1397–1455). Italian humanist who became Pope Nicholas V (from 1446); founded the Vatican Library and arranged for Bessarion to oversee the translation of Greek manuscripts there.

Lorenzo Valla (1407–57). Gifted Italian classicist and philologist; a protégé of the expatriate Byzantine humanist Cardinal Bessarion.

Marsilio Ficino (1433–99). Friend and associate of Cosimo and Lorenzo de Medici; founded the Platonic Academy in Florence after learning Greek.

THE ISLAMIC WORLD

Muhammad (c. 570–632). Prophet and founder of Islam.

Muawiyah (c. 602–80). Fifth caliph (from 661) and founder of Umayyad dynasty, based in the former Byzantine province of Syria.

Abd al-Malik (646–705). Umayyad caliph (from 685); restored Umayyad power; built the Dome of the Rock.

Al-Mansur (c. 710–75). Abbasid caliph (from 754) and founder of Baghdad; initiated Greco-Arabic translation movement.

Al-Mamun (786–833). Abbasid caliph (from 813); carried on Greco-Arabic translation movement; associated in later sources with "House of Wisdom."

Hunayn ibn Ishaq (808–73). Nestorian Christian translator of Greek medical and scientific texts into Arabic; traveled to former Byzantine territory to get texts.

THE SLAVIC WORLD

Boris I (?–907). Khan of Bulgaria (852–89); converted to Christianity in 865; adopted Slavonic liturgy of Cyril and Methodius.

Symeon the Great (c. 865–927). Boris' son and Bulgaria's first tsar (from 893); ardently Orthodox; carried out two major wars against Byzantium in an effort to capture Constantinople.

Stefan Nemanja (?–c. 1200). Ruler of medieval Serbia who brought it into the Byzantine Commonwealth; founded Serbia's ruling dynasty and numerous Orthodox monasteries; became a monk and an Orthodox saint.

Sava (1175–1235). Youngest son of Stefan Nemanja; became a monk at Mt. Athos; founded independent Serbian Orthodox Church; Orthodox saint.

Olga (?–c. 969). Russian princess and ruler (from 945) of Kiev; journeyed to Constantinople and converted to Orthodox Christianity.

Svyatoslav (c. 945–72). Russian prince of Kiev and son of Olga; a pagan warrior who was killed by the Petchenegs while crossing the Dnieper.

Vladimir the Great (c. 956–1015). Russian prince of Kiev and son of Svyatoslav; credited with converting his people to Orthodox Christianity; an Orthodox saint.

Yaroslav the Wise (978–1054). Russian prince of Kiev and son of Vladimir; rebuilt Kiev as an Orthodox capital and brought it to the height of its power.

Cyprian (c. 1330–1406). Bulgarian monk who, working with patriarch Philotheos, was the main exponent of Byzantine Hesychasm in Russia.

Sergius of Radonezh (1314–92). Russian Orthodox monk and saint; founder of Russian monasticism and promoter of Russian Hesychasm.

Euthymius of Turnovo (c. 1317–c. 1402). Bulgarian Hesychast monk and patriarch of Turnovo; founder of "second South Slavic" movement, the Hesychast revitalization of the Old Church Slavonic legacy.

Maxim Grek (c. 1470–1556). Born Michael Trivolis and educated in humanist circles in Florence before converting to Christianity; as the monk Maximos he spent a decade at Mt. Athos before going to Russia, where he was known as Maxim Grek, "Maxim the Greek."

CONCURRENT TIMELINE

Year	Byzantium	The West	The Islamic World	The Slavic World
330	Foundation of Constantinople			
C. 500		Goths in Italy; Boethius, Cassiodorus active		
500s	Justinian emperor (d. 565)	Reconquest of Italy	War between Byzantium and Persia	Slavs in Balkans
C. 575–640	Heraclius emperor (d. 641)	Lombards in Italy	Muhammad (d. 632) founds Islam	Avars allied with Slavs
C. 650–750	Dark Age begins	Rise of Franks	Umayyad dynasty	Bulgars arrive in Balkans
C. 750–850	Age of Iconoclasm	Papacy allies with Franks	Abbasid dynasty; foundation of Baghdad	Rise of Bulgaria
C. 860s	First Byzantine Renaissance under way; Photius active	Photian schism	Greco-Arabic translation movement flourishes; Hunayn ibn Ishaq active	Russians attack Constantinople; Cyril and Methodius active
C. 900s	Constantine VII Porphyrogenitus	Otto the Great	Abbasid decline begins	Symeon of Bulgaria (d. 927); rise of Kiev
C. 1000s	Basil II (d. 1025); Byzantine decline (after c. 1075)	Turks enter Asia Minor (after c. 1075)	Seljuk Turks	Vladimir the Great; conversion of Kievan Rus
C. 1100s	Comnenan emperors	Crusades begin	Decline of Arabic Enlightenment begins	Competing principalities in Russia
C. 1200s	Fourth Crusade (1204–61)		Mongols sack Baghdad	Golden Horde in Russia
C. 1320	Last Byzantine Renaissance; Theodore Metochites active	Giotto active; beginning of Italian Renaissance	Foundation of Ottoman Turkish state	Metropolitan Peter to Moscow (1326)
C. 1330–55	Hesychast controversy	Barlaam to Italy; Petrarch studies Greek	Rise of Ottoman power in Asia Minor	Philotheos promotes unity of Russian metropolitanate
C. 1350–C. 1400	Cydones, Philotheos active	Salutati active; Chrysoloras in Florence (1397–1400)	Ottomans conquer much of Balkans	Rise of Moscow; Battle of Kulikovo (1380); Cyprian active
C. 1400–C. 1480	Fall of Constantinople; end of Byzantine empire (1453)	Bessarion and others active in Italy; Council of Florence (1439)	Ottomans continue conquest of Balkans	Disintegration of Mongol power; expansion of Moscow

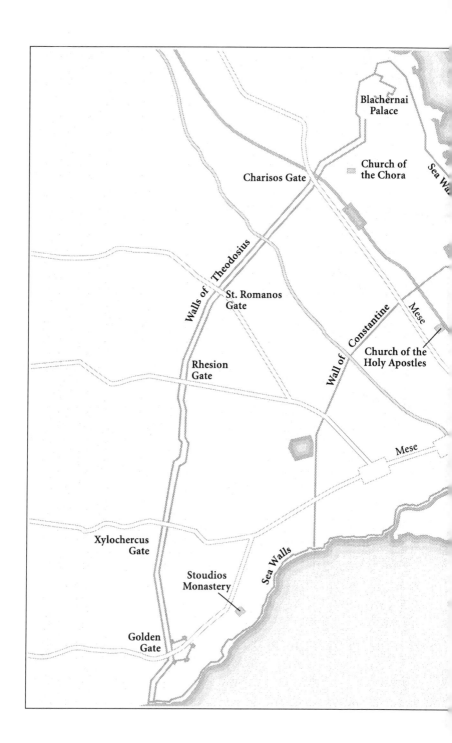

Blachernai
Palace

Church of
the Chora

Charisos Gate

Sea Wa

Walls of Theodosius

St. Romanos
Gate

Wall of Constantine

Mese

Church of the
Holy Apostles

Rhesion
Gate

Mese

Xylochercus
Gate

Sea Walls

Stoudios
Monastery

Golden
Gate

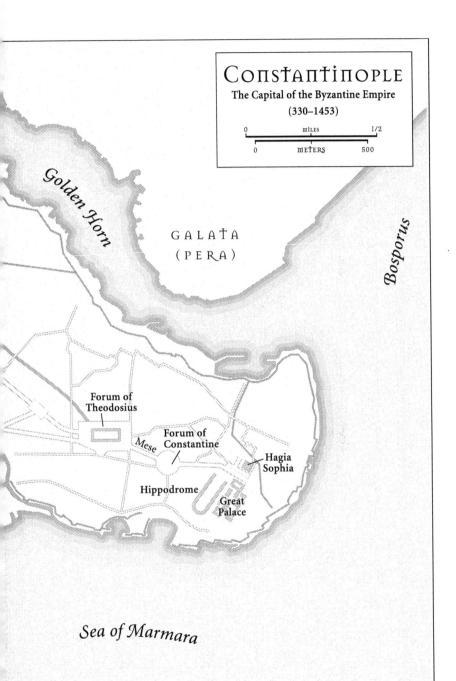

Constantinople

The Capital of the Byzantine Empire
(330–1453)

0   MILES   1/2

0   METERS   500

Golden Horn

GALATA

(PERA)

Bosporus

Forum of
Theodosius

Forum of
Constantine

Mese

Hippodrome

Hagia
Sophia

Great
Palace

Sea of Marmara

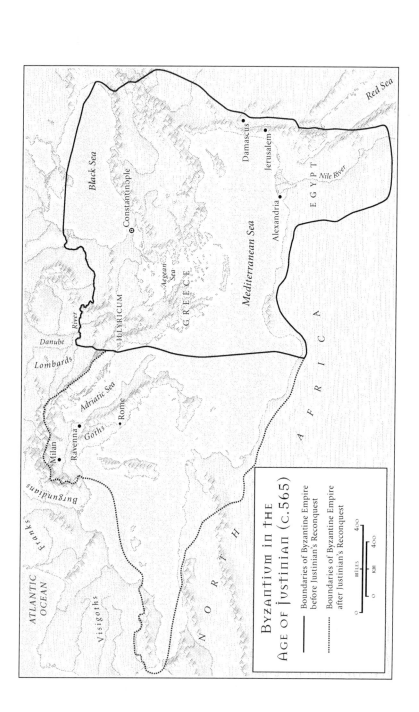

BYZANTIVM IN THE
AGE OF JVSTINIAN (C.565)

——— Boundaries of Byzantine Empire
before Justinian's Reconquest

·········· Boundaries of Byzantine Empire
after Justinian's Reconquest

MILES
0   400
KM
0   400

Red Sea

Black Sea

Damascus

Jerusalem

Nile River

E G Y P T

Alexandria

Constantinople

Mediterranean Sea

Aegean Sea

G R E E C E

ILLYRICUM

A F R I C A

River

Danube

Lombards

Adriatic Sea

Rome

Milan

Ravenna

Goths

Burgundians

Franks

ATLANTIC OCEAN

Visigoths

N O R T H

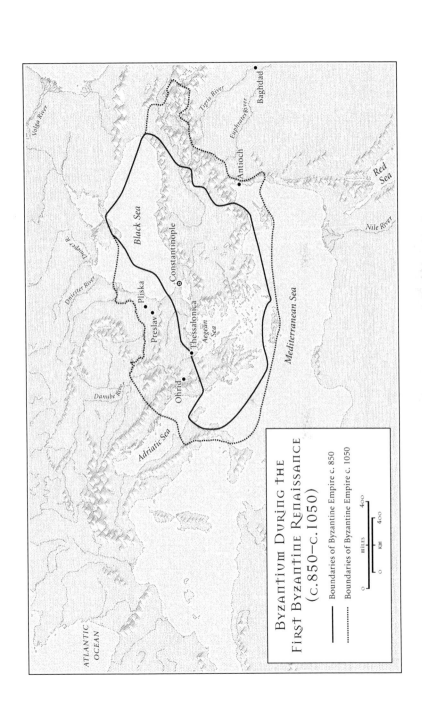

Byzantium During the
First Byzantine Renaissance
(c.850–c.1050)

——— Boundaries of Byzantine Empire c. 850
············ Boundaries of Byzantine Empire c. 1050

Volga River

Dnieper River

Dniester River

Danube River

Black Sea

Tigris River

Euphrates River

Baghdad

Antioch

Red Sea

Nile River

Mediterranean Sea

Constantinople

Pliska

Preslav

Thessalonica

Aegean Sea

Ohri

Adriatic Sea

ATLANTIC
OCEAN

MILES
KM
0   400
0   400

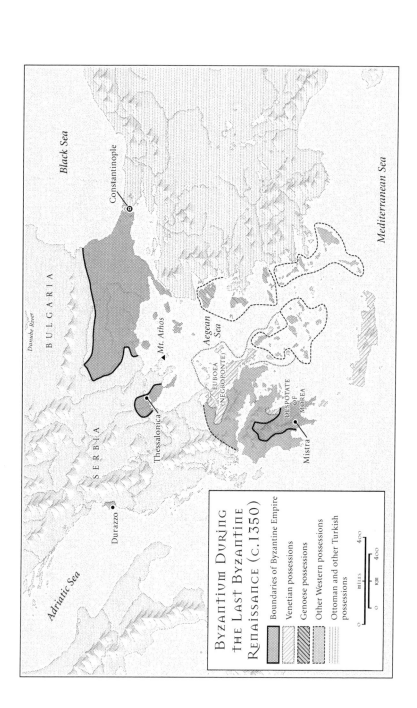

Black Sea

Constantinople

B U L G A R I A

Danube River

Mt. Athos

Thessalonica

Aegean
Sea

EUBOEA
(NEGROPONTE)

DESPOTATE
OF
MOREA

Mistra

Mediterranean Sea

S E R B I A

Durazzo

Adriatic Sea

BYZANTIUM DURING
THE LAST BYZANTINE
RENAISSANCE (C.1350)

Boundaries of Byzantine Empire
Venetian possessions
Genoese possessions
Other Western possessions
Ottoman and other Turkish
possessions

miles   400

0   KM   400

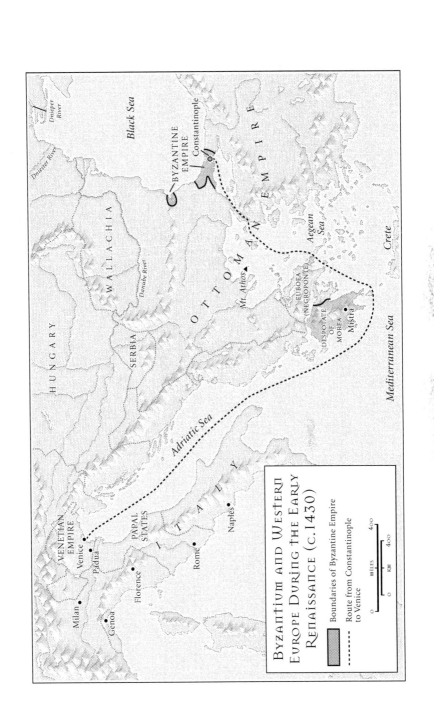

BYZANTIUM AND WESTERN
EUROPE DURING THE EARLY
RENAISSANCE (C.1430)

Boundaries of Byzantine Empire

Route from Constantinople
to Venice

0   MILES   400
0   KM   400

Dnieper River

Dniester River

Black Sea

BYZANTINE EMPIRE
Constantinople

OTTOMAN EMPIRE

Aegean Sea

Crete

WALLACHIA

Danube River

Mt. Athos

EUBOEA
(NEGROPONTE)

DESPOTATE
OF
MOREA
Mistra

HUNGARY

SERBIA

Mediterranean Sea

Adriatic Sea

VENETIAN
EMPIRE
Venice

Padua

PAPAL
STATES

I T A L Y

Rome

Naples

Florence

Milan

Genoa

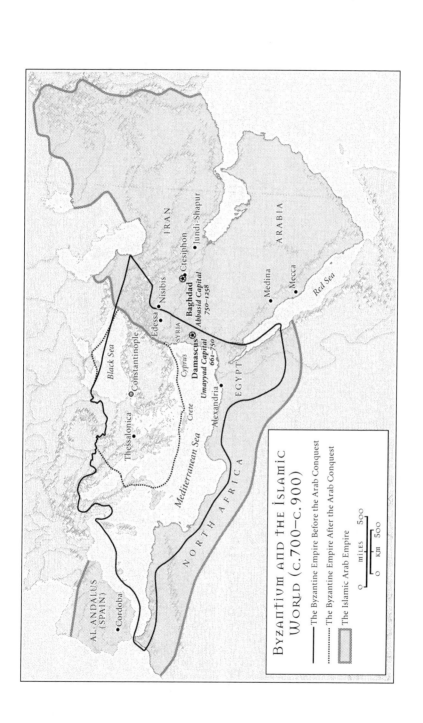

BYZANTIUM AND THE ISLAMIC
WORLD (c.700–c.900)

—— The Byzantine Empire Before the Arab Conquest
········· The Byzantine Empire After the Arab Conquest
▨ The Islamic Arab Empire

IRAN

ARABIA

Jundi-Shapur

Ctesiphon

Nisibis

Baghdad
Abbasid Capital
750–1258

Edessa

SYRIA

Medina

Mecca

Red Sea

Damascus
Umayyad Capital
661–750

Black Sea

Constantinople

Cyprus

EGYPT

Crete

Alexandria

Thessalonica

Mediterranean Sea

NORTH AFRICA

AL-ANDALUS
(SPAIN)

Cordoba

0   miles   500
0   km   500

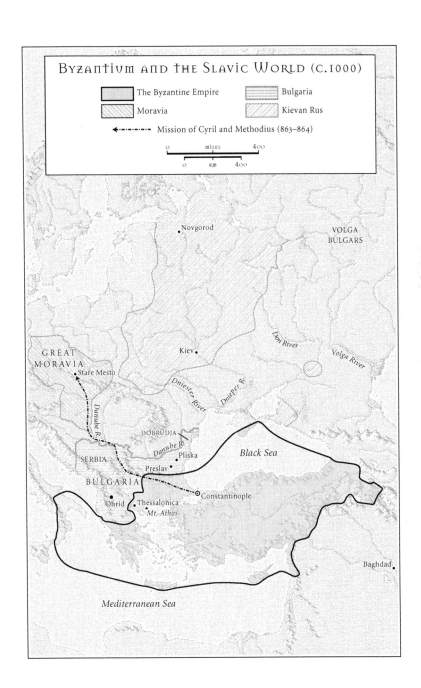

BYZANTIUM AND THE SLAVIC WORLD (C.1000)

- The Byzantine Empire
- Moravia
- Bulgaria
- Kievan Rus

◄·–·–·–· Mission of Cyril and Methodius (863–864)

	miles	
0		400

	km	
0		400

Novgorod

VOLGA BULGARS

GREAT MORAVIA

Stare Mesto

Kiev

Don River

Volga River

Dniester River

Dnieper R.

Danube R.

DOBRUDJA

Danube R.

Pliska

Black Sea

SERBIA

Preslav

BULGARIA

Ohrid

Thessalonica

Mt. Athos

Constantinople

Baghdad

Mediterranean Sea

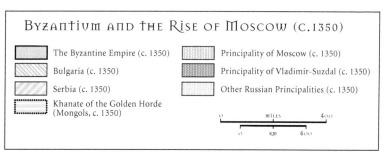

Byzantium and the Rise of Moscow (c.1350)

- The Byzantine Empire (c. 1350)
- Bulgaria (c. 1350)
- Serbia (c. 1350)
- Khanate of the Golden Horde (Mongols, c. 1350)
- Principality of Moscow (c. 1350)
- Principality of Vladimir-Suzdal (c. 1350)
- Other Russian Principalities (c. 1350)

MILES 0 400

KM 0 400

SWEDEN

NOVGOROD

Novgorod

ROSTOV

Tver

VLADIMIR-SUZDAL

Moscow

TEUTONIC ORDER

SMOLENSK

Smolensk

CHERNIGOV

Don River

Riazan

LITHUANIA

GOLDEN

Volga River

POLAND

Chernigov

Kiev

Dnieper River

HORDE

Dniester River

HUNGARY

GOLDEN

Danube

River

WALLACHIA

Black Sea

BYZANTINE EMPIRE OF TREBIZOND

Trnovo

SERBIA

BULGARIA

Ohrid

Constantinople

Thessalonica

Mt. Athos

TURKISH EMIRATES

DUCHY OF ATHENS

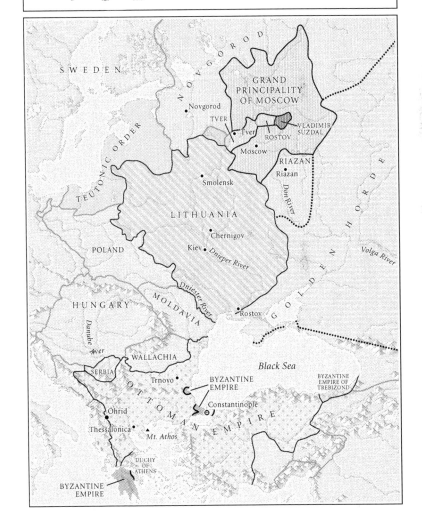

The Byzantine Empire (c. 1430)

Grand Principality of Moscow (c. 1430)

Serbia (c. 1350)

Lithuania (1430)

Ottoman Empire (c. 1430)

MILES   400

KM   400

SWEDEN

NOVGOROD

Novgorod

GRAND PRINCIPALITY OF MOSCOW

TVER

Tver

ROSTOV

VLADIMIR SUZDAL

TEUTONIC ORDER

Moscow

RIAZAN

Riazan

Smolensk

Don River

GOLDEN HORDE

LITHUANIA

Chernigov

POLAND

Kiev

Dnieper River

Volga River

Dniester River

HUNGARY

MOLDAVIA

Danube River

Rostov

WALLACHIA

Black Sea

SERBIA

Trnovo

BYZANTINE EMPIRE

BYZANTINE EMPIRE OF TREBIZOND

Ohrid

Constantinople

OTTOMAN EMPIRE

Thessalonica

Mt. Athos

DUCHY OF ATHENS

BYZANTINE EMPIRE

Introduction

The Byzantine empire was the medieval heir of ancient Greece and Rome, the continuation of the Roman empire in Greek territory and with Christianity as the state religion. It began in the early fourth century with the foundation of a new Christian capital, Constantinople, on the site of the old Greek city of Byzantium. It ended when the Ottoman Turks captured that city in 1453, making it the capital of their Islamic empire, which in territorial aspirations and imperial style essentially replaced the old Byzantine Greek empire.

Starting with Edward Gibbon's *Decline and Fall of the Roman Empire*, Western historians have until quite recently depicted the history of Byzantium as a long, unedifying tale of imperial decay. If the measure of empire is territory alone, this might appear to be true. From the once vast reaches of the old Roman empire, a millennium's worth of adversity reduced Byzantium in its final decades to little more than the city of Constantinople itself.

Measuring by cultural influence, however, more recent

historical research has revealed a story of lasting achievement and often vigorous expansion. *Sailing from Byzantium*
tells this story for the general reader.

The book's organization comes from two ideas that together offer an easy handle by which to grasp the Byzantine
cultural legacy. The first is the dual nature of that legacy,
which is reflected in its embrace of both Christian faith and
Greek culture. The book's second organizing idea is that the
beneficiaries of this dual legacy were the three younger civilizations that emerged at first in lands wrested from Byzantium: the Western, Islamic, and Slavic worlds. Each of these
three global civilizations was radically shaped by Byzantium—
but each was highly selective about the side of Byzantium it
chose to embrace. This book celebrates the energy and drive
of these younger cultures as well as the extraordinary richness of Byzantine culture.

Accordingly, *Sailing from Byzantium* is divided in three
parts. Part I, "Byzantium and the West," narrates the Byzantine legacy to Western civilization. This consists primarily in
the transmission of ancient Greek literature. As Latin West
and Greek East drifted apart during the Middle Ages, Byzantine scholars painstakingly preserved the ancient Greek classics. Then, at the dawn of the Renaissance, they came to Italy
and taught ancient Greek literature to the first Italian humanists, who were only then beginning to hunger for knowledge of Greco-Roman antiquity. Were it not for this small
but dynamic group of Byzantine humanist teachers, ancient
Greek literature might have been lost forever when the Turks
conquered Constantinople in 1453.*

---

* The terms *humanism* and *humanist* have been used in many ways since the mid-
fourteenth century, when the Italian poet Petrarch revived the ancient concept of *humanitas,* which the Roman author Cicero had used as an equivalent of the Greek *paideia,*

Part II, "Byzantium and the Islamic World," goes back in time to describe the rise of the Arab Islamic empire on former Byzantine lands in the Middle East. Long before the Italians rediscovered ancient Greece, the Arabs took up ancient Greek science, medicine, and philosophy, building on these works to found the Arabic Enlightenment commonly known as the golden age of Islamic science. Again, these texts ultimately came from Byzantium, as did the scholars who taught and translated them for the Arabs. The Islamic world eventually repudiated the ancient Greek legacy, as religious authorities suppressed the rationalistic inquiry on which ancient Greek science and philosophy were based.

Part III, "Byzantium and the Slavic World," explores the religious side of the Byzantine legacy. Over centuries of determined missionary work, the Byzantines turned the southern and eastern Slavs from uncivilized invaders into the great defenders of Orthodox Christianity. Converting first the Bulgarians, then the Serbs, and finally the Russians, Byzantine and Slavic monks worked together to create what a leading modern scholar has called "the Byzantine Commonwealth."* This pan-Slavic cultural entity transcended national boundaries, blending Orthodox monastic traditions of mystical contemplation with energetic missionary zeal to utterly reshape the world north of Byzantium's borders.

"education." By the late fifteenth century, teachers in Italian universities of the *studia humanitatis*—literally, "the study of humanity," a syllabus that included ancient grammar, rhetoric, and philosophy—were being called *humanistas*. In the nineteenth century, German scholars coined the term *humanismus* from this usage. Most Renaissance scholars would restrict the words to the study and the student of ancient Greek and Latin literature and civilization in the West beginning with Petrarch. In this book, the terms are applied to Byzantium and its classical scholars, before Petrarch as well as after. Some modern authorities have argued against such a usage, which risks both anachronism and the blurring of some important differences. Yet, it seems like a good way of emphasizing what the Byzantine "humanists" had in common with their Italian counterparts: a deep interest in the world of classical antiquity.
* The phrase is Dimitri Obolensky's.

Although these stories must be told separately, the reader should bear in mind that they happened, for the most part, concurrently. It has seemed best to tell them in the order in which they begin. Their climaxes fall in a different order. Part I begins with the sunset of Greco-Roman antiquity and moves forward to the humanistic rediscovery of that world in the fourteenth and fifteenth centuries. Part II focuses on the rise of Arab Islamic civilization in Byzantium's shadow from the seventh to ninth centuries. Part III has successive narrative peaks from the ninth to fifteenth centuries, as the Slavic world coalesced to take its place as Byzantium's truest heir. For an overview of developments in all three areas, the reader is referred to the concurrent timeline at the front of the book.

PROLOGUE

In a secluded corner of Istanbul, tucked under the old city's massive land walls near where they begin sweeping down to the Golden Horn, a small Orthodox church sits in a quiet square. Guidebooks call it Kariye Camii, which is the Turkish version of its older Byzantine Greek name, the Church of the Holy Savior in Chora. Roughly equivalent to the American slang expression "in the sticks," the tag "in Chora" reflects the church's remoteness from the busy urban heart of the old city. Vibrant, dirty, chaotic, thrilling, the modern city has spread far beyond the ancient land walls, but the Church of the Chora remains far removed from the herdpaths that shunt the bulk of tourists to bigger, better-known sites such as Hagia Sophia, the Blue Mosque, or Topkapi Palace.

The Chora's plain exterior has nothing about it to attract the eye from the charming and recently restored Ottoman-era houses fronting the square, one of which has been converted into a pleasant café and another into a hotel. Yet, those lucky enough to have it included in their tours do not soon forget the the graceful, delicate mosaics and bold, dynamic frescoes that cover its interior walls and ceilings. Painstakingly restored during the 1960s, they depict scenes and stories from the Old and New Testaments. Their quality and emotional impact offer eloquent testimony to the achievement of the vanished civilization that flowered in the city before the coming of the Turks.

The church itself and its associated monastery were probably founded as long ago as the sixth or seventh century, but after a number of restorations both had fallen into disrepair by the early fourteenth century. The monastery is long gone. As the church survives it is almost entirely the creation of one man, a wealthy Byzantine Greek named Theodore Metochites, who paid for and oversaw the complete renovation of both church and monastery between the years 1316 and 1321. It was during those years that the Chora's mosaics were assembled and its frescoes rapidly painted onto the still-wet plaster.

The Church of the Chora is the finest, most concentrated, and best-preserved example of Byzantine art surviving today. The Chora also reflects a startling new phase in the long history of Byzantine artistic expression. A thousand miles to the west, the Italian painter Giotto di Bondone— Metochites' nearly exact contemporary—had just completed his own cycle of frescoes at the Arena Chapel in Padua. That work, Giotto's masterpiece, is now recognized as having inaugurated the artistic revolution of the Italian Renaissance. Taking the clear family resemblance between the two fresco cycles as a cue, art historians have suggested that they share a common humanist aesthetic, a new interest in the realistic portrayal of the human figure. Some have traced this interest back to Byzantium, to the period of innovation in Byzantine art that culminated in the Chora and that helped spark the artistic revolution to follow in the West.

Byzantium in the era of Metochites' lifetime was enjoying a renaissance of its own, one that prefigured its better-known Italian counterpart. The brilliant Byzantinist Sir Steven Runciman, who died in 2000 at age ninety-seven, wrote a little gem of a book about it, *The Last Byzantine Renaissance*. Other historians usually call it the Paleologan Renaissance, Paleologos being the surname of the emperors whose dynasty ruled in the last two centuries of the empire's existence.

There are obvious and important differences between the two renaissances of Italy and Byzantium. It's highly significant that we know Giotto's name but not that of any artist who participated in the Chora restoration, for which all recognition went solely to the wealthy patron, Metochites. Italians were shaking off the medieval worldview in a way that the Byzantines never would before time ran out on them.

If Theodore Metochites had done nothing more than restore the Chora, his name would still be worthy of remembrance. But quite apart from his patronage, he is considered the founder of the Last Byzantine Renaissance. The leading intellectual of his time, Metochites was an impressively learned writer and philosopher as well as a powerful government official, serving as prime minister for nearly a quarter of a century under the Paleologan emperor Andronicus II.

Like most Byzantine literati, by modern standards Metochites was a grotesque windbag. Even the normally verbose Byzantines generally found his classicizing Greek prose repetitive, self-aggrandizing, and often downright impenetrable. All of his writings survive except his letters, which were destroyed by fire in 1671, a loss that likely comes as a sneaky relief to those struggling to wade through his work today: dense commentaries on Aristotle, astronomical treatises, flaccid poems, tepid lives of saints, pompous orations, and above all reams and reams of miscellaneous essays on Greek history and literature.

Yet, modern scholars have also discovered nuggets of originality and liberal open-mindedness, two qualities not usually held to be widespread among Byzantine writers. Metochites has even been called a humanist, and his literary interests have been seen as complementing the artistic values reflected in the Chora mosaics and frescoes. As with its Italian counterpart, the Last Byzantine Renaissance was a literary and intellectual movement as much as (or even more than) an artistic one, and both renaissances took their cues from the writings of the pre-Christian Greco-Roman world.

In his pious appreciation of the Chora's new artwork, Metochites was no more than lukewarmly conventional. By contrast, he waxed passionate and eloquent about the secular manuscripts, the classics of ancient Greek literature, with which he abundantly stocked the library of the Chora's monastery, making it the best in the city. It was his own personal collection, which he donated with the stipulation that it also serve as a public library. Metochites considered this to be a far more significant act of philanthropy on his part than any other, as he says explicitly in a long admonitory letter to the monks of the Chora: "For my sake," he pleads in conclusion, "keep the storehouses of the best wealth, namely the priceless books, in safety," preserving "these exquisite objects and treasures undiminished, as they will be much desired by men for all times to come."

When Andronicus II was overthrown by his rebellious grandson in 1328, Metochites found himself stripped of his power and wealth. After being briefly imprisoned and then exiled, in accordance with Byzantine retirement custom he himself entered the monastery of the Chora as a monk, taking the name Theoleptos. He died there a few years later, in his early sixties.

Although the fate of these specific books is unknown, in a larger sense Metochites' words could not have been more prophetic. Within a few decades, the West would begin its slow, halting rediscovery of ancient Greek literature, and the realization that these classic works were available only in Byzantium would lead men such as Petrarch, Boccaccio, and their successors to form an alliance with the Byzantine humanists who were Metochites' intellectual heirs. Over the span of about a century, as the remnants of their empire crumbled around them, the partnership between these Byzantine teachers and their Italian students literally saved ancient Greek literature from destruction at the hands of the conquering Turks. The Byzantine contribution of the Greek classics allowed the promise of Renaissance humanism to be fulfilled, by letting the West reclaim the body of literature that makes up the foundation of Western civilization. How frightening it is to contemplate a world without these works, and how unsettling to make out the slenderness of the thread by which they dangled over the void.

PART I

Byzantium
and the
West

T⊙WARD A PARTinG
⊙F THE WAYS

ravel to Italy, and you'll find that Byzantium is never more than a stone's throw away. Even that short distance is closed, discreetly but persistently, when you step into the painting galleries, the museums, and especially the churches. In these places Byzantium swirls gently around you like a mist, muting the hum of German, American, and Japanese voices: in Venice's Basilica di San Marco, for example, built with the help of Byzantine artisans, modeled on Constantinople's long-lost Church of the Holy Apostles, and adorned with loot from Venice's conquest of Constantinople during the Fourth Crusade; or in San Vitale at Ravenna, where the famous mosaics of the Byzantine emperor Justinian and his wife, the notorious stripper-turned-empress Theodora, each with their retinues, gaze limpidly at each other across fifteen yards of apse and as many centuries.

Byzantium comes to life in the monuments of Italy as nowhere else in Europe, and in the monuments of Ravenna as nowhere else in Italy. Venice certainly has more of a Byzantine feel today, but it's the feel of a much later period, and anyway Venice's Byzantium is generally either lifted or copied. Ravenna's Byzantium is primal. Built long before the Venetians sank their first piling, its swampy environs more easily defensible than Rome, Ravenna in the early Middle Ages was the capital of the Byzantine administration in Italy.

Then came the barbarians—Vandals, Goths, and others—whose turbulent arrival and usurpation of political power we know as "the fall of Rome." Determined to reclaim the lost territory, in the middle of the sixth century Justinian carried out a ruthless and grueling Reconquest of Italy and other parts of the Western empire. Having completed the long war, he built San Vitale to celebrate his victory.

A few minutes' walk from San Vitale, mosaics in the church of Sant'Apollinare Nuovo offer a very different message from the bland, assertive gaze of the imperial couple and their retinues. Built by the Gothic king and statesman Theoderic the Great just before Justinian came to the throne, Sant'Apollinare Nuovo precedes San Vitale by a generation. It proclaims in the most buoyant terms the Goths' arrival on the Roman scene. Two extended series of mosaics face each other on the church's long interior walls: a grand cityscape of Ravenna featuring Theoderic's palace on the south wall and a view of the nearby port of Classis on the north wall.

The cityscape on the south wall once included portraits of Goths, members of Theoderic's Amal dynasty or other nobles; after the Reconquest, just as they had painstakingly rooted the Goths out of Italy, the Byzantines prised out and replaced the mosaic stones constituting the Gothic figures. A visitor today can clearly make out the dappled areas where the new stones, which don't quite match, were applied. On the edges of columns depicted next to the palace, between which billowing curtains replaced the original Gothic figures leaning against them, you can still see a few fingers: they are remains left by the revision, too delicately embedded to chip away from the mosaic columns, so that it looks as if the last of the Goths hide there behind them, waiting to spring out through the curtains. On the wall nearby, what appears to be a portrait of Theoderic has had his name excised from the legend and that of Justinian written in.

Sant'Apollinare Nuovo reflected a widespread state of affairs in Europe at the time, a civilization really, but a clumpy one that scholars have given the name "sub-Roman": the part-Roman, part-barbarian cluster of cultures, like the Goths, that arose in the West over the fragmented course of the fourth and fifth centuries. These yeasty little worlds were the earliest signs of the Western Europe to come, and appeared first in the former Roman colonies from Spain through Gaul to Germany and down into the Balkans, and then eventually in Italy itself.

In Italy under the Goths, however, there wouldn't be time for the brew to ferment properly; the vessel would soon be shattered for good by Justinian's vain attempt to grab it back. Not only the Goths would suffer, for virtually the entire peninsula would be wrecked, its people deeply traumatized by what was theoretically their rescue.

It was not the barbarian invasions at all, but the havoc of this brutal Byzantine Reconquest that ended the ancient world in the West.

Yet, Theoderic's reign in Italy, which came right before the Reconquest, had an air of optimism. The early fifth century had been violent and unsettling in the West, with Roman rule petering out and the incoming barbarians taking over in uneasy partnership with the now rudderless Roman local elites: Vandals ending up in Africa, Visigoths in Spain, Franks in Gaul. Rome itself was twice laid open to barbarian armies, in 410 and again in 455. The crumbling of

Roman power had led a Christian bishop and writer from Roman Africa, one Augustine of Hippo, to turn away from the earthly landscape and point his readers toward the City of God, whose pristine invulnerability stood in splendid contrast to Rome's decay. However, within a few short decades the West turned a corner.

The year 476, later seen as the end of the empire in the West, in fact passed unremarked by contemporaries. The absence of imperial power had by then lost its fearsome aspect. In the last decade of the century, the Byzantines invited Theoderic—himself raised and more or less educated in Constantinople—to occupy Italy with his followers. The Goths set themselves up in an uneasy alliance with the old Roman senatorial elites, ruling Italy in the name of good government and of the "Roman" emperor in Byzantium.

Procopius, the main Byzantine historian of this era, describes Theoderic as popular and dignified. The Gothic king, we are told, "was exceedingly careful to observe justice, he preserved the laws on a sure basis, he protected the land and kept it safe from the barbarians dwelling round about, and attained the highest possible degree of wisdom and manliness." Though in time Theoderic himself could be considered "in name a tyrant," Procopius goes on, "in fact he was as truly an emperor as any who have distinguished themselves in this office from the beginning."

Procopius' description hints at a few of the intriguing ambiguities that characterize this shifting world. What made a barbarian? A tyrant? A king? Indeed, an emperor? Byzantines and Italians would soon begin to come up with conflicting answers to such questions as they slowly went their separate ways. The long divergence—marked by tiny, imperceptible steps rather than huge, irrevocable ones—stretched over the whole thousand-year history of Byzantium.

BOETHIUS AND CASSIODORUS

To start us on the path to this parting of the ways, we shall call on two learned Roman gentlemen of Theoderic's day, Boethius and Cassiodorus. Like double-faced Janus, the Roman god of arrivals and departures, each looks in two directions at once, harkening back to the fading world of antiquity and beckoning us forward into the emerging world of the Middle Ages.

Modern scholars invariably introduce Boethius as "the last of the Romans and the first of the Scholastics."* What this comes down to is that Boethius was the last Western European of cultural consequence to know Greek and Greek philosophy for a very long time. He wasn't the absolute last— there were a number of stragglers, certainly more than used to be thought—but he was the last heavyweight, at the very least until Thomas Aquinas and other Scholastics rediscovered Aristotle starting in the twelfth century, some seven centuries later. Even then few if any Scholastics had Boethius' knowledge of ancient Greek; knowledge on that level in the West would have to wait nearly a thousand years, for the Renaissance scholars of quattrocento Florence.†

It isn't certain how Boethius learned his Greek, or where he learned it, though it's possible from hints in the sources that he studied in Athens or Alexandria, or both, as a young man. If so, it wasn't much longer that such sojourns, once standard practice for a vanishing Mediterranean-wide

---

* Scholasticism was the major intellectual movement in Europe before the rise of humanism, and it, too, was stimulated by the discovery of ancient literature—in this case, the partial recovery of Aristotle's thought in the twelfth century. It is closely associated with the rise of universities or "schools." The greatest scholastic was St. Thomas Aquinas, whose thought was incorporated into Catholic doctrine after his death. Scholasticism stressed the use of reason and dialectical disputation in the formulation of theology.

† *Quattrocentro,* Italian for "four hundreds," refers to the fifteenth century and its cultural innovations in Italy.

upper class, would be possible. Boethius' father died when he was still a boy, and he was adopted by an older relative, Symmachus, a leading figure in Rome who also had strong ties to the literary culture of the Greek East. The refined Symmachus, it turns out, nursed an ambitious plan for restoring Italian familiarity with the Greek classics, and this may have been among his reasons for sponsoring his brilliant younger relative. Under Symmachus' guidance, Boethius undertook the almost unbelievably audacious project not only of translating into Latin the entire works of Plato and Aristotle, with commentary, but also of reconciling their often divergent philosophical views. And he planned to do this in his spare time, since from the age of about twenty he was writing prodigiously as well as filling increasingly important political positions for Theoderic.

Theoderic clearly valued Boethius' wide-ranging intellect, making it part of plans he had for revitalizing higher Roman culture and fixing in place its Gothic veneer. But he also had worldly reasons for promoting Greek learning in Italy. Boethius' learning had a practical side, and the king took full advantage of it in promoting his domestic and foreign prestige agendas: fulsomely flattering letters exist in which he asks Boethius to devise a tamper-proof system of weights and measures, to find a skilled harpist to send to Clovis, king of the Franks, and to come up with two timepieces, one a sundial and the other a water clock, as impressive gifts for Gundobad, king of the Burgundians. The letters present a pretty picture of peaceful coexistence, cooperation even, between the Roman senatorial class—of which Boethius was a member—and its new Gothic masters in Ravenna.

There was, however, a dark side to this happy kingdom. Modern scholars have generally followed Procopius in portraying Theoderic as an enlightened and liberal ruler, at least until the last few years of his reign. In particular, they point to his religious tolerance, for he and his Goths were Arian Christians, and as such they were not in communion with the main body of the church.* The Goths had been converted during the fourth century, when Arianism had powerful support, especially among the imperial heirs of the dynasty of Constantine. Arianism was later declared heretical, but not before the Goths and most of the other German tribes had adopted it. In an age in which religious persecution was almost a matter of course, Theoderic's policy was one of "separate but equal." In Ravenna today, next to Theoderic's Arian cathedral, visitors may find the charming Arian baptistery, where Goths received baptism, and which was built to balance the grander Orthodox baptistery adjoining the city's main cathedral.

The baptistery of the Orthodox was in fact the one used by the Romans. Since the church had not yet split along the lines that would later divide it, of Roman Catholic and Byzantine or Greek Orthodox, either term would do: *catholic* ("universal") and *orthodox* ("right-believing") were used freely in both Rome and Constantinople.

It was now that the earliest cracks appeared in the edifice. From 484 to 519, when Boethius was growing up and beginning his service in Theoderic's government, the church underwent its first East-West schism. It arose when the pope excommunicated the patriarch of Constantinople over the question of how to resolve another heresy, that of the Monophysites.† In Constantinople, the emperor sided with the

---

* Arians followed the teachings of Arius (c. 256–336), an Egyptian monk who denied Christ's divinity and emphasized his humanity.
† Monophysites emphasized Christ's divinity at the expense of his humanity, roughly the reverse of the Arian position. Monophysite views were especially popular in Egypt, the Holy Land, and Syria, all Byzantine provinces at this time.

patriarch, while in Rome the powers that be supported the pope, and so the whole controversy became highly political, alienating the remaining local Roman elites from the imperial government back in Constantinople.

Theoderic, whose constitutional position was at best ambiguous, benefited from the schism, for their hostility to Constantinople made the Roman elites much more willing to cozy up to the Arian Goths. As long as Theoderic could play Rome and Constantinople against each other, his position between them was relatively secure. In 518, however, a humble soldier named Justin was acclaimed as emperor. From the start, the power behind Justin's throne was his nephew Peter Sabbatius, who promptly took the name Justinian, and who seems to have engineered his uncle's elevation. Determined to restore unity, Justinian took part personally in the negotiations to end the schism, and his efforts bore fruit the following year. With pope and patriarch once more in communion, Theoderic suddenly found himself on shaky ground.

It was against this background—the successful resolution of the schism—that Theoderic decided to arrest, try, imprison, torture, and eventually execute his *magister officiorum*, his master of offices, the highest-ranking and most honored minister in his civil administration, his learned and versatile subject Boethius. The charge was treason, Procopius tells us, "setting about a revolution," a false accusation that Procopius claims was trumped up by other Romans, jealous of Boethius' wealth and standing, who managed to hoodwink the otherwise perspicacious Theoderic.

It's a typically vague reference, for Procopius tends to be long on action and short on insight. Boethius himself gives a fuller account in *The Consolation of Philosophy*, which he composed in prison as he awaited execution. Soon after

Boethius wrote this influential masterpiece—a complex and poignant mix of poetry and prose that would be second only to the Bible in its influence in the West during the Middle Ages—the sentence was carried out. Boethius, we're told, was first tortured by having a rope tightened around his forehead until his eyes began to pop out, and then he was clubbed to death.

As Procopius observes, the torture and execution of Boethius are difficult to square with Theoderic's reputation for enlightened liberality. While Procopius implies that Theoderic was manipulated by Boethius' enemies in the senate, many observers have found this explanation lame. One intriguing possibility is that the Gothic king executed Boethius quite deliberately, having learned that the Roman had taken part in a political conspiracy to reunite East and West under Byzantine rule by ending the schism. According to this scenario, Boethius' theological writings played a key part in the plot. Without religious rapprochement there wasn't a hope of political unity, and Boethius' theological tractates pushed reconciliation of the schism along exactly the lines proposed by Justinian, who was negotiating for the Byzantines. In effect, they were imperial propaganda written as part of a deliberate program to overthrow Gothic rule in Italy. Theoderic executed Boethius because Boethius, acting as a Byzantine agent, had betrayed the Gothic king.

As East and West drifted apart in succeeding centuries, in different ways each would be haunted by the uneasy ghost of Boethius. The loss of Greek came naturally, as Western Europe began to realign itself on a new axis, one that ran from north to south rather than east to west. The very fact that Boethius would be celebrated for knowing Greek (among the many other things he was celebrated for) is telling, as is his judgment that the most useful thing he could do vis-à-vis Greek philosophy was to translate it into Latin, which wouldn't have been as necessary in an earlier age.

If Boethius had lived long enough to carry out his plan of translating Aristotle and Plato, Western intellectual history would have been startlingly different. He never got to Plato at all. Of Aristotle's vast body of work, Boethius managed to render into Latin only the six pieces on logic known as the *Organon*, or the "Instrument." Essentially a set of rules for systematic thinking, the *Organon* lies at the heart of Aristotelian rationalism. It is here that Aristotle lays out for his readers such intellectual methods as the syllogism, which proceeds in careful steps from premise to conclusion: Socrates is a philosopher; all philosophers are human; therefore Socrates is human.

These translations, however, would be ignored for centuries. It was Boethius' other work that went a long way toward single-handedly fixing the educational curriculum that the West would follow throughout the Middle Ages: dense technical tracts on arithmetic, music theory, astronomy, rhetoric, philosophy, and theology. In contrast with the translations from Greek, these works of synthesis stayed in the mainstream and would become standard reading, the last word on their subjects up to and into the Renaissance.

Hidden in the work that fell by the wayside was the overarching concern that Boethius shared with the great thinker who would resume his work seven centuries later, Thomas Aquinas: *conjungere rationem fidemque*, to join faith and reason. Like the idea of reconciling Plato and Aristotle, in some ways parallel to it (for Plato's writings have strongly mystical elements), this need to harmonize cosmic epistemological opposites was an appetite that the West would lose and then rediscover in the centuries to come.

To replace Boethius as master of offices, Theoderic

promoted his court rhetorician Cassiodorus, who had written the fulsome letters requesting Boethius' services mentioned earlier. Writing such letters in the king's name was part of his job as royal rhetorician, a role he gracefully fulfilled while holding a number of political offices in the first decades of the sixth century. A collection of these urbane missives, carefully edited for publication by Cassiodorus later, survives and is one of the major sources for our picture of Italy in the age of Theoderic.

Boethius had sailed close to the wind, but Cassiodorus, a careful survivor if ever there was one, sailed squarely with it. All along Cassiodorus had endorsed the ruling Goths, concocting a *History of the Goths* meant to show how Roman they really were underneath it all. He lived and worked in Ravenna, breathing its atmosphere of eager collaboration, whereas Boethius had remained Roman geographically as well as culturally. Cassiodorus was a civil servant, not a philosopher, not so famous in his own times, and in all respects a more representative figure than the imposing Boethius. Cassiodorus' long life—he was said to have lived to one hundred—extended into the new age just as Boethius' was cut short at the edge of the old one.

Cassiodorus' service to the Goths was based on his considerable skills as a classically trained rhetorician. It wasn't for much longer that such skills would have a place in Italy. Theoderic himself died in 526, and Justinian put growing diplomatic pressure on the weakened Gothic government. His armies invaded Italy in 535, and in 540 his brilliant general Belisarius captured Ravenna. The collaborator Cassiodorus became, in effect, a prisoner of war. Replacing the Gothic administration with direct rule, the Byzantines spirited Cassiodorus off to Constantinople.

Though he went as a hostage, they were really doing

him a favor. After its strong start, Justinian's Reconquest of Italy bogged down, grinding on for another decade and a half of bitter, destructive fighting. By the time it ended in 553 the Goths had been wiped out and Italy itself devastated. Cassiodorus seems to have stayed in Constantinople the whole time. Although he left no record of his sojourn there, we can imagine how the city must have struck him. Italy was being blasted, but here was wealth and glitter, pomp and power, ceremony and civilization.

The city stands at the brink of Europe, on a blunt promontory whose hilly tip looks out toward Asia across the narrow Bosporus. According to legend, the Greek colonists who founded the city in archaic times named it after Byzas, their leader; the colonists who had already founded Chalcedon across the Bosporus were accused of blindness for passing up the site. Its southern edge lies on the Sea of Marmara, its northern edge on the Golden Horn, a deep tapered slice cut into the European shore of the Bosporus that gives the city one of the best natural harbors in the world. In the event of attack by sea, the Byzantines would hoist a heavy iron chain across the mouth of the harbor, sealing out the hostile ships.

Constantine's city was enlarged after a century by Theodosius, whose great double walls run for five miles, cutting the city off by the landward approach. The city's central artery, the Mese, opened onto the Augusteum, a complex of grand public spaces near the promontory's outer tip: the Hippodrome, where chariot races and games were held; numerous forums ringed about with columns, arches, and porticoes; the two ornate Senate Houses, built to symbolize the transfer of power from Rome, along with the vast complex of the Great Palace, where imperial business was transacted, and which overflowed onto the hillside toward the seawalls fronting the Bosporus. Constantinople bristled with commemorative columns, statues, churches, public bathhouses, monasteries, and palaces. In Justinian's day the belief was taking shape that God himself guarded it. It was the center of the world, a temporal version of the heavenly city, a great physical and metaphysical tortoise shell into which the Byzantines would tuck themselves over and over, weathering attack after attack by less civilized invaders.

To our modern ears its very name conjures the exotic, but since its earliest days it thrummed with foreign voices, for it lies at the convergence of trade routes from all points of the compass: north and south by water, between the Mediterranean and the grain-rich ports of the Black Sea; east and west by land, from Europe into farthest Asia. It always remained polyglot, a place where unknown tongues might constantly be heard striking bargains, offering wares, disputing urgent theological matters.

When Cassiodorus got there, the city was passing through a frenzy of construction. Less than a decade earlier, much of it had been torched in riots that began in the rowdiness of the games at the Hippodrome. Sweeping away the ruins of the old, Justinian had undertaken a spectacular building spree. Public baths, government buildings, porticoed palaces, and especially churches all arose in just a few years. In the city center, along the Mese, the Church of the Holy Apostles had survived the fires but was pulled down and rebuilt anyway, bigger and better, in the shape of a cross with five domes. Contruction was under way when Cassiodorus got there, and it was completed during his stay.*

---

* Already in ruins by 1453, the Church of the Holy Apostles was torn down to make way for the mosque complex of Mehmet the Conqueror, Fatih Camii in Turkish. The church probably looked very much like the Basilica di San Marco in Venice, which was modeled on it.

It would be the second biggest church in the city. Cassiodorus would have been able to visit the biggest right away, Justinian's great new church of Hagia Sophia, which replaced a burned-down original, and which the emperor's builders had recently finished. Surmounted by a broad, shallow celestial dome more than one hundred feet across, the squat, powerful brick structure commanded the heights near the Hippodrome at the farthest end of the Mese. Centuries earlier, the Romans had invented concrete, using it on its own or in combination with brick and stone to make buildings, aqueducts, monuments, roads. Such knowledge had faded in the West, where brickmaking, like ancient Greek, disappeared for almost a thousand years. It survived in Byzantium, where the bricks and mortar of Hagia Sophia mark the climax of late Roman building.

Only a few years later, though, the dome collapsed. Jostled from its perch by an earthquake, it had to be replaced by a steeper one. Less impressive to the observer inside, the new dome had the compensatory quality of staying put. The story makes a good allegory of Justinian's reign: grandiose designs bring down the house, which then has to be rebuilt with less grandiosity and more practicality.

The years that Cassiodorus spent in Constantinople fell precisely on the hinge connecting antiquity and the Middle Ages. The decade of the 540s is when things began to go badly for Justinian and Byzantium. Seemingly concluded with the capture of Ravenna, the war in the West reignited for its long, furious burn through the Italian peninsula. Even so, the Byzantines might have dealt with it, but starting a year or so after Cassiodorus arrived, Constantinople and other Byzantine cities were ravaged by a severe outbreak of bubonic plague, which carried off something like a quarter of Justinian's subjects. In coming decades, the outbreaks would recur over and over, depopulating the empire and putting huge strains on the army. Justinian had other wars to fight as well, having opened up hostilities on a second front in the East, against Persia. When Belisarius sent for reinforcements, none were available.

Byzantines began turning inward, and Cassiodorus did, too. Sometime around the beginning of the war, he had "converted," in the ancient sense of embracing a Christian life and Christian values more fully, even if already nominally Christian. Now he stepped completely into the world of the monks. It was probably while in Constantinople that he composed a voluminous commentary on the Psalms that later became the standard guide in the West to reading this text, which was an intimate, daily part of monastic life. By the time he returned to Italy, Cassiodorus was committed to that life.

Looking around at the wreck that was his homeland, Cassiodorus withdrew to his family's extensive estates in the south. There, near the windswept sea cliffs at Squillace, he established a monastery called Vivarium, "Fishpond." As monasteries go, it wasn't a powerhouse. It certainly didn't hold a candle to the great monastery of the age, Monte Cassino, which had been founded a couple of decades earlier by St. Benedict, the father of Western monasticism. What seems to ensure its place in history, however, is something its highly literary founder gave it: a scriptorium, a specially equipped room dedicated to the copying of manuscripts. While we can't be sure, it appears that the Vivarium's scriptorium was the first in the West, and that Cassiodorus brought the idea back with him from Byzantium, where such rooms already existed in monasteries as well as in the private homes of aristocratic literati.

Cassiodorus describes the Vivarium's scriptorium proudly

in his book *Institutions of Divine and Secular Letters,* a sort of monastic handbook cum encyclopedia that is probably his most influential work. It had a sundial for sunny days, a water clock for cloudy ones or nighttime, and "cleverly constructed lamps which . . . without human attendance abundantly maintain a very full clearness of most copious light." While the Vivarium foundered soon after Cassiodorus' death, the scriptorium caught on and became a standard feature of Western monasteries.

To go with the scriptorium, Cassiodorus gave his monastery an unusually beefy library, including a load of books he had brought back from Constantinople. Scholars used to depict Cassiodorus as the savior of pagan literature at the Vivarium. They now believe that he was interested almost exclusively in religious texts, and that goes as well for the Greek works he brought from Byzantium. It was a Christian library he created, and a Christian intellectual milieu that he fostered, aiming to replace, not to repair, the West's decayed centers of secular learning. He did include some texts of secular Latin authors, but his interest in them now was for purely linguistic instruction. The monks used them as models to improve their knowledge of classical Latin grammar and syntax, which they could then deploy for religious purposes. Outside the church, spoken Latin was turning into Italian, French, and Spanish. Cassiodorus' last work, written when he was in his nineties, was an elementary manual on Latin spelling, which he put together for the undereducated monks who manned the scriptorium.

It was a far cry from the secular historical works and high-flown rhetorical flourishes with which he'd begun. But that wide-open world was gone. The scale of things had shrunk. The rhythm and direction of Cassiodorus' career offer a handy epitome of the general drift in the West toward a church monopoly on learning, as life moved from the public arena to the closer confines of the private estate. There's no doubt that Cassiodorus was a chameleon of the first order, but one has to wonder whether the circumstances of his extreme old age might have brought this chameleon a touch of nostalgic pentimento.

THE PARTING

In the Dark Age that now began, Christendom slowly and organically split itself in two halves, a Latin Catholic half and a Byzantine Orthodox half. One rested on a foundation of Latin church writings, the other on Greek. For centuries both upheld the façade of a single unified church. But the cracks in that façade grew ever wider.

It wasn't just the church. Justinian's Reconquest crumbled away with the emperor's passing, and into the depopulated Italian peninsula poured a new group of barbarians, the Lombards, who unlike the Goths cared nothing for the prestige of the Roman past. Isolated by the collapse of Byzantine power and under threat from the Lombards, the popes eventually turned north for protection, to the rising power of the Franks. The union was consummated on Christmas Day in the year 800, when Pope Leo III crowned the Frankish king Charlemagne "emperor" of a restored Roman empire. This was a deep affront to the Byzantines when they heard about it. At the time, the empress Irene ruled in Constantinople, and one of the pope's rationales for appropriating the title was that a woman could never be considered the rightful Roman ruler. Byzantine indignation was sharpened by underlying suspicion that the pope was correct.* Byzantines started lumping all Westerners together as Frangoi (Franks), perceiving them as an undifferentiated and dangerous barbarian horde.

In the years, decades, and centuries to come, wrangling over the title *emperor of the Romans* assumed almost comically exaggerated proportions. With a steadfastness that at times approached the delusional, the Byzantines always insisted that they alone were the true "Romans" and that only their emperor could claim the title, maintaining the fiction that Byzantine sway was universal among Christians and that Western kings ruled at their pleasure. But the reality fell short, even though Byzantium began to recover in the early ninth century. By then, the West's isolation had bred self-reliance—among its scrappy and ambitious feudal kings, the most powerful of whom, following the example of Charlemagne, couldn't help but covet the ultimate title, emperor of the Romans; and in the papacy, which, accustomed to standing alone, reserved the right to bestow that title.

Westerner and Byzantine no longer knew each other, and when introduced they busily erected walls of mutual contempt. Fortune has given us an illuminating window into this estrangement in the figure of Liudprand, a Lombard noble and diplomat who made two visits to Constantinople around the middle of the tenth century, in 949 and 968. The first was in the service of the Burgundian king; the second was on behalf of Liudprand's new master Otto the Great, duke of Saxony, German king, and eventually (inevitably, one might say) "emperor of the Romans." Between these

---

* Few Byzantines would have openly shared such doubts with the empress herself, a formidable ruler who had just deposed her son and reigning co-emperor by having him blinded, rendering him ineligible to rule. The procedure was badly executed, and he died of the wounds.

visits, both of which the prolific Liudprand wrote about in copious detail, Otto appointed him bishop of Cremona, and so he is known to history as Liudprand of Cremona.

On his first visit he was favorably impressed by the Byzantine emperor Romanus I, and his descriptions dwell on the magnificence of Constantinople's palaces and court ritual, both of which far outshone anything in the West. Like the caliphs of Baghdad, the Byzantines deployed sophisticated devices at court to create an impression of awe-inspiring majesty. A gilded bronze tree stood next to the emperor's throne, with mechanical birds, also gilded, on its branches. Each bird sang the song appropriate to its species. Romanus himself sat on a huge throne guarded by mechanical golden lions, "who beat the ground with their tails and gave a dreadful roar with an open mouth and quivering tongue" as the visitor approached. Then, in a final demonstration of supernatural omnipotence, the throne itself rose magically into the air, up to ceiling level, emperor and all.* When it descended seconds later the emperor was wearing a new, elaborate costume. Distance prevented any direct interaction, and the emperor communicated through a secretary with the now thoroughly softened-up visitor.

Two decades later, Liudprand was beyond being cowed by such tricks. Now he was bishop of Cremona, representing a rival emperor of the Romans. Romanus was gone, and the Byzantine ruler was Nicephorus II, upon whom the disenchanted Liudprand heaps the most delicious invective. "A monstrosity of a man, a dwarf, fat-headed and with tiny mole's eyes," he begins, going on from there in a similar vein. In fact, Nicephorus was one of Byzantium's most impressive

---

* In the twentieth century, these images inspired William Butler Yeats, whose poems "Sailing to Byzantium" and "Byzantium" use them as metaphors for incorruptible intellect and timeless beauty.

warrior-emperors, the veteran of numerous campaigns against the Arabs and Slavs. But he had refused to acknowledge Otto as "emperor of the Romans," which stuck in Liudprand's craw.

So did everything else on this visit, including (literally) the food, which "smelt strongly of garlic and onions and was filthy with oil and fish sauce." Byzantine customs had become very un-Roman, as Liudprand pointedly observes. With their long-sleeved robes, flowing hair, and jewelry, the Byzantines themselves were wily and effeminate, "idle liars of neither gender." The Byzantine emperor drank bathwater; Otto was manly and honest, and he didn't eat smelly food.

The growing cultural divide found religious expression in the eleventh century, when, in a fit of pique, a supremely arrogant papal envoy named Humbert took it upon himself to excommunicate the patriarch of Constantinople. Humbert's temper tantrum, which happened in the year 1054, would later harden into final schism between the two churches, revealing that deeper things were at work than one inflated ego. One of them was Rome's addition of the *filioque** to the Latin creed earlier in the century: Catholics now professed that the Holy Spirit proceeded "from the Son" as well as from the Father. The Orthodox, meanwhile, clung to the original formulation that it proceeded only from the Father. Since 1054 the pope and the patriarch of Constantinople have not been in communion.

Strategically, too, the eleventh century proved, like the sixth, to be a fulcrum. When it began, Byzantium was at the height of its medieval prosperity and the West played second

---

* Latin for "and from the Son." The word was added to the Nicene Creed by the Western church at the insistence of the Franks. Eventually, the procession of the Holy Spirit became the major point of doctrinal difference between the Catholic and Orthodox churches.

fiddle. When it ended, Byzantium was in disarray and the West had embarked on a period of explosive growth.

The most visible sign was the launching of the First Crusade at the end of that century, to recover the Holy Land from the Muslim Turks. These raucous expeditions brought Frangoi and Byzantines into close contact, because the route to the Muslim lands went through Byzantium. The Byzantines assumed that the conquered territory would be returned to Byzantine rule. The Crusaders had other ideas. Conquering Jerusalem, Antioch, and other former Byzantine cities, they set up Crusader kingdoms that didn't answer to the emperor in Constantinople.

Over the next century, through three Crusades, the increasingly desperate Byzantines (theoretically the hosts) managed to keep the disruptive Frangoi (theoretically the guests) under a semblance of control. But the gap between East and West had grown too wide. The façade of a Christian alliance would soon self-destruct in the most dramatic way imaginable.

THE FOURTH CRUSADE

On a fine spring morning in the year 1203, a vast invasion force assembled itself in and around the island port of Corfu, off the Adriatic coast of northern Greece. Unfurling their sails to a mild, favorable breeze, the ships began moving off southward. Those watching found it exhilarating. The fleet spread out on the glinting water as far as they could see. Leading the way were the ponderous but deadly warships, followed by transports laden with men and horses, then swift galleys rowed by slaves and prisoners of war. Scores of merchantmen with provisions and other goods kept pace with the fleet. It was Saturday, May 24, the eve of Pentecost, and the fleet's objective, the fabled city of Constantinople, lay some five hundred miles to the east.

The ships belonged to the wealthy maritime republic of Venice, formerly a Byzantine province but now a rival. They carried about ten thousand Christian Crusaders from Western Europe, French and Norman knights mostly, who had hired the Venetian ships at an exorbitant sum. Constantinople was to be a supply stop for the pious knights of this Fourth Crusade, whose stated purpose was to overthrow the Muslim rulers of Egypt.

Leaving Venice late the previous summer, the Crusaders had proceeded south along the Dalmatian coast. That autumn they had conquered the Dalmatian port of Zara, a Christian city, but one controlled by Venice's rival, Hungary. The Venetians had demanded its capture in exchange for letting the Crusaders postpone paying off the huge fee the Venetians were charging for transportation. This cynical deal was struck by Venice's elderly, ambitious, and utterly unscrupulous doge, Enrico Dandolo. Crusaders, of course, weren't supposed to attack fellow Christians, and Pope Innocent III was duly outraged. He had already warned against such impious behavior, suspecting correctly that Dandolo coveted a much greater prize than Zara. The Crusaders had wintered in Zara before sailing southward to Corfu, picking up stragglers along the way.

The journey from Corfu to Constantinople took a month. In late June 1203, the Crusaders anchored for the first time within view of the Byzantine capital.

The sight of the city left them stunned. Nothing in Western Europe could have prepared them for Constantinople's size and magnificence. The largest city in the West at this time was probably Venice, whose population most likely stood at around one hundred thousand. London and Paris, even Rome itself, were backwaters by comparison, with populations of perhaps twenty thousand to forty thousand. Going on figures he got from from Byzantine officials, the French knight Geoffroy de Villehardouin later estimated Constantinople's population at four hundred thousand. It was therefore something on the order of ten to twenty times larger than Paris.

"All those who had never seen Constantinople," Geoffroy tells us in his chronicle of the Fourth Crusade, "gazed very intently at the city, never having imagined there could be so fine a place in all the world." During the approach through the Sea of Marmara, as the Crusaders' ships drew closer, the long, high, gray stone seawalls—which still crouch right at the edge of the rocky shoreline—had slowly grown from a dark smudge on the horizon to fill their sight. The walls continued as the ships rounded the promontory, and now on the hillside behind the walls the graceful porticoes and columns of the Great Palace complex came into view. Farther along were more sea walls and then the mighty, humped presence of Hagia Sophia, crowning the city's high ground, plainly visible from the Bosporus. "There was indeed," Geoffroy continues, "no man so brave and daring that his flesh did not shudder at the sight."

Despite its staggering opulence and the continued prosperity of its trade—trade on which the Venetians' own wealth depended, and which they longed to control—Constantinople and its empire had suffered decades of political instability and turmoil. Byzantium's sacred throne had been seized by one usurper after another, and internal dissension wracked the governing class and the imperial administration. The Crusaders rapidly found out the soft spot in the city's defenses. Westerners had traditionally been quartered across the Golden Horn, in the Galata district. It was there, from the heights of the Galata Tower, that the great chain was winched up to seal off the harbor. By storming the tower, the Crusaders—led by the Venetians—were able to lower the chain and attack where the walls were weakest, deep inside the Golden Horn.* Within weeks of arriving, they had occupied the city and installed their own puppet on the throne, Alexius IV, the son of a former emperor who had been overthrown some years earlier.

For the rest of that summer and fall, the Crusaders waited in Constantinople with their Venetian escorts as Alexius IV failed to meet his obligations to them—in particular, the payment of the huge fortune he'd agreed to fork over in return for the throne, money the Crusaders owed in turn to the Venetians. During this time, Alexius IV grew increasingly unpopular with his Byzantine subjects, who resented the Crusaders' rough and imposing presence. Skirmishes broke out between rowdy Western knights and sullen Byzantine soldiers stationed in the city.

At length the popular resentment bubbled over, and in January 1204, Alexius IV was overthrown and executed by a leader of the Byzantine resistance, an elderly but energetic aristocrat named Alexius Ducas. Also known as Murtzuphlus or Bushybrow, he assumed the throne as Alexius V.

The Crusaders stepped up their demands for payment, but the new emperor refused them flatly. He would have been unable to cooperate even had he wished to do so, since (as his predecessor had discovered) the imperial treasury was empty. But the Crusaders needed to pay off the implacable Venetians, who threatened to simply sail away. The obvious

---

* Crucially, the Byzantines had recently disbanded their navy, which had sheltered in the Golden Horn during previous sieges and prevented earlier attackers from using the tactic here employed by the Crusaders.

solution, as the wily Dandolo had foreseen, was for the Crusaders to capture and plunder the city for themselves.

They launched their offensive in early April. Though the desperate and demoralized Byzantines managed to drive back the first attack, psychologically the Frangoi had already made the conquest. Byzantine defenses crumbled a few days later, on April 13, when the Crusaders again breached the seawalls at their weakest point, near the inner tip of the Golden Horn. They set fire to the city. Alexius V gave up and fled with most of the Byzantine aristocracy on his heels. The Crusaders poured in.

The mayhem that followed is unique in history. For three days and nights, the Crusaders murdered, raped, looted, or destroyed everyone and everything they could get their hands on. Untold thousands perished; many more were brutalized, maimed, left homeless. The Byzantine historian Nicetas Choniates witnessed it all before escaping the city two days after the pillage ended. The streets were filled with the screams and moans of the dying and wounded, he wrote later, as men were slain, women and girls raped, the elderly beaten, and the wealthy robbed. "Thus it was in the squares, thus it was in the temples, thus it was in the hiding places; for there was no place that could escape detection or that could offer asylum to those who came streaming in."

Tragic as the human cost was, this isn't what makes the sack of Constantinople unique. The city had stood inviolate as the capital of Christendom for nearly nine centuries, since its founding as the New Rome in the early fourth century. A peerless collection of fine art, religious relics, and irreplaceable manuscripts filled its churches, monasteries, libraries, and palatial homes. Mosaics, icons, frescoes, ancient bronze and marble statues, precious metalwork, jeweled artifacts, silken wall hangings, painstakingly copied works of ancient and medieval Greek literature—the scale of what the world lost in those three days can only be guessed, never known.

The mercilessly acquisitive Venetians specialized in removal. The most famous examples of their booty are the four bronze horses that adorn the Basilica di San Marco, but countless other art treasures were carried off to grace the churches, palazzos, and piazzas of the Serenissima. The less sophisticated French went in more for wholesale drunken demolition, though gold, silver, and jewels were easy enough to spot and grab. In the great church of Hagia Sophia, Nicetas Choniates tells us, looters stripped the silken wall hangings, smashed the icons, tore apart the gold and silver furnishings, and then brought mules inside to load with booty. Some of the mules slipped and fell, unable to regain their footing on the blood-slicked marble floor. Their guts were slashed with knives so that shit oozing from their wounds mixed with the blood on the marble. A drunken whore sat on the patriarch's throne and sang obscene songs before kicking up her heels in a burlesque dance.

Even the Muslim infidels, Choniates continues, treated Christian captives better. The Westerners' atrocities against both humanity and God revealed their depraved and demonic natures for all to see. As for Constantinople itself, Choniates laments, the city's majesty has been forever despoiled: "O City, formerly enthroned on high, striding far and wide, magnificent in comeliness and more becoming in stature; now thy luxurious garments and elegant royal veils are rent and torn; thy flashing eye has grown dark."

The Crusaders didn't make it to Egypt. Instead, they set up a "Latin Empire of Constantinople" complete with a Western "emperor." But they had overextended themselves. The Byzantines proved resilient enough to regroup, first into several rival governments in exile, then into a single Byzantine rump state. Led by the emperor Michael VIII Paleologos, who styled himself the "New Constantine," they recaptured Constantinople in 1261.

The emotional chasm between East and West was now fixed in place, deep and wide. Byzantium never forgave or forgot the outrage of Fourth Crusade, nursing a hatred of the West that it would take to the grave. And though the empire lasted a further two centuries, it never recovered its former strength and political influence.

Yet, it was during this final stage that Byzantine civilization shone most brilliantly. Nicetas Choniates could never have known it, but far from growing dark, Byzantium's flashing eye would light the world as never before.

CHAPTER TWO

BETWEEN ATHENS
AND JERUSALEM

What has Athens to do with Jerusalem?" asked the second-century Christian writer Tertullian. Hostile to the secular wisdom of the ancients, Tertullian meant to evoke the answer "Nothing at all," but others asked the question with sincere curiosity. Boethius asked it, essentially, in his quest to join faith and reason. After him, the West forgot to ask it with any seriousness.

In Byzantium, things were different. Tertullian's question didn't ever go away entirely, and it serves as a prism through which we may glimpse the outlines of Byzantine civilization. Somehow, through all the centuries, Byzantium kept a tight grip on the literature of ancient Greece, yet held it firmly at arm's length. Their ancient pagan literature was at once too barbed with secular reason and other dangers for the Christian Byzantines to embrace too closely, yet too imposing, too downright gorgeous to dismiss altogether. Athens sparkled at one pole of the Byzantine consciousness, Jerusalem glowed softly at the other.

Ever adept at compartmentalizing, the Byzantines drew a clear and crucially revealing line between ancient Greek literature, which they called the Outside Wisdom, and Christian literature, which they called the Inside Wisdom. The distinction was codified in the fourth century by an Eastern Church Father, St. Basil of Caesaria, in his famous essay *To Young Men, On How They Might Derive Profit from Pagan Literature*, which remained one of the most widely read works in Byzantium. This short book would do much to keep the peace between Athens and Jerusalem in the coming millennium.

When Basil was writing, controversy raged throughout the Greco-Roman world over Tertullian's question. Attempting to still the waters, Basil affirmed for Christians the moral utility of "the wisdom drawn from the outside," at least insofar as its precepts could be shown to be in agreement with Christianity's. Ancient poets, historians, and especially philosophers all praised virtue, he wrote, so their works properly deserve a place in the education of Christians. True, they also depict patricide, fratricide, incest, lust, cruelty, gluttony, and other sinful goings-on, not to mention the bickering and multiple gods of the pagan pantheon. Readers must therefore exercise due diligence in weeding out the bad passages from the good, storing up the moral lessons as they go, just as bees make honey through judicious visits to fragrant and colorful—but otherwise useless—flowers.

Over time, Basil's approach was adopted as the mainstream attitude in the Byzantine East. As such, it remained in force for more than a millennium: a thousand years later Theodore Metochites would explicitly echo it in his letter to the monks of the Chora. Even in Basil's day, however, there were those who took a harder line toward Greece's secular, rationalistic pagan heritage, including his friend, the only slightly less esteemed theologian St. Gregory of Nazianzus. The hostility and suspicion of these Christian hard-liners—almost always they were monks—toward the classics would never go away. At times it would simmer quietly, while at other times it would boil over into open controversy.

Despite the monks' hostility, this most Christian of societies always retained a secular educational system based on the Outside Wisdom, which it had inherited from its pre-Christian past. This sharply distinguishes the Byzantine East from the Latin West. As Christianity triumphed throughout the empire over the fourth to sixth centuries, various forces—doctrinal disputes, barbarian invasions, and in the seventh century the rise of Islam—shattered the old unity of the Greco-Roman world. Both East and West entered Dark Ages in which the classics came as close to vanishing as they ever would. In the Latin West, the future Catholic world, the break with the past was severe. In the Byzantine East, the future Orthodox world, continuity prevailed—after a fashion. Rome and the West fell to incoming barbarians, but Constantinople and the East endured, though not without suffering their own travails.

The Dark Age of Byzantium

By the seventh century, when those travails were at their worst, Greek had replaced Latin as the language of government, reflecting the new capital's Greek milieu. By that time, too, the long struggle between Christianity and paganism was drawing to a close. A landmark came in 529, when the emperor Justinian closed the last major stronghold of pagan philosophy, the venerable Platonic Academy in Athens. There

Neoplatonist writers and teachers had struggled to stem the Christian tide by developing and codifying Platonic doctrine.*

A century after Justinian closed the Platonic Academy, the Dark Age of Byzantium began. For the next 150 years, Byzantium suffered a break in its secular traditions of cultivated literacy and higher education in the pagan classics. The remaining academies closed, and no longer did Byzantine historians, for example, schooled in the craft of Herodotus and Thucydides, practice their reasoned inquiries into human activities. Pressed in the east by the Arab conquests that followed the rise of Islam and in the north by the incursions of Slavs into the Balkans as far as southern Greece itself, the Byzantines lacked the resources, the leisure, and above all the will to indulge in such pursuits.

Still, there is dark, and there is dark. While classical learning died off in the West, in Byzantium it merely lay ill, ignored and unloved by a society in desperate need of the unity and simple comfort that Christianity offered. Even during Byzantium's Dark Age, which began later and ended earlier than the West's, a strong central state survived, which cannot be said of the West. Homer, Aeschylus, Sophocles, Herodotus, Thucydides, Plato, Aristotle, and the other ancient authors continued to be read in school. They may also have been taught privately on a higher level by a handful of learned individuals, though no names of any such teachers survive. Meanwhile, like Italian, spoken Greek had long been evolving into simpler forms: reading and especially writing

---

* Platonism refers to the ideas of Plato, while Neoplatonism refers to the interpretation and augmentation of Plato's ideas by later philosophers. Often described as "emanationist," Platonic and Neoplatonic theory hold that meaning emanates from a single divine source, that the material world is unreal, and that true reality resides in immaterial "forms" or "ideas." Plato also taught that the soul is immortal. Plato and his later interpreters had a huge impact on the development of Christian theology.

ancient Greek required hard study even for Byzantines who were native Greek-speakers. Byzantine humanists were always a tiny minority. Even at the best of times, the leisure to pursue the Outside Wisdom was reserved for wealthy elites. In the Dark Age, if the humanists were there at all, their numbers were so small as to have left no impression.*

Despite the breakdown in higher education, Homer was always "the poet" to Byzantine schoolchildren—and his works, the beginnings of Western literature, survive today because they stayed on the Byzantine educational curriculum. The same holds true for other ancient Greek authors. Like the bones of dinosaurs, ancient Greek literature survived by becoming fossilized.

The end of the Dark Age and the revival of interest in ancient Greek learning came during a period of expansion and renewed prosperity that for convenience (and in homage to Sir Steven) we'll call the First Byzantine Renaissance.† Byzantinists know it as the Macedonian Renaissance, after the imperial dynasty that presided over it.

THE FIRST BYZANTINE RENAISSANCE

This was the age in which visitors such as Liudprand of Cremona beheld with awe the throne of Byzantine emperors. Byzantine prestige provided the model of imperial Christian

---

* The continuity of classical literature during the Dark Age remains a controversial question in Byzantine studies. Little is known, and much remains speculative. A few leading scholars have argued that the break was severe. Yet, it seems hard to believe that the mastery of ancient Greek demonstrated by the Byzantine humanists of the ninth century could have arisen from a complete void.
† Sir Steven Runciman, who until his death in 2000 was the grand old man of English Byzantinists. His book *The Last Byzantine Renaissance* was mentioned in the Prologue.

rule for the West, even if Western kings like Otto the Great chafed to outdo it. Byzantium was also an art school, a repository of techniques old and new, lost or never known, that the West now began discovering. From Hungary and Austria to Spain and Portugal, from Sicily and Naples to Britain and France, Byzantine artists (and art objects) traveled to European courts. With them came precious knowledge of mosaic, painting, carving, book illumination, and other techniques. Cloisonné enamel came to Limoges from Byzantium.

Within a newly confident, outward-looking Byzantine society, secular learning and Christian piety now embarked upon the period of their closest and most fruitful partnership. An aristocratic mastery of classical Greek literary style reasserted itself as the criterion for service in the imperial bureaucracy (Byzantium's overeducated civil servants are often compared to the Confucian mandarins of imperial China). Byzantium's historians again took up the pen, doing their utmost to imitate the dense, rationalistic Thucydidean style. The scribes and scholars of this era preserved everything we have of ancient Greek literature, for the oldest surviving manuscripts were copied in these years. The collaboration also resulted in Orthodoxy's farthest-reaching victory, the conversion of the eastern and southern Slavs.

In the eleventh century, internal and external difficulties again beset the empire. Weakened by social divisions that the strong emperors of the Macedonian era had held in check, Byzantium suddenly faced incursions by fierce enemies on all its borders. Petchenegs raided from the north; Normans (still just Frangoi to the Byzantines) invaded from southern Italy; and the populous Seljuk Turks, in the process of displacing the Arabs as leaders of the Islamic world, began pouring into Asia Minor from the east.*

Desperate measures ensued, and under the inspired leadership of a brilliant emperor, Alexius I Comnenus, who founded a new imperial dynasty in the late eleventh century, the empire managed to survive. Much was owed to Alexius' fortitude and determination, as his talented daughter and chronicler, the historian Anna Comnena, makes clear in her paean to him, the *Alexiad*. On the run and cobbling together one rabble army after another from scratch, Alexius endured a series of blistering thrashings at the hands of the Normans. Much was owed also to his skillful negotiations with the Venetians, former Byzantine subjects from whom Alexius secured military aid in exchange for valuable trade privileges in Constantinople. It must have seemed like a winning proposition then, and no doubt it was, although at a time not too far distant the Venetians would extract their pound of flesh, and more, from the empire's flagging body.

Survival would exact another price, as the partnership between secular learning and Christian piety, between reason and faith, began to crumble under the burden of social and military disintegration. Taking advantage of the prevailing uncertainty, and of the monks' traditional suspicion of the humanist intellectuals, Alexius browbeat a reluctant church administration into condemning a critic of his, the philosopher John Italus, for heretical Neoplatonic beliefs. Other such trials would follow. Historians have associated them with an upsurge of mysticism in the Byzantine monastic community. The example of John Italus weighed heavily on Byzantine humanists of succeeding generations, and for

---

* A loose confederation of Turkic tribes that had migrated westward from Central Asia, the Seljuks ruled from Baghdad.

centuries his fate essentially closed the door on the independent pursuit of Greek philosophical ideas within Byzantine society.

The stand taken against such inquiry by Byzantium's powerful monks was soon reinforced by a succession of historical circumstances that further stressed the empire's already tattered social fabric. The worst of these was the Fourth Crusade, when the Latins occupied Constantinople for over half a century. Under the house of Paleologos the Byzantines recovered some of their morale with their capital in 1261, and for a few short decades Athens and Jerusalem found harmony again.

Then, as Seljuk power waned around the turn of the fourteenth century, an aggressive new Turkish power arose along the Byzantine border in western Asia Minor. Named for its founder, Osman, the growing Osmanli or Ottoman state soon pushed the Byzantines onto the defensive for the last time.

THE LAST BYZANTINE RENAISSANCE

Several times in the fourteenth century, crippling civil wars wracked the dwindling Byzantine empire. Often there were multiple claimants to the throne, with the Venetians and Genoese each sponsoring their own competing members of the Paleologan dynasty, and the Turks acting as kingmakers. In strategic terms, the last part of Byzantine history makes a dreary tale, as Genoese, Venetians, Turks, and others contentiously scavenged what they could from the remains of the empire.

Paradoxically, Byzantium's culture seemed to flower more insistently each time its military power was pruned back. This defiant cultural florescence was the Paleologan or Last Byzantine Renaissance, in which Theodore Metochites played such an important part. We have now described a circle, back to the springboard from which Byzantium's humanists launched the ancient Greek classics on their westward trajectory.

In the century or so before the fall of Constantinople, Theodore Metochites and his successors made a partial comeback within Byzantium. Yet, this time there would be no fruitful partnership with the monks. In the mid-fourteenth century, even as the humanists gathered momentum, the monks enjoyed their own renewal. It deliberately excluded the literary humanism of Metochites' intellectual heirs. Championed by the monks, a spiritual resurgence ultimately invigorated the whole Byzantine church, whose authority and power seemed to grow as those of the imperial government diminished. This great awakening is known as Hesychasm, and it, too, was a vital part of the Last Byzantine Renaissance.

The name comes from the Greek noun *hesychia,* originally simply "quiet," later "holy quiet," "peace," and "solitude" rolled into one; the Hesychast monks believed that meditation with controlled breathing and repetitious prayer could lead to *theosis,* "divinification," mystical union with the Godhead, bathing its practitioners in the same divine light that had bathed Christ at Mt. Tabor in the transfiguration. The Hesychasts would eventually win dominance of the Orthodox church, and religious scholars today view their movement as the last major phase in the development of Orthodox theology.

Byzantium's humanists found themselves once again opposed by its monks, this time in the monks' new Hesychast incarnation. They boldly challenged the monks in a bitter public dispute that historians call the Hesychast controversy.

The humanists were more conscious of shared history and eventually became more open to the West, which reciprocated with a flattering interest in their beloved ancient literature. Many would convert to Catholicism. To them, Christian solidarity seemed the reasonable, obvious—indeed only—way to escape political extinction at Turkish hands, and appeared to be attainable only if the Orthodox church was willing to compromise with the Catholics.

But they were out of step with the Byzantine mainstream and its champions, the monks. A devout people with its back to the wall can be pushed deeper and deeper into hardening religious nativism, in the end even preferring national suicide to religious compromise. This is what happened to the Byzantines. In that sense, Byzantium chose its fate. Military conquest by the Turks was less of an evil than spiritual submission to the hated Catholics. Without strict adherence to Orthodoxy there could be no hope of spiritual salvation, and spiritual salvation came before political survival.

As their empire edged closer to extinction, the Hesychasts and the humanists became often bitter ideological enemies, in a spectacular clash of values and beliefs that frequently spilled over into politics. It was not a simple situation, and much of the time there were no clearly marked lines of separation between the factions. There was much common ground. Both were patriots who wished to save Byzantium and its heritage. The question, inevitably, became which heritage, classical or Christian, and at what price? With tragic inexorability, the antagonists came to act as if the price of survival for one tradition must be the death of the other.

Now we can grasp Theodore Metochites' ultimate significance. His life, which lasted from 1270 to 1332, spanned the years of good morale, the last hurrah that came with Constantinople's recovery. Metochites lived during the last historical moment when Athens and Jerusalem would coexist peacefully with each other in Byzantine civilization.

In the decades after Metochites' death, what was originally a doctrinal dispute snowballed into a culture war to the death. At times the monks and humanists seemed to put their differences aside, but more often they ignored the common ground and treated each other with contemptuous inflexibility. Under the stresses of the looming Turkish conquest, the great rift between the pagan Greek and Christian Greek traditions—a fault line that rumbled ominously through Byzantium for long centuries—burst to the surface with a vengeance. The Hesychast controversy contributed to the civil wars of the mid-fourteenth century, at a time when unity was Byzantium's only hope of hanging on against the Turks.

Yet, this very tension drove the gears that spread Byzantine influences abroad, even as the Turks closed in at home. For this reason, the Hesychast controversy proved as fertile for us as it was destructive for the Byzantines. That strange and complex process lies at the heart of the story that follows, as the Byzantine champions of Athens and Jerusalem each found new horizons beyond a dying empire.

CHAPTER THREE

HOW PETRARCH AND BOCCACCIO FLUNKED GREEK

The Byzantine humanist who triggered the Hesychast controversy was a brilliant but sharp-tongued Greek from southern Italy named Barlaam. An Orthodox monk himself (though he later converted to Catholicism), Barlaam was also thoroughly versed in the classics, an astronomer and mathematician as well as a philosopher and theologian. Unfortunately for him, his formidable learning was coupled with an arrogant, sarcastic manner, so caustic at times that he put off even his friends and allies.

Born about 1290 in Calabria in southern Italy, Barlaam came to Constantinople in the 1320s.* His learning immediately won him a wide reputation and a post as abbot of an important monastery. In 1334, two Catholic missionary bishops in Constantinople on their way from Genoa to the Crimea challenged the patriarch to a public disputation.

---

* Greek dialects are still spoken in isolated pockets of southern Italy, which retained its Byzantine culture long after being lost to the empire.

Such debates were a common and favorite spectacle. Not willing to take on the bishops himself, the patriarch turned to Barlaam.

Barlaam's assignment was to defend the Orthodox position that the Holy Spirit proceeded only from the Father and not from the Son. He chose an approach that was aggressively rationalistic, invoking Aristotelian logic to argue that matters concerning God could never actually be demonstrated but could only be rationally inferred. Even at the time, Barlaam's rationalism antagonized some in the crowd; afterward he wrote several tracts in the same vein.

Barlaam's arguments drew the attention of a stern Hesychast monk named Gregory Palamas. In particular, Barlaam's use of pagan philosophy—which Palamas likened to snake poison—inflamed Palamas, who attacked Barlaam in tracts of his own. The problem with Barlaam's rational position was that although he meant it to refute the Catholics, it went equally against the beliefs of the Orthodox. In Barlaam's hands, Aristotelian rationalism was a double-edged sword.

Provoked, Barlaam now loosed his considerable powers of invective not merely on Palamas, which he might have gotten away with, but on Hesychasm itself and, most outrageously, on the revered monks of Mt. Athos, the community of monasteries in northern Greece where Hesychasm was strongest.* The Hesychasts' meditative practices included gazing at their navels as a way of focusing their contemplative powers. Barlaam singled out this practice for his derision, calling the monks *omphalopsychoi*, which might be loosely translated as "navelheads." He also attacked them on

---

* The reader will find a brief description and history of Mt. Athos in Chapter Twelve.

doctrinal grounds. Palamas leapt to the Hesychasts' defense, incidentally sharpening Hesychast doctrine as he defended it against Barlaam's attacks.

In responding to Barlaam, Palamas drew an important distinction between God's "essence" and His "energy." This distinction, implicit in earlier Orthodox theology but never fully ironed out, was necessary in order to defend the Hesychasts' mystical approach, because to suggest the possibility of human participation in God's essence would be heretical. It was not reason that was the key to enlightenment, Palamas' argument went, but the possibility of partaking in God's divine energy directly, through meditation, controlled breathing, and repetitive prayer. God could indeed be demonstrated, Palamas said, but not rationally known, experienced but not articulated—roughly the reverse of the position taken by the rational Barlaam and his followers. Posing mystical spirituality against human reason, this balanced antithesis of belief was the knot at the heart of the matter.

BARLAAM, BOCCACCIO, AND PETRARCH

At that point, perhaps partly to defuse a touchy situation, the emperor Andronicus III sent Barlaam on his first diplomatic mission west. The emperor's goal was military aid against the Turks, not a new Crusade (by this time, the Byzantines had had quite enough of Crusades) but an expedition of professional soldiers from the West. Barlaam's first stop was Naples, where he got on well at the humanist court of the Neapolitan king Robert the Wise, a curious and intelligent patron of culture whose entourage included the Florentine expatriate writer Boccaccio. Arriving toward the end of spring, Barlaam stayed for a few weeks before moving on to Paris and the French court, and finally to the papal curia at Avignon, where the pope kept his shaky grip on power with French support.*

The price the Greeks wished to avoid paying for aid was submission to the pope. Union, possibly; outright submission was out of the question. But how one without the other?

Barlaam brought his own plan for resolving this dilemma. A long address to the pope in Latin, it aptly summarized the whole intractable situation. The Orthodox position was (and still is, for that matter) that the pope may be first in prestige among Christian bishops, but he is not the final authority: they allow him primacy, in other words, but not supremacy. The Orthodox have always held that important issues must be decided by a council of bishops, like those held in the early centuries of the Christian era. But by the fourteenth century that era was long over, and the popes were accustomed to unchallenged rule in the Western church.

Barlaam's proposal was to call a joint church council in the East, in Greek territory, with representation by the Orthodox patriarchs and papal envoys. There was no other way, Barlaam argued, that the Greek populace would accept a unionist decree. And before anything else the pope must press for an expedition to clear the Turks from Asia Minor. Yet, constrained by his own dicey political situation, the pope could never make the first concession—as Barlaam must have known. In one form or another, over the rest of Byzantium's life this same spin cycle would make the issue of Western aid into an ongoing farce: neither side would deliver what the other demanded before being promised what the other side couldn't deliver anyway.

---

* Driven out of Rome by factional violence, the papacy resided at Avignon from 1309 to 1377.

So it's hardly surprising that nothing concrete came of Barlaam's negotiations, and that in diplomatic terms the trip was a failure. On top of that, Palamas had taken advantage of Barlaam's absence to strengthen his position. Ever rash, on returning Barlaam accused Palamas of heresy. But at the resulting church council, on June 10, 1341, with the patriarch, the heavy-hitting monks of Mt. Athos, and the loudly anti-Western populace lined up carefully behind him, Palamas had no trouble defending himself. Barlaam was not the only anti-Hesychast around, as events would prove shortly thereafter, but as a south Italian Greek he was suspect. Anti-Western feelings saturated the city; the council ended up condemning Barlaam himself.

A mere five days later, Andronicus III died, leaving a nine-year-old son, John V, plus a number of intimates and other rivals who wished to claim the powerful role of regent until the young emperor came of age.

Barlaam protested briefly against the council's ruling, but he soon realized that it had ended his prospects in the East. His trip two years earlier, however, had won him real friends in the West. In late summer he returned to Italy, stopping in Calabria and then Naples, where once more he was welcomed by King Robert and the humanist circle at the Neapolitan court. The Kingdom of Naples, which included Sicily, was a fascinating melange of Byzantine, Arab, Italian, and Norman influences. Its Norman rulers liked to keep the pot bubbling; Robert the Wise was merely one in a long line of enlightened kings.

Boccaccio, reclaimed by his family after his father's death, had moved back to his native Florence, but Barlaam renewed his relationship with Robert's court librarian, Paul of Perugia. Barlaam helped Paul arrange the Greek manuscripts in Robert's growing library. He also assisted with the

Greek parts of Paul's own book on classical mythology, *The Collections*. The two were rough contemporaries. Paul, Boccaccio wrote, "enjoyed peculiar friendship with Barlaam, and though it could not be based on common interests in Latin culture, it was a means by which Paul drank deeply of Greek lore." Barlaam stayed in Naples from late summer 1341 to early 1342, and sometime during his stay he converted. It was as a Roman Catholic that he journeyed to Avignon in the spring of 1342.

In Avignon waited Petrarch, who worked in close association with the Avignonese papacy, and whose beloved villa was nearby at Vaucluse. It's unclear whether he and Barlaam had met on Barlaam's earlier visit, but they became friends this time at least. Petrarch had managed to get his hands on a Greek manuscript of Homer from a Byzantine diplomat in Avignon. His letters show it to be one of his most prized possessions; he was dying to be able to read it.

Paul of Perugia, Boccaccio, Petrarch—these pioneering humanists were just starting to rediscover the glorious Roman past, along with the Latin authors who had memorialized it. However, it is impossible to read those authors for long without realizing that reading classical Latin literature with any sensitivity requires familiarity with ancient Greek literature.

This goes further than mere influence or inspiration: in self-consciously forging a national literature, classical Latin authors based virtually all their works on Greek models. Virgil is the most commonly cited example, and one obviously of great relevance to Petrarch and Boccaccio. The *Aeneid* (imitating Homer's *Iliad*) was only the last such work Virgil wrote; in his two earlier works, the *Eclogues* and the *Georgics*, Virgil imitated the Greek authors Theocritus and Hesiod, respectively. In his letters and speeches, Cicero, too, whom Petrarch and many of his successors idolized above all, constantly refers to his own Greek models and sources (an important one being, for example, the Athenian orator Demosthenes).

Because these Greek texts survived only in Byzantium, the Italians found themselves cut off from the works that had not only inspired but almost *dictated* the Latin literature they were in the process of rediscovering. Learned Byzantines such as Barlaam offered the only access. "Not infrequently I quote Barlaam," Boccaccio wrote later in *The Genealogy of the Gods*. "Though his body was slight, he stood higher than others in learning. Shall I not do well to trust him, particularly in all that pertains to Greek?"

Barlaam stayed in Avignon from mid-May to mid-November 1342. He went on the curia's payroll in August, receiving fifty-three florins and twenty shillings for eighty-one days' "lecturing in Greek in the curia." This probably refers to the famous lessons he gave Petrarch. However, it turned out there was little time, for at Petrarch's own request, Barlaam was given a bishopric in Gerace in Calabria, far to the south.

Time wasn't the only factor. Lectures in Eastern languages were not unknown at the curia, but ancient Greek is difficult. Without the teaching aids that eventually became common, such as grammar books, exercises, vocabulary lists, and above all bilingual Greek and Latin texts (which later humanists would particularly come to favor), the odds were stacked against Petrarch. "I wasn't so lucky as to learn Greek," he wrote. "I'd thrown myself into the work with eager hope and keen desire, but the newness of a strange tongue and the early departure of my teacher frustrated me in my purpose."

After several unhappy years in Gerace and a brief and even more unhappy visit to Constantinople on behalf of the pope, Barlaam returned for a third time to Avignon in 1347.

He gave more lessons to Petrarch, but this visit, again of only six months' duration, was also too short to be productive. Boccaccio, urged on by Petrarch, would have slightly better luck in the 1350s, under the tutelage of Barlaam's student Leonzio Pilato, who had also briefly tutored Petrarch. Pilato, like Barlaam a Calabrian Greek who had sojourned in Constantinople and Thessalonica, was a less than ideal teacher—in Boccaccio's words, "a man of uncouth appearance, ugly features, long beard, and black hair, forever lost in thought, rough in manners and behavior."

For almost three years, according to an impressively game Boccaccio, they stumbled through Homer together in Greek. Boccaccio even secured for Pilato a position teaching Greek in Florence in the early 1360s, but nothing came of it. It was simply too early for interest to have spread from standouts such as Petrarch and Boccaccio, Renaissance humanism's founders, after all, to their followers. The Italian humanists needed the pressure of greater numbers—and they needed, too, a teacher of Greek who could supply real teaching and the deep inspiration that goes with it. Both were coming, but not for a while yet.

CYDONES TRANSLATES THOMAS AQUINAS

Barlaam, despite his abrasiveness, was missed by Byzantium's younger intellectuals. In 1347, the year that he made his second attempt with Petrarch, Barlaam entered into a brief correspondence on theological matters with a talented young Byzantine named Demetrius Cydones, whom he had met on his last visit to Constantinople.

When he met Barlaam, Cydones had recently arrived in Constantinople to seek his fortune. In his early twenties, he had been born to a noble and recently impoverished family in Thessalonica, the empire's second city. His father, an ally of Andronicus III, had undertaken several sensitive diplomatic missions for the emperor, but Andronicus had died only days after the council condemning Barlaam had adjourned. A bloody and exhausting six-year civil war ensued between Andronicus' best friend and prime minister, John Cantacuzenos, and an alliance between the patriarch and Andronicus' widow, Anne of Savoy, an unpopular Western princess who managed to hold power in Constantinople for much of the war's duration. Cantacuzenos eventually won the war, although the political infighting festered for decades. Cydones' family had supported Cantacuzenos but lost everything in violent riots in Thessalonica against Cantacuzenos' side.

Cydones was a master of the flowery classical rhetoric prized by the aristocratic Byzantine literati, and in a letter to Barlaam after Barlaam's departure he laments the void it left in Constantinople's intellectual circles. There follow pages and pages of detailed theological discussion; Cydones is clearly eager for Barlaam's reply. Barlaam, still arguing passionately for union between the two churches, died in spring 1348, shortly after writing it. By that time Cydones had entered the service of the victorious Cantacuzenos, who had had himself crowned as John VI soon after winning the civil war.

The new emperor was a complex and subtle man whose career embraced a bundle of contradictions. Grimly realistic politician, brilliant statesman, able general, aristocratic magnate, devout Hesychast, accomplished man of letters— Cantacuzenos was immune to the obscurantism that so often attached itself to Hesychast beliefs, as his earlier patronage of Barlaam shows. A book lover, Cantacuzenos opened himself wide to theological speculation, even searched it out. When forced from office less than a decade later, he would become a monk and devote himself to literature in the classical mode, writing a history of his times in the style of Thucydides. The Hesychasts' suspicions notwithstanding, imitation of classical Greek authors was always the height of literary aspiration for educated Byzantines, and Cydones, too, would win great fame for his mastery of it.

Cydones began his employment as the emperor's chief secretary in charge of appointments, and rapidly made himself indispensable as both secretary and friend. Brilliant and prolific (his surviving letters, some 450 of them, take up three volumes of Greek and are a major historical source for late-fourteenth-century Byzantium), Cydones would walk in Barlaam's anti-Hesychast footsteps. In contrast with Barlaam's heavy tread, Cydones' humanist slippers rustled softly through the corridors of power, even in the palace of a confirmed Hesychast such as Cantacuzenos. In a fifty-odd-year political career, Demetrius Cydones stayed light on his feet and nimble in dodging blows from the shadows.

Not all would be so lucky, and there were many others in the humanist camp who shared fates similar to Barlaam's. The Hesychasts had another friend of Barlaam's excommunicated, the erudite Simon Atumano, who made his way west and converted to Catholicism in time to succeed his friend as bishop of Gerace; also like Barlaam, he briefly but unsuccessfully tutored some Italians in ancient Greek. The theologian Gregory Akindynos, a friend of both Barlaam and Palamas, began by trying to mediate between them but was soon persuaded on purely theological grounds to support Barlaam.

Akindynos was more typical of the early anti-Hesychasts than Barlaam and Atumano, in that his wide classical learning did not instill in him any affinity for the Latins. Condemned with Barlaam in 1341 and excommunicated by another church council in 1347, Akindynos went into exile in the East and died soon afterward. Leadership of the anti-Hesychast group then fell to the polymath and historian Nicephoras Gregoras, also no friend of the Latins, who was condemned by a church council in 1351 and placed under house arrest in Constantinople.

It was at this point—with the civil war over, Cantacuzenos still in power, and Palamas' orthodoxy confirmed by several church councils—that Palamas can be considered to have won the controversy. From now on Hesychasts dominated the official structure of the Byzantine Orthodox Church. When Palamas died in 1358, he was widely mourned and quickly canonized; when Gregoras died sometime around 1360, his corpse was dragged through the city's streets to be jeered at by the devout populace.

Byzantium had now made its choice. After long centuries, it had rejected the Outside Wisdom. Palamas' victory had turned Barlaam away from Byzantium and toward the West, where his humanism was welcomed, not condemned. The pattern would repeat itself in coming decades, as Byzantine humanists found themselves less and less in sympathy with the direction Byzantium had chosen.

Only after Hesychasm's victory was secure and it rose to control the church did humanistic opposition to it become more firmly associated with Western sympathies. Demetrius Cydones illustrates this, for his anti-Hesychasm—already clear in his letters to Barlaam in the 1340s—preceded his interest in the West, which arose after the church council that endorsed Hesychasm in 1351.

His "Defense of His Own Faith," written later, after his conversion to Catholicism, tells the story. In conducting the emperor's affairs, Cydones found himself encountering the

Westerners on a daily basis. Merchants especially, but also diplomats, papal legates, mercenaries, even the odd touring noble—the West's presence at the imperial court had grown insistent. Deluged by petitions for this or that imperial favor, each of which had to be translated from Latin, Cydones soon grew frustrated with the lame attempts of the court translators to keep up with it all. He realized he had little choice but to learn Latin himself. Among the Western presence in Constantinople were Franciscan and Dominican friars, and it was a Dominican whom he knew from the Genoese quarter at Pera, across the Golden Horn, that Cydones found to instruct him.

Despite his heavy workload, Cydones tells us, he made rapid progress (like Barlaam, he didn't suffer from false modesty), and soon he was as fluent "as if trained by my parents from childhood." So to give him something he could really get his teeth into, his delighted teacher presented him with "a little book" to work on, the *Summa Contra Gentiles* of Thomas Aquinas, one of two works in which Aquinas lays out his plan for reconciling the faith of the theologians with the reason of the philosophers.* Reading the West's Angelic Doctor was like coming home, Cydones tells us, and it ultimately set him on the path to conversion. "Having tasted the lotus," he says, he couldn't hold back; Aquinas came as a progressive revelation as he read and translated further. As he stacked the Latins up against the Greeks who attempted to refute them, it was the Greeks who seemed to come up short, blindly parroting old arguments that didn't address the detailed and sophisticated reasoning of a writer such as Aquinas.

---

* The title can be translated as *Summary Against the Gentiles*. The other work was the *Summa Theologiae*, or *Summary of Theology*.

In 1353, by which time he himself had been elevated to the position of prime minister, Cydones decided to write out a translation of the whole book. In doing so he caused quite a stir, for he made no secret of his new fascination. The emperor himself took an interest, supporting Cydones' efforts as beneficial to Byzantine culture—and of course to Cantacuzenos' own avid theological curiosity.

The last part of Cydones' manuscript of the translation, written out by his secretary with notes in Cydones' own hand, survives in the Vatican library. At the end, Cydones left a celebratory note in Latin, no less. Its immediacy (not to mention its sentiment, familiar to any classics student) spans centuries: "The book is finished, may praise and glory be to Christ. Demetrius of Thessalonika, servant of Christ, translated this book from Latin into Greek. He worked at it for one year, finishing at 3 P.M., December 24, 1354."

Only a month before, Cantacuzenos had abdicated in favor of John V, now in his early twenties and married to Cantacuzenos' daughter Helena. With time on his hands now, Cydones says, Cantacuzenos copied out the manuscript himself, which certainly must have taken some effort. He also passed it on to others, creating a most unexpected ripple of Thomism in the highest circles of Byzantine power.

In conjunction with his younger brother Prochorus, whom (though he doesn't say) it seems likely he may have tutored in Latin himself, Cydones went on to make Greek translations of many of Aquinas' works, as well as works of various other Latin theologians. Both made translations of St. Augustine, and Prochorus also translated some of Boethius' theological writings. Of the two, Prochorus Cydones was the more strident anti-Hesychast, although he himself was a monk in one of the monasteries of Mt. Athos and (unlike Demetrius) never converted to Catholicism. Demetrius would not always be able to shield him from persecution, and the Hesychasts succeeded in having Prochorus anathematized in 1368. He went into exile and died shortly thereafter. Demetrius himself would be similarly anathematized, but only after his own death.

The Cydones brothers' enthusiasm for Aquinas reveals the temperament that the Byzantine humanists shared with the Catholics, whose church was moving toward rationalism just as the Orthodox church was moving toward mysticism. Like Boethius so long before, Aquinas strove above all to find a place for Aristotelian rationalism in Christian faith. As the Hesychasts well knew, Aquinas' thought had recently been officially embraced by the pope. Just as Hesychasm completed Orthodoxy, so did Thomism complete Catholicism; Palamas and Aquinas were mirror images of each other.

Demetrius Cydones' translation work gave him not only a growing enthusiasm for Aquinas and Catholic theology but also a new receptivity to the Westerners with whom he increasingly came in contact. His home became a gathering place for Westerners who had texts that needed translation. For their part, the Frangoi were pleased to be seen in a new light, to show off achievements with which no Byzantine would earlier have been willing to credit them. "For the whole race," says Cydones, "was judged only by the sojourners, and anyone speaking of things Latin would mention nothing more than sails, oars, and other things needed for a sea journey." Byzantines, he continues, had carried over the old Greek habit of "dividing all mankind into Hellenes and barbarians, with the barbarians assumed to be stupid and gauche."

Now the barbarians appeared to have pulled ahead, and in theology, the queen of the sciences, no less. Entranced by the vigor of the new Latin theology, Cydones embarked on a determined crusade to break down his countrymen's ancient prejudice—and, like Barlaam before him, to effect the all-important reconciliation between the two churches. He managed to keep his place despite Cantacuzenos' fall from power and soon made himself equally indispensable to the new emperor, John V Paleologus, who held power on and off over the next few decades, his own rule disturbed by periodic struggles with his sons. Cydones remained in office most of that time, eventually becoming the Byzantines' most respected elder statesman. A trip to Venice in 1353 was his first venture abroad; eventually, others would follow as he deepened his contacts in Venice, in Rome, and finally in Florence.

Engrossed in politics, diplomacy, and his Thomistic studies, Cydones let a further fifteen years go by before returning to Italy; in the interim, he converted to Catholicism. In 1369 he journeyed to Rome with John V, who at Cydones' urging now took the drastic step of himself professing the Catholic faith in hopes of papal support against the Turks.

It is a reflection of John's general weasliness that his conversion was completely ignored by the Orthodox hierarchy at home in Constantinople, and indeed by pretty much everyone else, too. For his part, Cydones enjoyed hobnobbing at the papal curia, but his letters of the period teeter between hope and despair when it came to the ever elusive goal of Western aid. Western promises had become so empty, he writes at one point, that "even the Turks ask with laughter if anyone has word of the expedition."

It's unlikely there was much the West could do anyway. In retrospect the point of no return was probably reached sometime around the middle of the century, with the dreadful civil war between Cantacuzenos and Anne of Savoy; after that, it seems impossible that any mere expeditionary force could have turned back the rising power of the Ottomans, who continued conquering more and more lands in Asia Minor and, after 1347, in Europe as well.

The thirty-odd-year reign of John V Paleologos saw a rapid and catastrophic loss of territory to the Turkish juggernaut, which rolled right into the Balkans, smashing the culturally Byzantinized kingdoms of Serbia and Bulgaria. Ottoman rule in the Balkans would last until the modern period. By the 1380s, little remained of the Byzantine "empire" but a few cities and their environs: Constantinople, Thessalonica, Trebizond, bits and pieces of the Peloponnesus. The amazing thing is that Byzantines held on as long as they did.

After a close call when the Ottoman sultan Bayezid blockaded Constantinople for eight years starting in 1394, Byzantium would owe its half-century reprieve only to the fearsome Mongol conqueror Tamerlane. He devastated Bayezid's army at Ankara in 1402 before withdrawing to the East, where he died a few years later. The Ottomans' brutal defeat at Ankara proved a temporary setback, but—for the survival of Greek literature—a crucial one. As the Turks regrouped, siege craft would again rumble toward the big walls of the Queen of Cities.

IN VENICE WITH CHRYSOLORAS

For two decades, as the Turkish tide washed into the Balkans, political concerns thwarted Cydones' oft-expressed desire to return to the West. Throughout his letters—always, modern scholars point out, written with an eye toward publication—he mentions or congratulates friends, younger men who had made overtures to the West and its culture, either learning

Latin or actually traveling themselves to Italy or France. Plans for his own return were continually laid and put off. Finally, by the late 1380s, conditions for a trip began improving, as Cydones' advancing age (he was now in his mid-sixties) and his open affection for John's ambitious if loyal son Manuel combined to reduce his involvement at court. In late 1389, Cydones set out for Venice, again to seek aid against the Turks.

Cydones' second trip to Venice lasted just under a year and a half, during which he cemented his ties to this most Byzantine-flavored of Italian cities. In January 1391, a few months before Cydones ended his sojourn, the Venetian doge Antonio Venerio granted him honorary citizenship. The document, still in the Venetian state archives, confers upon "the noble and extraordinarily wise man, Lord Demetrius Cydones, now resident among the Venetians . . . all the rights, benefits, immunities, and honors now enjoyed by other Venetian citizens."

Perhaps, if they had known the eventual fruits of Demetrius' residence among them, the Venetians might have gone even further. Cydones' traveling companion was his student, friend, and compatriot Manuel Chrysoloras, and it was sometime in 1390 that Cydones put Chrysoloras in touch with an Italian, Roberto Rossi, who wished to learn some Greek. Barlaam may have failed with Petrarch, but over the succeeding decades the remarkable Manuel Chrysoloras would redeem that failure, and much more.

The chances for an Italian seeking to learn Greek were becoming better than in Petrarch's and Boccaccio's day, a generation or two earlier. For one thing, it was someone like Rossi who now had the desire: not a pioneering genius, but a more representative figure, bright and talented certainly but

one of a growing crowd. This development is directly attrib-
utable to one man, the Florentine chancellor and renowned
humanist teacher Coluccio Salutati.

Greekless himself, and destined to remain so despite his
later efforts, Salutati nonetheless inspired an energetic enthusiasm for Greek literature among the wide circle of trendy
young intellectuals in Florence who looked on him as their
mentor. Rossi was one of this group of young Florentines
(actually Rossi himelf was not so young; around forty, he was
Chrysoloras' rough contemporary). Historians believe that it
was at Salutati's urging that Rossi came to Venice in the first
place, expressly to seek out instruction from either Cydones
or Chrysoloras, both of whom were well known. Rossi would
probably have told the two Byzantines about Salutati; on returning to Florence, he certainly told Salutati all about them.
Be that as it may, Cydones arranged for Rossi's lessons, and
those lessons were the first link between Chrysoloras and
Florence—an association that would, in the end, become legendary.

Cydones, Chrysoloras, and Rossi all went home in 1391,
the two Byzantines to Constantinople and Rossi to Florence.
For the aging Cydones, the next few years seem to have been
rewarding ones. Manuel II Paleologos—a Platonic "philosopher king," Cydones calls him in a congratulatory letter—
had succeeded to the throne shortly before Cydones'
departure from Venice. Once again taking a hand in affairs of
state, Cydones immersed himself in Manuel's desperate attempts to treat with the Turks.

Meanwhile, back in Florence, Rossi gave Chrysoloras
enthusiastic reviews both to his teacher Salutati and to his
fellow students in Salutati's circle. One of them, Jacopo
Angeli da Scarperia, eventually grew so excited by Rossi's

tales that in 1395 he took the simplest step he could to emu-late him—simple, maybe, but dangerous, for the Turks were even then laying siege to the city. Yet, Angeli possessed bold-ness to match his enthusiasm. He went to Constantinople to find Chrysoloras and learn Greek.

CHAPTER FOUR

CHRYSOLORAS IN FLORENCE

acopo Angeli da Scarperia had been born in a small town north of Florence around 1360. His father had died when Angeli was a boy, and his mother had brought him to the city, where she had remarried. It isn't known how he first came to Salutati's attention, but the older man had taken a special liking to Angeli early on. Though never a humanist of the first rank, the affable Angeli would remain one of Salutati's favorite pupils, and received the honor of being asked to stand as godfather for one of Salutati's own children.

Salutati had urged Angeli to make the journey to Constantinople, having already conceived the idea of inviting Chrysoloras to teach in Florence. The plan was for Salutati to lobby Florence's main governing council, the signoria, to issue an official invitation; meanwhile Angeli would do everything he could to tempt Chrysoloras into accepting the offer when it came.

To reach the Byzantine capital, Angeli probably followed the standard route, the same one, for example, the knights of the Fourth Crusade had used nearly two centuries earlier—that is, traveling overland to Venice, from there sailing down the Adriatic coast and thence eastward through the Aegean. We don't know exactly when he left Italy. But he most likely entered Constantinople sometime in the late fall, evading the Turkish blockade of the besieged city. He also almost certainly carried letters of introduction from Salutati and Rossi, along with instructions from Salutati to be on the lookout for alluring manuscripts of ancient Greek works.

The discovery of lost books, usually from monastery libraries, had been a main humanist occupation ever since Petrarch, who had recovered Cicero's seminally important *Letters to Atticus* (in which the Roman author glorifies Greek culture), among other works. Along with the desire to learn ancient Greek, the attraction of acquiring important undiscovered Greek works would play a large role in bringing other Italians to Constantinople in Angeli's footsteps. Many more books would be brought to the West by Chrysoloras and the Byzantine humanist teachers who came in *his* footsteps. A letter survives from Salutati to Angeli in spring 1396, when Angeli had been in the East for several months, in which Salutati gives a list of specific titles and authors he wants Angeli to look for and try to bring back to Florence. In Byzantium as in the West, books were very expensive and hard to find. Each one still had to be laboriously copied by hand; the arrival of printing still lay more than half a century off. Salutati assures Angeli that a sponsor has been found for buying the books, and that whatever money was needed would be rapidly accessible to facilitate speedy purchase.

Arriving in Constantinople in the fall of 1395, Angeli looked up Cydones and Chrysoloras, making a good impression on both older men and beginning his study of Greek with the latter. Chrysoloras introduced Angeli around, and soon the gregarious Italian had struck up friendships with other leading Byzantine humanists and intellectuals. Under Chrysoloras' tutelage, he progressed well in his Greek studies, although it would be some time before he could read Greek without his teacher's assistance. This was only to be expected. Students today commonly use cribs, or helpful translations, well into their third or fourth year of ancient Greek, and often longer if the text is especially difficult, as many are. Such translations weren't available to Angeli—for the simple reason that it would be he and his future fellow students back in Italy who would make most of the first ones.

Along the way, Angeli naturally took every opportunity with his teacher to play up Florence's attractions and Salutati's sterling qualities. In truth, though, Chrysoloras needed little convincing. As will become clear, he had compelling reasons of his own for accepting the offer. The official invitation from the signoria was duly forthcoming, along with a respectable stipend, as Salutati announced happily to Chrysoloras in a letter dated March 1396. Sometime around late summer or early fall that year, Chrysoloras and Angeli left Constantinople for Italy, traveling together with Chrysoloras' old friend Demetrius Cydones. Angeli's highly successful visit to the Byzantine capital had lasted just under a year.

Florence, Salutati, and Civic Humanism

The city that Chrysoloras was traveling to wasn't yet the city familiar to the modern tourist. If transported back in time to admire the Florentine skyline as Chrysoloras would have seen it, the first thing we would notice would be the gaping absence of Brunelleschi's dome; the Duomo or cathedral, under construction since 1296, was still unfinished, its great size having baffled all attempts to design a dome for it. More than two decades would elapse before Brunelleschi would draw up his innovative plans for what would be the first large dome built in Italy since before Boethius' day.

Drawing closer, we might also remark on the city's extraordinary spikiness. Florence had once been a forest of towers. Many were pulled down by the fourteenth century, but earlier paintings of the city make it look like a quiver packed full of arrows. Enough survived to be noticeable, interspersed with the ruined stubs of others. As we entered the central part of the city itself, we would feel shut in by the dark, narrow streets, no more than alleys really, winding through canyons of solid masonry, only occasionally opening onto tiny piazzas and courtyards. This claustrophobic sense would lift slowly during the Renaissance, giving way to broader streets and wide-open public spaces. Already the city fathers had planning on their minds, though the characteristic odors of the medieval city would linger awhile yet. A few months after Chrysoloras got there, Florentine officials fined three residents 10 lire each for failing to dig a cesspool as ordered and instead letting their sewage flow into the street.

Most times, then as now, life was fast and sharp. The marketplace up the street from the Ponte Vecchio was a daily throng of activity, with meat, fish, fruit, vegetables, exotic delicacies, and dry goods all laid out in profusion. Pack-horses and delivery carts vied with shoppers; wealthy men alertly shepherded their elaborately decked-out wives past thieves, gamblers, drunks, and whores. Verbal quips filled the air, punctuated now and then by the clash of steel on steel. It was not a safe place, Florence. It overflowed with energy, which expressed itself in constant factional strife and politi-cal experimentation. After dark a curfew was in effect—being caught out at night could bring a fine or worse.

In winter, when Chrysoloras arrived, life slowed some-what as the damp Tuscan chill settled in the bones. But winter or not, Florence was the most exciting place on earth. Florence's anarchic feel came from the fact that the city was ruled by its people; the towers had been there to protect the politically disenfranchised Florentine nobility from the peo-ple's wrath, until the people pulled them down. Not since classical Athens had such a place existed.

Florence at the moment of Chrysoloras' arrival was in the middle of a long, intoxicating, and ultimately rather dan-gerous flirtation with history. Even the Black Death, which struck repeatedly starting in 1348, had failed to dampen the city's spirit despite cutting down nearly half its population. By the turn of the quattrocento, Florence was poised to be-come, for just a few decades, the undisputed literary and artistic capital of the West. Chrysoloras was about to find himself in a June garden, which he himself would bring to rich harvest. And its prize products would owe their germi-nation to the movement known as humanism. Though simi-lar shoots were sprouting up elsewhere in Italy (in places such as Naples and Padua, for example), it was in Florence that the fruits of humanism ripened first.

Florence was not much of a university town. In this it differed from self-important centers of Scholastic learning such as Paris, Oxford, Bologna, or Padua, where the great universities—the "schools"—had arisen starting in the twelfth century. Founded only in the 1320s, Florence's *studio* (as the Italians called a university) was small and backward—when it existed at all, which it didn't for long stretches of time over the fourteenth century and well into the fifteenth, much to the wealthy Florentines' embarrassment.

At the same time, Florence's wealth was based on activities (such as international banking, which the Florentines basically invented in the fourteenth century, but also manufacture and trade) that encouraged literacy, with the result that its citizens were likely the most literate in Europe. They may have had a poor university, but their elementary education was superb. Besides, Florentines could easily travel to nearby Bologna or Padua to attend university if they wished. And even at these universities, with their professional outlooks (they specialized in law and medicine, respectively), Scholasticism hadn't attained the monopoly it enjoyed in the northern schools such as Paris and Oxford. It was a northern European invention anyway, as has often been observed, an import from Paris and Oxford that had never sat comfortably in Italy in the first place. In Florence it was less comfortable still.

All this made Italy in general and Florence in particular a promising place for literary and intellectual innovation. It was natural for that innovation to be inspired by Italy's rich Roman past, which remained immediate not just in the pages of Virgil and Cicero but more visibly in the ancient ruins present in many Italian cities and towns. In Florence's case, the city's Roman foundation would play a big role in its not inconsiderable humanistic self-regard.

In 1375, the year of Boccaccio's death, Coluccio Salutati was appointed chancellor of Florence. Petrarch himself, Salutati's correspondent and mentor, had died the year before. Petrarch was the first to recover the idea of *humanitas,* the ancient Roman idea that carefully tended, well-rounded literacy can enhance one's humanity. But while Petrarch mentions *humanitas* a number of times in his writings, it was Salutati who really turned it into the programmatic catchword that it eventually became.

Born in 1331 in the Tuscan town of Stignano, Salutati had studied law in Bologna as a young man, but he'd soon abandoned legal studies in favor of an apprenticeship as a notary. His notarial skills had served him well, combined of course with his love of classical literature, and he'd been chancellor in several other towns before accepting the position in Florence. A chancellor (*cancelarius*, or first secretary) was the head of a city's official bureaucracy. In Florence the job was unusually prominent and well paid, and it brought Salutati great wealth, prestige, and power. Salutati would never again leave his adopted city. He served as chancellor until his death in 1406, upon which the city honored him with a magnificent state funeral. Florence's republican constitution ordained that elective offices on the various governing councils be filled only by members of the commercial guilds or business associations, who were also the only ones allowed to vote. In contrast with the enfranchised and often wealthy merchant class, both upper-class "magnates" (the old aristocracy) and lower-class workers were traditionally excluded from official power. But spots on the governing councils could be held only for very short periods, usually just a few months. This meant that Florence's bureaucracy furnished the only continuity in its public administration. As head bureaucrat, for decades Salutati was the city's most recognizable public figure and political leader.

By the 1390s, Salutati had gathered a following of talented younger men, often but not always aristocrats, who emulated his interest in Greco-Roman antiquity. Most of them would study Greek under Chrysoloras, and the two brightest stars among them, Leonardo Bruni and Poggio Braccolini, would succeed Salutati in the office of chancellor. As a humanist, Salutati wasn't alone in his generation. Nor was he the only older Florentine humanist with a following of younger students. But he was certainly the most prominent.

Salutati's prestige and his value to Florence were all the greater because his tenure as chancellor coincided with a series of acute crises for the republic. The gravest threat came precisely in the late 1390s, when Florence faced the military might of its dangerous and aggressive rival Milan. Salutati turned the conflict with Milan into more than just a case of a powerful militaristic city-state waging war against a smaller, less militarized neighbor. Under the autocratic rule of Gian Galeazzo Visconti, Milan stood in sharp contrast to the traditional Florentine values of liberty and republican freedom, values that Salutati forcefully championed in public letters against the Milanese "tyrant."

It was a role Salutati relished, a role much like Winston Churchill's in the early years of the Second World War, with Salutati's widely circulated letters serving the same purpose as Churchill's defiant broadcast speeches. And as with Churchill in the dark days after Dunkirk, stirring rhetoric was Salutati's best—almost his only—weapon. At one point Visconti himself paid tribute to his adversary's eloquence, remarking famously that a single letter from Salutati was worth a thousand horsemen. Despite the vaunted power of Salutati's rhetoric, Florence would be delivered at its moment of peril only by Visconti's sudden, unexpected death in 1402.

The keystone of Salutati's rhetorical campaign against Milan—indeed of his chancellorship as a whole—was the identification of republican Florence with the virtues and values of republican Rome, especially *libertas*. This elaborate propaganda effort was just reaching its climax as Chrysoloras arrived. It ultimately gave birth to a mini-movement of its own, which historians call civic humanism.*

In civic humanism, the Florentines embarked upon Italian humanism's second stage, after its Petrarchan first stage. Civic humanism determined which books Salutati and his followers most wanted to read and write about. Though still ultimately inspired by Petrarch, they took less interest in subjects like poetry, and more in political theory and especially history. The shift arose directly from the sense of civic crisis caused in Florence by the struggle with Milan. So if humanism as a whole made up the larger setting for Chrysoloras' teaching, the birth of civic humanism supplied its immediate context, as Chrysoloras journeyed from besieged Constantinople to embattled Florence at the dawn of the quattrocento.

CHRYSOLORAS' NEW TEACHING

Setting out from the Byzantine capital in late 1396, Cydones, Chrysoloras, and Angeli stopped over in Venice for several months. There the elderly Cydones remained, no doubt happily, as the other two friends continued on the overland leg of their trip, arriving in Florence on February 2, 1397. Welcomed enthusiastically by Salutati and his coterie of younger humanists, Chrysoloras assumed his teaching duties at the Florentine *studio* almost immediately.

For someone who played such a crucial and celebrated role in the history of Western civilization, Manuel Chrysoloras remains a curiously elusive figure. He wrote little. Just a

---

* After Hans Baron, in *The Crisis of the Early Italian Renaissance*.

handful of letters and a few other brief writings survive. Though modern historians have characterized those few works as exceptionally important, they tell us next to nothing about Chrysoloras the man.

What little we know about Chrysoloras comes mostly from the writings of his students, some of whom quite simply idolized him. They describe a man of charm and magnetism, a warm and gifted communicator, widely cultivated if not an unusually learned scholar. He was physically impressive. Though only medium in size, he had a strikingly healthy complexion. Over a reddish beard worn long in the Byzantine style, his eyes suggested an outlook at once grave and lighthearted. In a modern American university, Chrysoloras would be the popular classroom performer rather than the scholarly researcher—but one whose graduate students turn out to be conspicuous for the brilliance of their later achievements, as well as the depth of their teacher's influence on them.

The roster of Chrysoloras' pupils reads like a who's who of early Renaissance humanism. And because his pupils went on to teach their own students, and so on, Chrysoloras' pedagogic legacy spread out and was still dominating the humanist landscape generations after his death.

Chrysoloras' teaching methods were innovative, even revolutionary, yet what's more striking is the way they were so perfectly in tune with the needs and values of the humanist milieu he encountered in Florence.

On a basic level, Chrysoloras boiled down the mind-numbingly complex Greek-language textbooks used in Byzantine classrooms to a clear and concise form, producing an elementary, user-friendly primer of ancient Greek called *Questions*. The title was less original, being the traditional one for such books in Byzantium, but Chrysoloras' *Questions* would remain the Western student's standard introduction to ancient Greek for well over a century. Its radical streamlining of Greek grammar had a huge practical impact. Where one traditional version made just a few years earlier offered Byzantine students fifty-six types of noun to memorize, for example, Chrysoloras' new one reduced it to just ten. A measure of the book's importance is that when printing came along later in the quattrocento, Chrysoloras' *Questions* was among the very first books printed.

That was innovation, and brought great advances in a hands-on, daily-grind kind of way. Revolution came in more profound realms of nuance and sensibility, and is best illustrated by Chrysoloras' approach to the deceptively complex problem of translation. Medieval Scholastic scholars, when they had translated from Greek into Latin at all, had practiced a method called *verbum ad verbum*—literally, "word for word." This is exactly what it sounds like: a mechanical, word-by-word substitution of one language for another. At its best, this resulted in clumsy, graceless Latin. At its worst, as Chrysoloras pointed out, it could change the meaning of the original completely. Chrysoloras abandoned the old method. Instead, he taught his students to stick as closely as possible to the sense of the Greek, but to convert it into Latin that was as elegant, fluent, and idiomatic as the original.*

The Italian humanists—who aspired above all to write perfect if rather sterile Ciceronian Latin—took up the new technique with gusto. It was perfectly in keeping with their literary values, and a logical outgrowth of the humanistic

---

* Some recent scholars have defended the Scholastic translations as being better than the humanists maintained (and even better than the humanists' translations). Regardless of who was better, the humanists had very different aims and interests. The differing aims of the two groups are probably more revealing than a subjective comparison of their skills.

program. Indeed, Salutati probably had similar ideas already, since Cicero himself had also condemned word-for-word translations for their stiffness. Chryoloras' students soon began undertaking humanistic translations on a grand scale, and for the first time accurate and graceful Latin versions of important Greek works started appearing rapidly in the West.

The famed Leonardo Bruni, the most prolific translator among Chrysoloras' students, exemplified the new approach. Commenting on his own criteria in translating Plato, Bruni wrote about the Greek author as if he were a good friend who was still alive: "I translate him in a way that I understand will give him most pleasure. . . . [B]eing the most elegant of writers in the Greek, he will not wish to appear lacking in taste in Latin." Bruni, incidentally, was the first to use the word *translation* (*translatio*, literally "carrying across") in this way, for the rendering of one language into another.

As Salutati had so clearly intuited, Chrysoloras in Florence at the turn of the quattrocento was truly the right man in the right place at the right time—in other words, the perfect teacher for the daunting educational task at hand. This is why Renaissance scholars agree that, despite Salutati's many accomplishments, his greatest contribution to humanism lay simply in bringing Chrysoloras to Florence.

CHRYSOLORAS' STUDENTS IN FLORENCE

Chrysoloras stayed in Florence for only three years, leaving in March 1400. In that short space of time, he ensured that the study of ancient Greek put down permanent roots in the West. His Florentine students represent the first true generation of classical Greek scholars in Western Europe:

- *Leonardo Bruni (1370–1444).* Born in the town of Arezzo (and therefore sometimes known as Aretino), Bruni was the most renowned Florentine humanist of the first half of the quattrocento. Interested mainly in history and political theory, he was the leading exponent of civic humanism.* Bruni's many polished translations include Aristotle's *Politics* and *Ethics,* several *Lives* of illustrious Greeks and Romans by the ancient biographer Plutarch (a favorite of the early humanists, Plutarch would later be a rich source for Shakespeare), and rhetorical works by the Greek orators Demosthenes and Aeschines. Salutati had compared Florence with republican Rome; Bruni extended the comparison to include Athens as well. In 1401 Bruni published his famous encomium *In Praise of the City of Florence,* basing it on Greek models such as Aelius Aristides' encomium of Athens. Later he wrote the pioneer work of Renaissance historiography, *The History of the Florentine People,* in which he revived the critical, secularizing methods of the ancient historians. Like many of his friends, Bruni spent time working at the Vatican, which also became a major center of humanist learning. His humanist skills brought him wealth and celebrity, and like his teacher Salutati he served as Florentine chancellor (from 1427 until his death).

- *Poggio Bracciolini (1380–1459).* Poggio was a teenager when Chrysoloras arrived in Florence, and he may have been too young to be officially included among Chrysoloras' students. He never mastered Greek and

---

* Through Bruni's writings, civic humanism has been credited with influencing the English, American, and French revolutions, among other epoch-making events of the modern world.

was probably more of a young hanger-on than a full-fledged student when Chrysoloras was teaching. Perhaps because of this situation, Poggio hero-worshipped Chrysoloras more than the other Florentines. However, at times he later appears mildly dismissive of Greek learning, which may reveal a touch of sour grapes after his youthful exclusion by the others. Regardless, he was certainly well accepted in Salutati's circle by 1400, winning his spurs as a superb Latinist and (with his older friend Niccolò Niccoli) eventually becoming the most celebrated discoverer of lost Latin manuscripts. Poggio's long and productive humanist career extended into the era when Medici absolutism ended the republican system in Florence. Unusually quarrelsome even for a humanist, he spent most of his career in Rome. He returned to Florence as an old man in 1453, when (following in Salutati's and Bruni's footsteps) he accepted the city's invitation to take up the post of chancellor.

- *Niccolò Niccoli (1364–1437)*. Like Chrysoloras himself, Niccoli wrote next to nothing and therefore remains a rather cryptic character. Yet, it's clear from the writings of his fellow humanists that Niccoli was a highly influential figure of central importance to the movement. Even more quarrelsome than Poggio (which is perhaps why the two of them got along), the eccentric Niccoli was the most avant-garde of the humanists in his attitude of extreme classicism. A bit of a poser, he ostentatiously courted financial ruin in order to devote himself solely to his studies. Unlike Bruni, his other close friend, Niccoli was an aristocrat. Also unlike Bruni, Niccoli shared with Chrysoloras an intense interest in ancient art. An avid book collector, he also pioneered the study of ancient coins, inscriptions, and other artifacts. After his death Niccoli's magnificent book collection became the nucleus of the public library founded at San Marco in Florence by Cosimo de Medici.

• *Pier Paulo Vergerio (1370–1444).* Born in Capodistria and educated at Padua, where he was professor of logic from 1390 to 1406, Vergerio was visiting Florence in 1398 when he heard about Chrysoloras and joined the group. Like Poggio and Bruni, he would also do humanist work for the Vatican, but Vergerio is best known as a teacher and pioneering educational theorist. He championed a liberal, humanist education that broke sharply with medieval traditions and attempted to recreate the *encyclios paidea* of the Greeks.* His book *On Gentlemanly Manners and Liberal Studies for Youth,* probably written a couple of years after Chrysoloras left Florence, was the first and the most influential work of Renaissance educational theory. It cites many Greek sources and seems to owe much to Chrysoloras' ideas and example.

• *Roberto Rossi (c. 1355–1417).* While lacking the genius of some of his friends, Rossi mastered Greek and acquired a fine collection of Greek manuscripts. But he's mainly notable first for his trip to Venice in 1390–91 (when he met Cydones and Chrysoloras), and second because he later tutored the scions of many leading

---

* The "all-round education" of the ancient Greeks, stressing the development of the whole person, and including subjects such as sports and music.

Florentine families in Latin and Greek. His students included the young Cosimo de Medici.

These were the standouts among Chrysoloras' Florentine students of Greek. The brilliant threesome of Bruni, Poggio, and Niccoli made up the core group of friends, though there were others whose humanist credentials were perfectly respectable. The aristocratic Palla Strozzi, an exceedingly wealthy and well-connected patron of the arts and letters, had taken the lead in helping Salutati arrange for Chrysoloras' invitation. It was he who paid for the Greek books that Chrysoloras used in teaching, and for having copies made for the other students. Antonio Corbinelli, another wealthy aristocrat in the group, eventually acquired one of the best classical libraries in Europe, the Greek portion of which included Homer, Plutarch, Herodotus, Thucydides, Polybius, Plato, Aristotle, Euclid, Aeschylus, Euripides, Sophocles, Aristophanes, Demosthenes, Aeschines, Theocritus, and Pindar.

And of course there was Jacopo Angeli da Scarperia, who kept up with his Greek after escorting Chrysoloras back to Florence, and who ultimately made a number of workmanlike translations of his own (including several of Plutarch's *Lives*). After Chrysoloras left in 1400, Angeli took a mid-level secretarial position at the Vatican, which enabled him to continue his humanist studies. Neither unusually talented nor terribly ambitious, he remained hardworking and openhanded, sharing his own hard-to-find Greek books with Salutati and the others. He did have an uncharacteristic collision with Bruni in 1405, in which he ungallantly tried to beat out the younger but more brilliant man for a prestigious post that had become available at the papal curia, and for which

Bruni had applied. Angeli, who had shown no interest in the position before Bruni made his move, was goaded by friends who thought he would be shamed if the younger man, a former fellow student, got the better job. When the pope had them each write a sample letter in Latin, Bruni won hands down despite his youth.

Yet, Angeli had a contribution to history left to make after Chrysoloras' departure. When Chrysoloras left, he passed on to Angeli an unfinished translation he had been working on. The book was Ptolemy's *Geography*, the key geographical text of the ancient world, which Chrysoloras had brought with him from Constantinople. Angeli completed the translation Chrysoloras had started, making this highly sought-after work available to the West for the first time. Numerous copies of it began appearing rapidly, along with maps based on the information in the text. In fact, that "information" was inaccurate. Ptolemy's *Geography* greatly underestimated the distance between Europe and Asia. And so when, decades later, this widely distributed and pregnantly mistaken ancient authority found its way into the hands of a Genoan sailor named Christopher Columbus, it implanted in him a firm (and ultimately marketable) conviction that sailing westward to the Indies was likely to be a piece of cake.

CHRYSOLORAS MOVES ON

Chrysoloras had contracted to stay in Florence for five years, and his abrupt departure two years shy of fulfilling that agreement has raised scholarly eyebrows ever since. Even more surprising than the departure itself was the destination.

Of all the places for Chrysoloras to move on to, he chose the absolute last one you would expect: Milan. In March 1400, he went from Florence straight into the arms of the city's deadly enemy, the Milanese tyrant Gian Galeazzo Visconti, and right in the midst of Visconti's bitter campaign against Florence. Moreover, there isn't the slightest hint from any of the Florentines that they ever held this against Chrysoloras in even the mildest way. Years later they were still praising him to the skies.

To understand Chrysoloras' apparently baffling behavior, it will help to keep our eyes on the big picture. Chrysoloras was an aristocrat, a high-level diplomat, and a Byzantine patriot. He was also the contemporary, relative by marriage, and close personal friend of the Byzantine emperor Manuel II Paleologos.* Chrysoloras' visit to Venice in 1390–91 had been made at his friend's behest—not with the goal of teaching ancient Greek to Roberto Rossi or anyone else, but with the express mission of securing aid against the Turks.

Chrysoloras and Manuel II probably saw the Florentine invitation as another opening for this ongoing effort. Chrysoloras' motives would likely have been common knowledge to his Italian friends, which would explain why they felt no resentment against him for leaving. If Chrysoloras' main interest had been to teach ancient Greek to young Florentines, he would have stayed out his contract. But his diplomatic aims came first. When after three years it became clear that the Florentines (like so many later Westerners) were more interested in ancient Greeks than in

---

* Manuel II, who ruled from 1391 to 1425, was the son of John V Paleologos and John VI Cantacuzenos' daughter Helena. He was the same highly literate emperor whom the reader will recall Demetrius Cydones praising as a Platonic "philosopher king" at the end of the last chapter.

contempory ones, Chrysoloras moved on to what he no doubt hoped would be greener pastures with no real hard feelings on either side. Hence the attraction of Milan, a major military power under Visconti. Hence also Chrysoloras' departure from Milan, and Italy, soon after Visconti's sudden and unexpected death in 1402 temporarily plunged the city's power into decline.

A slew of details supports this interpretation, which in retrospect seems an almost obvious one.* It explains the movements not just of Chrysoloras himself but also those of his friend Manuel II. For during this same period—that is, from 1400 to 1403—the Byzantine emperor himself was touring the power centers of the West in hopes of drumming up money and support against the Turks.

In fact, he arrived in Venice in April 1400, shortly after Chrysoloras had left Florence. From there Manuel II went to Padua, Vicenza, Pavia, and Milan, where he and Chrysoloras celebrated their reunion as the fêted guests of Gian Galeazzo Visconti. Manuel II would continue on to Paris, living there as the guest of King Charles VI for over a year, and London. He was a big hit in the English capital, where King Henry IV and his subjects gave him a magnificent reception and were for their part deeply impressed by the emperor's regal presence. Significantly, Manuel II did not visit Florence. It's hard not to see some degree of coordination at work between the two Byzantines, especially when you consider that the rest of Chrysoloras' own career would be taken up with similar diplomatic journeys in the ongoing quest to stave off the Turkish advance.

---

* First argued by Ian Thomson in 1966, it has been widely accepted by other scholars.

SCHOOLING THE SCHOOLMASTERS

Interwoven with these diplomatic initiatives in the years after Florence was Chrysoloras' burgeoning relationship with a new Italian pupil, Guarino of Verona. Born in that northern Italian city in 1374, the son of a metalworker who died when he was 12, Guarino was educated there as a boy. As a promising young humanist he had gone on during the 1390s to nearby Padua, studying there under Pier Paolo Vergerio, the Paduan teacher (four years Guarino's senior) who joined Chrysoloras' classes in Florence. Unable to go to Florence himself, Guarino heard about the Byzantine's teaching from Vergerio, who by the early 1400s was conceiving and writing his pioneer educational work, *On Gentlemanly Manners and Liberal Studies for Youth.*

Vergerio's ideas, backed once again by Chrysoloras' instruction and personal example, would inspire Guarino's own coming achievements. Over the next several decades Guarino would rise to become the quattrocento's most prominent humanist educator, and thus ultimately Chrysoloras' most influential student. All that lay in the future in 1403, when the young Guarino found himself in Venice, for which its smaller neighbor Padua acted as university town (Venice would officially absorb Padua in 1405). Chrysoloras, having quit Milan the previous year, had just accompanied the emperor Manuel II back to Constantinople. Like Angeli nearly a decade earlier, Guarino—who had still not met Chrysoloras—now decided to journey to the Byzantine capital, to seek Chrysoloras out and to study Greek with him. He traveled with a wealthy Venetian merchant named Paolo Zane, who made his trip possible by offering Guarino employment, along with generous encouragement and advice.

Welcomed into Chrysoloras' household, Guarino stayed

in Constantinople for more than two years, mastering Greek and acquiring a good number of manuscripts. He then spent some time traveling around the Aegean, perhaps as Zane's secretary, visiting Rhodes and Chios and possibly the Greek mainland as well. Guarino's main teacher during his enviable Constantinopolitan sojourn was not Chrysoloras himself but Chrysoloras' nephew John, who was much sought after as a tutor to aristocratic young Byzantines. Manuel remained busy with diplomatic missions, traveling back and forth between Constantinople and Italy, though he spent most of 1405 in the Byzantine capital and kept close tabs on Guarino's studies throughout.

Chrysoloras was in Constantinople when he followed his intellectual forebears Barlaam and Cydones in converting to Catholicism. Shortly after that he left on a mission to Italy, though he was back again by the end of 1406. Before another year was out, however, Chrysoloras left Constantinople for the last time, moving permanently to the West. He spent the next few years trekking around Europe trying to drum up aid against the Turks and working, like Barlaam and Cydones before him, toward reuniting the Catholic and Orthodox churches.

By this time, Catholic leaders had succeeded in their push for church councils to heal the decades-long Western schism between the rival popes in Avignon and Rome.* Chrysoloras, now one of the most famous and revered men in Italy, took part in this process, which also included an effort to reunite Catholic and Orthodox Christians. Indeed, when Chrysoloras died in 1415, he was representing the Orthodox in these negotiations, at Constance, Switzerland. At

---

* The schism between rival popes began in 1378 and was healed by the Council of Constance, 1414–18.

the time of his death, Vergerio tells us in his epitaph for Chrysoloras, everyone considered him a leading contender for election as pope, no less.

Guarino, meanwhile, had returned to Italy, though he continued to keep in touch with Chrysoloras until his master's death. Teaching in Florence, Bologna, Venice, Verona, and during the last three decades of his life for the ruling Este family in Ferrara, Guarino acted with Vergerio as the pipeline through which Chrysoloras' teaching changed the face of Italian and then European education. To take but a single example, their most successful protégé, Vittorino da Feltre, applied their ideas in establishing what seems to have been the first European boarding school, La Casa Giocosa—the House of Laughter—at the humanist court of the Gonzaga dynasty in Mantua.

At the heart of this education revolution lay the revival of the *encyclios paidea,* the "all-round education" of the ancient Greeks. Combining a broad academic curriculum with music, physical fitness, and moral instruction to produce a fully rounded individual, *encyclios paidea* was the Greek model that inspired the Roman ideal of *humanitas*. Resurrecting it was the most important step forward in education since the invention of universities, and the values that Chrysoloras ushered in at the beginning of the quattrocento still profoundly shape the way we think about such matters today.

CHRYSOLORIANA AND BEYOND

Of all Chrysoloras' students, Guarino had stood closest to Chrysoloras emotionally, as well as being his most enthusiastic and devoted admirer among the Italians. It was primarily through passionate tributes by Guarino and his son Battista, written long decades after Chrysoloras' death, that Chrysoloras would take on the golden aura of a legendary figure. A body of literature, the so-called Chrysoloriana, arose among later generations of humanist scholars, celebrating Chrysoloras and his achievements in Italy.

In modern times, too, Chrysoloras has exerted a seemingly irresistible fascination on Renaissance historians, who have vied with each other to credit him with the most glamorous developments of the Italian Renaissance. One scholarly book suggests that his broad-based teaching gave rise to the idea of the Renaissance man; another that his aesthetic sophistication stimulated the invention of linear perspective and pictorial composition in painting; still another that his inspiring classicism introduced the first glimmerings of a secular outlook in the West. Such speculations are attractive and must of course be taken seriously—but perhaps not too much so. It is enough that so many have seen so much in the man.

CHAPTER FIVE

BYZANTINE ÉMIGRÉS
IN THE QUATTROCENTO

Tamerlane's devastating defeat of the Ottomans at Ankara in 1402 offered a last reprieve for the beleaguered Byzantine empire, as the sons of the fallen sultan Bayezid fought each other for control of the shattered Ottoman state. The eventual winner of that contest, Mehmed I, owed his victory to the adroit assistance of Manuel II, who—in the best Byzantine tradition—took full advantage of the Ottomans' disarray to play the diplomatic odds. When Mehmed finally dispatched his brother Musa in 1413, it was with the backing of Byzantine and Serbian troops. From that day forward, Mehmed swore gratefully, he would be like a son and obedient subject to his father the emperor. He was true to his word. Mehmed's gratitude, and his apparently genuine friendship with Manuel, lasted as long as Mehmed lived.

Aware that the obligation was personal and temporary, Manuel used the opportunity to prepare as best he could for the onslaught that he knew would be renewed after Mehmed's death. Leaving aside defenses in Constantinople itself for the moment, Manuel focused on the southern part of the Greek mainland, which had become one of the most vital outposts of Byzantine culture during the Paleologan Renaissance.

This broad peninsula, connected to the rest of the mainland by the narrow isthmus of Corinth, was called the Peloponnesus in ancient times, but Byzantines knew it as the Morea. Administered from the city of Mistra, near ancient Sparta, the Despotate of the Morea was ruled by a close relative of the emperor, usually a son or younger brother. Now Manuel rebuilt the ancient wall called the Hexamilion, across the narrow isthmus of Corinth, fortifying it with 153 towers and a castle at either end. Manuel's rebuilt Hexamilion protected the Morea against a land invasion from the north and was said to have been completed in less than a month.*

Pletho and His Students

The Morea was home to the man who was one of the most eccentric and original thinkers in the Byzantine humanist tradition, George Gemistos Pletho. Philosopher, lay theologian, and advisor to both Manuel II and his son and successor John VIII, Pletho had been born simply George Gemistos. Later, during his pivotal visit to Florence in 1439, he would take the surname Pletho (a synonym for Gemistos, meaning "abundant") because it sounded like the name of the philosopher he most revered, Plato.

Born and educated in Constantinople, Pletho taught there for many years, but eventually got in trouble for

---

* The area remains an exciting place to visit, not least because the monasteries and churches of Mistra and nearby Monemvasia boast some of the finest surviving Paleologan artwork, rivaling that of the Chora.

promoting pagan beliefs. Sometime around 1410, when Pletho was about 50, Manuel II felt compelled to exile Pletho to Mistra, where he promptly founded a philosophical academy, a commune essentially, that continued to promote those same heretical beliefs.

As Manuel had no doubt seen, Pletho's unusual, even unique approach fit better in Mistra's esoteric intellectual climate than in Constantinople's more conservative religious one. Using Platonic doctrine as a springboard, Pletho eventually turned his back on Christianity altogether, calling on his compatriots to reinstate Zeus and the Olympian pantheon, and conceiving a comprehensive program of organized paganism that recalled the emperor Julian's more than a millennium earlier.* Unlike Julian's, however, Pletho's pagan system incorporated a strong element of Greek patriotism, easier now that the empire had been shorn of all its former non-Greek lands (and most of its Greek lands, too, for that matter).

Harkening back to Hellenic Outside Wisdom and to glorious martial traditions such as those of ancient Sparta, Pletho proposed social and military reforms that he hoped would strengthen Byzantine society and the Byzantine army against the Turks. Pletho went so far as to denounce the very institution of monasticism, painting the monks as useless parasites who contributed nothing to society. However, Pletho would not make these views public until very near the end of his life, after his visit to the West, publishing them in his *Book of Laws*.

In so flagrantly abandoning Orthodox Byzantium for

---

* A nephew of Constantine's, the emperor Julian (ruled 361–63) was the only pagan to rule the empire after Constantine. Known as Julian the Apostate, he tried to reinstate paganism, but was killed on campaign against Persia before his efforts could gain any traction.

ancient Greece, Pletho represents an extreme version of the classicizing tendency that had helped drive the humanists further and further from the Byzantine mainstream. Most Byzantines had already paid their money and taken their choice, and that choice was not Pletho's. Their most urgent priority was to save their immortal souls, not to preserve what was now an essentially Greek state. Imbued with Hesychasm's somber, otherworldly tones, the mainstream of Byzantine civilization had already turned toward a better life in the next world while resigning itself to Turkish captivity in this one. For his self-reliant stand against the Turks Pletho has been called the first Greek nationalist—so ardent was he, in fact, that he argued against church union not for religious reasons but for patriotic ones, preferring to find strength from within.

Surprisingly, Pletho numbered among his students and friends not only the humanists but also the Hesychast leaders who would later figure most prominently in Byzantium's short future. While those who became Hesychasts ultimately rejected his values, among the Byzantine humanists he stimulated a new interest in the works of Plato. Not that any of them endorsed his wilder fantasies, but they all respected him immensely. Like those of Cantacuzenos a century earlier, Pletho's relations with both sides reflect the complexities of the cultural gulf still dividing the Byzantines as they sank slowly beneath the quicksand of history.

The Council of Florence

Hellenic patriotism could hold only limited interest for the Florentines, sympathetic though they might be. Plato, however, proved a different story. Once exposed to Pletho's enthusiasm, Florence, like Byzantium, answered with a zeal of its own. In this new incarnation of Florentine humanism, Plato, an ancient Greek, replaced Cicero, an ancient Roman, as the Florentine humanists' biggest hero.

The event that triggered this shift came more than two decades after Chrysoloras' death, when some of his brightest Florentine alumni took part in a momentous gathering that brought Pletho and other learned Byzantines to Italy. This was the Council of Florence, a full-scale church council called in Ferrara in 1438 to negotiate the union of the Eastern and Western churches, and moved early the following year to nearby Florence.

Events meantime in both East and West had unfolded in such a way as to favor the old idea of union. By the 1430s Byzantium was clearly nearing the end of its rope. The previous decade had seen the deaths of Mehmed I and Manuel II, who were succeeded by their sons Murad II and John VIII Paleologos, respectively. Eager to resume the attack, in 1430 Murad captured Thessalonica. In desperation John VIII turned to Rome.

On their side, the Catholics, too, had new reasons. For decades, rivalry between the papacy and the conciliarist movement had split the Western church.* The conciliarists believed that church doctrine should be decided by church councils rather than dictated by the pope, and in 1431 the rebellious Council of Basel repudiated the newly elected pope, Eugenius IV. Eugenius was driven from Rome by hostile mobs and forced to take refuge in Florence, where he stayed with his court for nearly a decade. Acknowledgment of papal

---

* The conciliarist movement originated in the church councils that were held to heal the schism between rival popes (1378–1418). Though the conciliarists had much in common with the Orthodox outlook, ultimately the Byzantines decided they were better off negotiating with the pope.

supremacy by the Orthodox would be just the thing to sub-
due the conciliarist rebels.

As far back as Barlaam, a council had been seen as essential by Byzantine pro-unionists if any union were to win real
support among the Byzantine public. Ideally it would be held
in the East—Eugenius offered to come to Constantinople—
but the Turkish presence obviously made that impossible,
and the Byzantines in turn accepted the need to go to the
West. As it was, Eugenius agreed to foot the bill for everything,
including travel and accommodations for the Byzantines.

In November 1437, on ships supplied by Eugenius, the
Byzantine delegation of some seven hundred church and lay
dignitaries embarked for Italy. Led by the emperor himself,
John VIII, and by the elderly patriarch of Constantinople,
Joseph II, it included twenty metropolitans along with numerous other bishops, monks, and learned scholars.* Most
of the prelates oversaw flocks who now lived outside of
Byzantine control, which took some of the edge off their lus-
ter. Still, never before had emperor and patriarch journeyed
to the West together in this way, much less with such a substantial and distinguished retinue.

After a long and uncomfortable voyage (both John and
Joseph were ill for much of it), the Byzantines anchored off
the Lido at Venice on the morning of February 8, 1438. Carefully negotiating the tricky shoals of protocol—compared to
which any actual shoals dwindled to insignificance—the emperor, the patriarch, and the Venetian doge greeted each
other amid the greatest pomp and pageantry the Venetians
could lay on. This was considerable, since the Venetians,
whose commercial empire was then close to the height of its

---

* In Orthodox hierarchy, a metropolitan is the bishop of a city officially designated a
"metropolis," or mother city.

power, had learned pomp and pageantry from the Byzantines. The climax came late the next morning, when the doge's magnificent state barge *Bucentaur* approached the emperor's ship so that the doge might present himself and his son to the emperor.

From Venice the delegation made the short trip to Ferrara, where Eugenius, the papal court, and assorted Catholic archbishops, bishops, abbots, and scholars awaited them, including Leonardo Bruni (chancellor of Florence at this time), Poggio Bracciolini, Pier Paolo Vergerio, and Guarino of Verona, who was teaching in Ferrara in the employment of the ruling d'Este family. There were further daunting complexities of protocol, such as deciding whether the patriarch would submit to the customary kissing of the pope's foot. (No, he would not. But he would bow to the pope and kiss his cheek—a fine adjustment that perfectly captures the Orthodox attitude to the papacy.) An additional delay of several weeks ensued because the emperor insisted on waiting—in vain, as it turned out—to see if Western rulers would show up. Finally, on April 9, the full combined council opened with a solemn ceremony.

In the negotiations that followed, the two delegates who can be securely identified as Pletho's former students, John Bessarion and Mark of Ephesus, quickly emerged as the Byzantines' leading spokesmen—on opposite sides.

Born in the Black Sea port of Trebizond, which like Mistra was a nominally independent outpost of Byzantine civilization, John Bessarion would, after Chrysoloras, become the most influential Byzantine émigré scholar, a teacher, friend, or patron to virtually every major humanist, Byzantine or Italian, of his day. He had studied with Pletho in the 1430s before being appointed metropolitan of Nicaea. Eloquent for the Orthodox position at the start, he spoke less and less as the council wore on. In fact, as the discussions progressed Bessarion found himself more and more persuaded by the Latins' theology. In Ferrara and then in Florence, he went through a conversion process that, like those of Barlaam and Demetrius Cydones in the previous century, was spurred by theological argument and possessed dimensions that spanned both intellect and spirit. Bessarion's openness to Latin theology apparently began with doubts he had about the doctrinal correctness of Hesychasm, which he expressed before the council in correspondence with a Greek archbishop of the Latin rite. By the time the council officially closed, Bessarion wore the hat of a Catholic cardinal, and except for a brief visit home he would live out the rest of his extraordinarily fruitful life in Italy.

By the council's middle stages, Mark Eugenicus, metropolitan of Ephesus, had taken over as the primary speaker on the Greek side as well as the main defender of the hard-line Orthodox position. Learned in the pagan classics as well as in Christian literature, Mark had studied with Pletho as a boy in Constantinople. He went on to write important theological tracts defending Hesychast doctrine. As a Hesychast, he could hardly be counted as a disciple of Pletho's, but—unlike the other hard-line monks—he was an unusually cultivated man and generally remained on friendly or at least civil terms with Pletho and the others. This is all the more remarkable considering that Mark of Ephesus would be the only prelate among the Byzantines who refused to sign the proclamation of union that was the council's ultimate product. As the sole holdout, he was later hailed as a great hero by the Orthodox faithful, and would be canonized as an Orthodox saint in 1456.

Despite their differing positions on union, Mark refused to condemn John VIII, and the emperor returned the favor. Even in the heat of the debates, the emperor never tried to coerce Mark, leaving him free to follow the dictates of his conscience. It's a measure of Mark's reputation and ability that he continued to be trusted as the Greeks' main speaker even when it became clear that he was isolated among the other prelates in his views.

In January 1439, after plague struck in Ferrara, the council moved to Florence, at the urging of the newly ascendant Cosimo de Medici, who had lobbied for Florence as the council's site from the beginning. On July 6, a decree of union affirming the Latin positions on every major issue was signed by all Greek prelates but Mark of Ephesus. Good for his side of the bargain, Eugenius called on Western rulers to mount an expedition against the Turks.

Several years later, the resulting effort, called the Crusade of Varna, set out from Hungary with an army of twenty-five thousand to relieve the Byzantine capital. After some success in the Balkans, the Crusaders' army was shattered by a much larger Ottoman force at Varna in Bulgaria in November 1444.

Strategically, this was Byzantium's last hope, and it proved a forlorn one. In ecclesiastical terms, too, the council failed utterly, since the carefully negotiated reunion that it proclaimed was even then in the process of being rejected by the intractable Byzantines, who pilloried their own returning delegates as having sold them down the river. Most of the prelates who had signed ended up recanting.

The most dramatic reversal was that of George Scholarios, a humanist who had supported union in Florence but ended up inheriting Mark's role as leading anti-unionist after the latter's death. First a friend of Pletho's, later a Hesychast leader and Pletho's bitter enemy, Scholarios underwent a "conversion" in the opposite direction from those of Barlaam,

Cydones, Chrysoloras, Bessarion, and the others. As the monk Gennadios, he would eventually be chosen as the first patriarch of Constantinople to serve under an Ottoman sultan.

The council's official sessions had been taken up with endless bickering over questions such as papal supremacy, the procession of the Holy Spirit, and the leavening of bread. Between those sessions, though, the council turned into an ongoing, informal colloquium on ancient Greek civilization, literature, and especially philosophy, a dialogue in which the flattered Byzantine humanists were the teachers and the avid Italians the students. The hottest speaker—though taking only a minor role in the official negotiations—was George Gemistos Pletho, now around eighty years old, whose talks on Plato absolutely electrified the Florentines.

Since Pletho likely knew no Latin, it was probably Bruni who served as his interpreter during these salons, which remain rather mysterious owing to a tantalizing lack of specific information about them. Though many Italians later referred to Pletho's lectures in gushing general terms, we know only two names for sure of those who actually attended them. One was a relative unknown named Grigorio Tifernate. The other, however, was Cosimo de Medici.

PLATO COMES ALIVE

Like Chrysoloras, Pletho came to Florence at exactly the right time. The generation of Bruni and Poggio was passing away and with it the concerns of civic humanism. A new era was emerging, peopled by a new generation with a new set of interests.

Bruni and the others had looked askance at philosophy,

seeing Aristotle and Plato as a sideline and focusing on them primarily for what they had to say on subjects such as the state or ethics. They thought Aristotle was passé, the standard authority of the old school, while the often mystical Plato, relatively unknown, hardly appeared central to the concerns of civic humanism.

The new generation, apolitical but comparatively devout, would see esoteric philosophy as the main attraction, and would mine Plato especially for what he had to say about the soul. The Florentine humanist ideal was turning from the *vita activa* to the *vita contemplativa*, from the active life to the contemplative, and Cicero the striving republican orator was about to give way to Plato the metaphysical theorist. Nor was it entirely coincidental that Plato's anti-democratic political views (which had dismayed Bruni) were much more in line with the emerging system of one-man rule in Florence. No doubt much of the attraction for Cosimo stemmed from his own aspirations in the way of being a Platonic philosopher king or some other such enlightened despot.

As a young man of broad humanist interests, Cosimo had been tutored in Greek by Roberto Rossi, who had played such a big role in bringing Chrysoloras to Florence. Then, during the Council of Constance in the 1410s, Cosimo had wandered the monasteries of northern Europe with the great Poggio, searching out classical Latin manuscripts. His family's immense wealth had been founded by Cosimo's father, Giovanni, and was based on banking. Giovanni died in 1429, and it was Cosimo who consolidated the family's political power thereafter, ending the Florentine republic in fact if not in name. This watershed in Florence's history was coming precisely in the years before, during, and after the council. Exiled by his oligarchic rivals in 1433, Cosimo had returned in triumph the following year, establishing a dynastic rule that was populist in flavor and preserved republican appearances, but soon concentrated power in Medici hands.

Of course, political status in Renaissance Florence demanded patronage of the arts and culture, and Cosimo—energetic, inquisitive, thrusting—prided himself in being on the cutting edge. He knew everybody. Cosimo hosted lavish banquets during the council at which the luminaries on both sides mingled, and these congenial gatherings provided a venue in which Pletho held forth on his favorite subject. Though we only have two names for sure, it's likely that Cosimo's large humanist circle was involved as well.

With fewer opportunities for Florentine humanists to exercise political influence, Florentine humanism itself became more academic—literally as well as figuratively. More than two decades after the fact, the great Florentine Neoplatonist Marsilio Ficino would recall how Pletho's lectures fired Cosimo de Medici with enthusiasm. "At the time of the council between the Greeks and the Latins at Florence," Ficino recounts, Cosimo "frequently heard a Greek philosopher Gemistus Pletho disputing about the Platonic mysteries. He was so inspired by his fervent utterance that he conceived the idea of an Academy."

The nature of Cosimo's famous Platonic Academy has aroused great interest among modern scholars. It used to be thought that Cosimo founded a formal institution, located at the magnificent Medici villa in Careggi, near Florence, and staffed by the most learned Greek scholars he could find. More recent historians have described the Academy as more of an informal circle of friends around Marsilio Ficino. It began around 1460, when Cosimo gave Ficino a villa near his own at Careggi and commissioned him to translate the entire corpus of Plato, along with many Neoplatonic writings, which Ficino proceeded to do with extreme competence.

Moving in the opposite direction from the secularism of Bruni's generation, Ficino's mystical philosophy fused Platonic and Neoplatonic ideas with Christianity. The result would have a huge impact not just on European philosophy but also on arts and literature, from paintings such as Botticelli's *Birth of Venus* (depicted according to Neoplatonic iconography) to the resounding concept of Platonic love.

Yet, by Ficino's own account, when Cosimo first "conceived the idea of an Academy" Ficino himself was a boy of about six or seven. Twenty-odd years lay between the conception and the execution—a gap that can be explained only by considering the last and most controversial stage of George Gemistos Pletho's already long and controversial career.

Immediately following the Council of Florence, Pletho returned to Mistra, where for the Italians' benefit he wrote a summary of his lectures entitled *On the Differences of Aristotle from Plato*. However, in composing this helpful explanation Pletho also revived a long-standing controversy among Byzantine philosophers over which of the two ancients was the greater philosopher. With his summary for the Italians, Pletho was seen by the others as getting in a sneaky blow in this old grudge match, which was as ancient as Byzantium itself.

Virtually the whole community of Byzantine émigré scholars in Italy eventually got involved in the celebrated, spectacular—and at times spectacularly stupid—proxy battle that ensued. At first the Italians could only look on in uncomprehending amazement. By the end, however, the best of them could follow the arcane and nuanced disputation, and a few even contributed competently themselves.

More telling were the contributions of the most respected of the Byzantine émigrés, Pletho's former student

Cardinal Bessarion. In 1459, Bessarion responded to one of the Byzantine Aristotelians' vituperative blasts with a masterful book-length essay called *Against the Calumniator of Plato*. Balanced, judicious, authoritative, insightful, the book aimed less at tearing down Aristotle than at providing a clear and systematic exposition of Platonic and Neoplatonic thought, and at showing how, in Bessarion's view, Plato had much (though certainly not everything) in common with Christianity. Coming a decade after Pletho's book, Bessarion's further stimulated the Florentines in their Platonic studies.

Influential though it was, Bessarion's *Against the Calumniator of Plato* didn't extinguish the controversy, which sputtered on for a decade or so before blowing itself out in the early 1470s. By then it had served the useful purpose of focusing the Italians' attention on the original Greek texts of both philosophers, as an essential first step toward understanding their ideas. Only then were they finally brought into the humanistic mainstream. By then, indeed, with the help of a growing crowd of Byzantine teachers, the Italians were up to speed, most of them choosing to align themselves with Plato.

Aristotle had been the philosopher par excellence of the Scholastics; Plato now became the philosopher par excellence of the humanists. Yet, Plato didn't fully dislodge Aristotle (just as humanism didn't fully dislodge Scholasticism). Aristotle, too, was rediscovered, in the sense that while sharing the stage now with Plato, he still retained much of his old prestige, but was read more fully and in more authentic versions than during medieval times.

Those authentic Greek texts—along with the ability to read, translate, and comment on them—also came courtesy of the Byzantine humanists. In reclaiming the two great philosophers of antiquity, and in mastering the ability to read them in the original Greek, the Italians opened up for themselves a new chapter in Western philosophy.

NEW DIRECTIONS

A new generation of Byzantine humanists was arriving to carry on the teaching that Chrysoloras had begun, and to take it in the fresh directions dictated by the Italians' curiosity. This wave of émigré scholars was further boosted by the fall of Constantinople in 1453, an event of such consequence for humanism that at one time it was widely held to have started the Renaissance itself. Settling not just in Florence but elsewhere as well, the Byzantine émigrés enabled other cities—first Rome, then Venice, with its university at Padua—successfully to challenge Florence for leadership of the humanist world.

One of the first after Chrysoloras was George of Trebizond, who had emigrated as a young man in 1417, studying Latin with Guarino and Vittorino da Feltre, and converting to Catholicism before attending the Council of Florence. A quarrelsome man, he had been the "calumniator of Plato" whom Bessarion had addressed in his book.

Another Byzantine Aristotelian, George's rival Theodore Gaza, was at least as good a scholar and was more easygoing to boot. Theodore had come to Italy in the mid-1430s, a few years before the Council of Florence, and had also studied Latin with Vittorino da Feltre in Mantua, exchanging Latin lessons for tutelage of Vittorino in Greek. Theodore would turn out to be one of the more influential Byzantine teachers, and with Bessarion and George of Trebizond one of the few to learn Latin really well. Theodore attended the Council of Florence, afterward teaching Greek in

Ferrara. In 1447, he declined an invitation from Cosimo to assume Chrysoloras' old chair in Florence, but a couple of years later he moved to Rome, joining a circle of humanists, Byzantine and Italian, that arose around Bessarion at the papal curia. A warm personal and intellectual friendship arose between Theodore, the moderate Aristotelian, and Bessarion, the moderate Platonist.

John Argyropoulos, who also learned Latin, was another of Pletho's and Bessarion's younger émigré friends. A native Constantinopolitan still only in his twenties when he attended the Council of Florence, Argyropoulos studied Latin and medicine in Padua in the early 1440s before returning to Constantinople, where he converted to Catholicism. He was there when the city fell, losing everything— including, temporarily, his wife and children, who were captured by the Turks. Only after several years of unstinting effort did Argyropoulos succeed in ransoming them from captivity. He then returned to Florence for more than a decade, where he accepted from Cosimo de Medici the prestigious post that Theodore Gaza had turned down, occupying Chrysoloras' old chair in Greek studies at the Florentine *studio*.

Born the year Chrysoloras died, Argyropoulos proved a worthy successor, and he played a comparable role in the ongoing development of Florentine humanism. Like Chrysoloras, he was a strong classroom performer who energized his students. He taught Aristotle by day but, responding to the Italians' curiosity, offered private lessons in Plato in the evenings. Ultimately, it was Argyropoulos who fulfilled the hunger for Platonic knowledge that Pletho had aroused during the Council of Florence.

It's not known for sure whether Argyropoulos formally taught the young Marsilio Ficino, though it seems likely.

Certainly his teaching and his magnetic presence did much to influence Ficino and his circle, the group that would become the Platonic Academy. But unlike many of his fellow émigrés, Argyropoulos steered clear of the controversy over Plato and Aristotle. He taught both and sought to reconcile the two sides in the dispute. His students included Cosimo's grandson Lorenzo de Medici ("the Magnificent"), the young aristocrat Donato Acciaiuoli (who with Cosimo had helped bring Argyropoulos to Florence, and whose family ruled the Florentine Duchy of Athens), and the prodigious Angelo Poliziano, known in English as Politian, a talented linguist associated with Ficino's circle but whose interests ran more to philology and poetry than to Neoplatonism.

Unchallenged leadership of the humanistic world had passed away from Florence by the middle of the quattrocento. There were two main reasons for this: the return to Rome from Florence of a newly independent and influential papacy, and the Byzantine humanist diaspora to other places in Italy after the Council of Florence and the fall of Constantinople. Most cities in northern Italy worth their salt had humanist schools of some description by mid-century, headed by Byzantine-trained Italian humanists. We've seen such schools, for example, in Milan, Ferrara, and Mantua.

Florence itself certainly remained a vibrant center of Greek studies, as other Byzantine protégés of Bessarion succeeded Argyropoulos in the Florentine *studio*. But two other cities, first Rome and then Venice, would enjoy periods of primacy before the lead in Renaissance humanism moved outside the borders of Italy, finding new centers in northern Europe by the early fifteenth century.

ROME, BESSARION, AND THE HUMANIST POPE

In 1397, the year that Chrysoloras came to Florence, Tommaso Parentucelli, the son of a poor doctor, was born in the small Tuscan town of Sarzana, near Carrara. As a young man he was forced by poverty to abandon his studies at the University of Bologna. Making his way to Florence, he found work as a tutor for the children of two of Cosimo de Medici's aristocratic rivals. One was Palla Strozzi, the student of Salutati and Chrysoloras who had helped bring Chrysoloras to Florence. Parentucelli's other employer was Rinaldo degli Albizzi, head of the family that would engineer Cosimo's exile in 1433. Both were enthusiastic humanists, and through his job as tutor to their children Parentucelli gained entry into the Florentine humanist world.

Returning to Bologna and completing his studies, Tommaso entered the service of Bologna's Cardinal Albergati, whom he served faithfully for two decades. He was with Albergati when the cardinal accompanied the papal curia on its Florentine exile. In Florence again, Tommaso took up his old humanist connections, joining the group around Bruni and Poggio as they gathered for conversation outside the Palazzo della Signoria in the mornings and evenings. He also formed a lasting friendship with Cosimo at this time, despite his earlier links with Cosimo's rivals. Assuming a leading role at the Council of Florence, Tommaso was made bishop of Bologna on Albergati's death and elevated to cardinal in 1446. A few months later, he was elected pope, taking the name Nicholas V.

A diminutive, stoop-shouldered scholar, friendly and witty, Nicholas V was the first of several popes with a strong humanist outlook. Previous popes had used humanists for secretarial purposes; Nicholas *was* a humanist, and actively promoted a humanist agenda. His gentle, nonconfrontational style belied a determination to transform the Vatican into a progressive center of humanist learning and culture, which he believed was the best way to strengthen the role of the papacy in Europe's expanding civilization. An adroit diplomat, he placated the conciliarists with mild concessions, ending their insurrection against papal power once and for all. With Cosimo as his banker, he also adorned Rome with spectacular art and architecture. He relied on his friendships with the Florentines, many of whom had worked for his predecessors, but he went the earlier popes one better by placing ancient Greek, rather than Latin, at the center of his program. In the Vatican of this first humanist pope, as in Florence after Chrysoloras, we see the Italians using the tools the Byzantines had given them to create a vibrant new intellectual world.

His great passion was books and book collecting, and it is as the founder of the Vatican Library that Nicholas V is best remembered. As the new library's crowning glory, Nicholas decided to commission Latin translations of Greek literature, including both classical and Christian texts. Quite possibly he envisioned translating all of the available Greek corpus. If so, he died long before that grandiose scheme could be accomplished, though he made a good start. To oversee the project he chose Cardinal Bessarion, giving him a blank check to attract the best Greek scholars, both Byzantine and Italian.

In addition to hiring his fellow Byzantines, George of Trebizond and Theodore Gaza, and performing many translations himself, Bessarion lured a brilliant native Roman scholar named Lorenzo Valla back to Rome from the humanist court at Naples, where Valla had worked for over a decade. His first education had been in Rome, where he'd lived until his early twenties, till the jealous hostility of the Florentines who dominated the papal curia shut him out from employment there. One of the most gifted classicists of the Renaissance, and the most important figure among Bessarion's circle in Rome, Valla is thought by some scholars to have studied Greek with Guarino of Verona.

Valla's treatment by the Florentines made him skeptical toward the papacy, and his skepticism is perfectly exemplified by his most celebrated achievement. While still at Naples (where the king was no friend of the pope), Valla had used his Latin expertise to demonstrate that the famous Donation of Constantine, a crucial document used to support the papacy's claims to temporal power since medieval times, was in fact a forgery. Then he came to Rome, where Nicholas V's unflinching support of such a papal critic as Valla shows the humanist pope's broad-mindedness, especially considering the charges of heresy that plagued Valla throughout his life— and beyond, since the church ultimately banned many of his works.

Nicholas commissioned the landmark work that modern scholars find Valla's most impressive, the first complete translation into Latin of the Greek historian Thucydides. Later, in 1453, Nicholas commissioned Valla to translate the other great historian from the Greek classical period, Herodotus, though, owing partly to Thucydides' far greater difficulty, the earlier translation is rated higher by posterity.*

With both translations but especially with the Thucydides, Valla made valuable textual emendations, proposing corrections in places where the manuscripts seemed corrupt. Many of Valla's emendations stand today, and modern textual critics would bust their bifocals to know exactly how

---

*The date of Valla's Herodotus translation, 1453, is ironic. Herodotus had chronicled the ancient Greeks' finest hour: their odds-against victory over the Persians, the classical Greek world's equivalent of the Ottomans.

much Bessarion helped with them. For his (presumed) deftness in proposing such corrections, Valla, who died in Rome a few years later at age fifty, is hailed as a major figure in the history of textual criticism, as well as a founder of the discipline of philology.

His early friction with Poggio went on for the rest of Valla's short life, since the long-lived Poggio survived Valla by several years. The last of the old Florentine school, Poggio was in Rome when Valla arrived, and he remained there until 1453, when he returned to Florence to take up the chancellorship of his native city, which he held until his death at age seventy-nine. While still in Rome, Poggio had also quarreled several times with George of Trebizond, no stranger to controversy himself. But Poggio's squabbles with Lorenzo Valla and George of Trebizond, both of whom he continued to denounce after returning to Florence, reflect more than just standard humanistic crustiness. Like Poggio's departure from Rome, they betray his impatience with a new generation that put competence in Greek above all else. Poggio, once too young to study with Chrysoloras, was now too old to fit in with Bessarion.

Times had changed, and knowledge of Greek was no longer merely a fashionable accessory, without which an unusually brilliant Latinist such as Poggio might survive and prosper. Instead, Greek now lay at the heart of the humanistic curriculum. This shift was part of what allowed the rise of a group like Marsilio Ficino's Platonic Academy, with its subtly nuanced interpretations of complex Greek philosophical texts. But nowhere was the change better illustrated than in the Rome of Pope Nicholas V, who initiated it, and his chief humanist, Cardinal Bessarion, who carried it out. That it took place in the bosom of the Latin church is but one ironic aspect of a situation that glints with irony from almost every angle.

"Another Byzantium"

Despite his long-standing connections with Rome, it was to Venice that Cardinal Bessarion chose to bequeath his own priceless personal library of some six hundred Greek manuscripts. The collection came second only to that of the Vatican Library, which Bessarion had helped Nicholas V create in Rome. Bessarion handed most of the books over in 1468, four years before he died, and they formed the nucleus of what became the Biblioteca Marciana, the Library of St. Mark.

Like Theodore Metochites, who had made a similar bequest to the Chora nearly 150 years earlier, Bessarion knew well the value that posterity would place on these books. For Chrysoloras, teaching ancient Greek had come second to saving Byzantium, which still seemed a possibility. For Bessarion, after the Council of Florence, salvaging the Outside Wisdom was the best he realistically could hope for. He'd built his collection over many years, at times almost desperately, but resolved always that as many of the classics as he could lay his hands on would survive the catastrophe of the Turkish conquest. Conscious and deliberate, his generosity was, with the rest of his life's work, part of a determined campaign to save ancient Greek literature by transplanting it to the West. There, he hoped, it might even promote a fusion of Greek East and Latin West that would re-create the cosmopolitan world of antiquity.

If this alluring vision turned out to be overly optimistic, Bessarion still had good reason to choose Venice as the beneficiary of his largesse. The Fourth Crusade notwithstanding,

Venice had always enjoyed a special relationship with Byzantium, although over the centuries the balance had shifted in Venice's favor as the Serene Republic progressed from Byzantine province and offshoot to Byzantine creditor and overlord. And of all Italian cities, Venice stood to lose the most by the Turkish advance. With its extensive commercial empire in former Byzantine lands throughout the Aegean, the city's economic and cultural ties to the Byzantine world remained pervasive and strong, if often rancorous.

So although little love was lost between Venetians and Greeks, during the quarter century after the fall of Constantinople, Venice attracted more Byzantine refugees than any other Western city. By the last quarter of the quattrocento it held a Greek immigrant community of more than four thousand. *Alterum Byzantium,* "another Byzantium," Bessarion called Venice in a letter to the doge explaining why he'd chosen to entrust his precious books to the city.

At first hardheaded Venice had showed comparatively little interest in Byzantium's ancient Greek heritage, lacking the classical past of a Rome or a Florence and being more exclusively concerned with practical matters such as trade. Only in 1463 did the university at Padua establish a chair in Greek, its first occupant being one of Bessarion's Byzantine protégés, Demetrius Chalcondyles. He taught there for a decade before leaving to succeed John Argyropoulos in Florence. By the time Chalcondyles went to Florence, humanism had established itself strongly enough in Venice and Padua to justify Bessarion's choice.

In both Venice and Florence, one of Chalcondyles' students was a Venetian-born Greek named Nicolaus Leonicus Tomaeus, who eventually returned to Venice to teach Greek himself. His lucky students were among the first to benefit from a hugely significant advantage that no earlier generation anywhere had shared: printed texts in Greek. Invented in Germany by Johannes Gutenberg around 1450, the printing press had come to Italy by 1465. In the 1480s, a Roman humanist and printer named Aldus Manutius arrived in Venice. Aldus had studied Greek and Latin with Guarino of Verona, Chrysoloras' closest student, and in 1495 Aldus' Venetian publishing house, the Aldine Press, began printing its famous Greek first editions. Specializing in inexpensive, high-quality editions of the Greek and Latin classics, the prodigious Aldine Press soon turned Venice into the printing capital not just of Italy but of all Europe.

Aldus' highest priority was Greek, and to edit his Greek texts he chose another Byzantine student of Demetrius Chalcondyles' named Marcus Musurus. A Cretan who has been called "the Renaissance's greatest Hellenist," Musurus had come from Crete first to Rome and then to Padua, where he succeeded Chalcondyles in the chair of Greek. Now he took a leading role in the "New Academy" of mostly Byzantine scholars that Aldus formed to act as an informal editorial board, selecting which Greek works to publish, comparing manuscripts, and painstakingly preparing the texts.

Though not the first Greek books printed in Venice (someone else had already published a popular edition of Chrysoloras' *Questions,* for example), the Aldine editions brought Greek literature in the original language before a wide reading public in the West for the first time. Aldus' Greek publications included Aristotle, Plato, Homer, Herodotus, Thucydides, Aristophanes, Sophocles, Aeschylus, Pausanias, and the ever-popular Plutarch. In addition, Aldus published numerous groundbreaking anthologies of Greek poetry and other works, helpful commentaries and reference books by Hellenistic and Byzantine writers, and a number of religious texts by the Greek Church Fathers. The Aldine Press issued some thirty Greek editions and some 130 editions in all before Aldus' death in 1515.

By that time, the combined efforts of the Byzantine and Italian humanists had achieved the goal that so many of them shared, of perpetuating ancient Greek literature. If the technological advance of printing allowed Greek texts to reach new audiences, equally important was the educational framework essential for comprehending those texts. The Byzantine humanists hadn't merely preserved the past, they had shown their Western students how to approach it and grasp it as well. Barely a century separates Barlaam's failed tutelage of Petrarch from the fall of Constantinople. The Italians' eagerness to learn came in the nick of time—as, in a lucky conjunction, did the Byzantines' to teach.

Northern Europe had taken an interest now, too, and its scholars had begun journeying to Italy, where many of them studied with the same Byzantine teachers as the Italians. The Dutch scholar who was the greatest of the northern humanists, Desiderius Erasmus, learned Greek in Venice with Marcus Musurus. Erasmus' English friend Thomas Linacre, a doctor and classicist who founded London's Royal College of Physicians, spent more than a decade in Italy studying Greek with Demetrius Chalcondyles and Politian, and winning his degree in medicine from the university of Padua. Linacre was Erasmus' and Sir Thomas More's doctor, and the close friend of another English humanist, John Colet, who had also studied in Italy. The German humanist Johannes Reuchlin had come to Italy in the 1480s, where he studied Greek with John Argyropoulos in Rome.

Another key figure was John Lascaris, a Byzantine who worked as Lorenzo de Medici's librarian, traveled widely in Ottoman lands to locate ancient Greek texts, and made his way to France, where he was appointed French ambassador to Venice in 1503. In Venice, he helped Aldus prepare an important edition of the Greek orators. John Lascaris is credited with bringing the Renaissance to France, where he befriended the early French humanists Guillaume Budé and Lefèvre d'Etaples, who had also studied with Argyropoulos in Rome in the 1480s. Even after 1453, Byzantine tides surged onto new shores in Western Europe.

PART II

Byzantium
and the
Islamic
World

CHAPTER SIX

A New Byzantium

Near the end of the seventh century, the caliph Abd al-Malik decided to build a great monument to the Arab conquests of the previous half century, and to the new monotheistic faith of Islam that had powered those conquests. Abd al-Malik was the ninth caliph to rule after the prophet Muhammad, and the fifth in the Umayyad dynasty.* He had just succeded to the caliphate, during a time of troubles in which numerous rebel Arab commanders had raised armies against the Umayyads. He was determined to restore Umayyad power, which was based not in Arabia but far to the north, in the Syrian city of Damascus.

Dark-complected and stocky, Abd al-Malik was known to his subjects as "Dew of the Stone" for his legendary stinginess. This latter trait, however, would be in marked abeyance when it came to the project he had in mind now, a magnificent

---

* The caliph (*khalifa*, meaning "successor" in Arabic) was the successor of the prophet Muhammad and claimed religious and political leadership of the Muslims.

marble octagon crowned by a gleaming golden dome some sixty feet across.

As the site for his memorial, Abd al-Malik chose not Mecca or Medina, Islam's holiest cities, but the ancient city of Jerusalem, long holy to Jews and Christians, formerly the religious centerpiece of the Byzantine empire and one of the first objects of the Arab conquests. Known to the world as the Dome of the Rock, Abd al-Malik's monument is Islam's oldest surviving public building, and to many observers its most splendid. From the top of Mount Moriah, the Temple Mount so central to Jewish history, the Dome of the Rock still dominates the old city's skyline, its swollen, shining cupola lording it over the comparatively drab remains of Jewish and Christian sites. Below it lie two of those sites, the Western or Wailing Wall, which represents the last remains of the Second Temple, and a bit farther west the Church of the Holy Sepulcher, originally built by Constantine the Great, though destroyed and rebuilt many times since. Next to it is the smaller al-Aqsa Mosque, built by Abd al-Malik's son and successor al-Walid.

Like Sant'Apollinare Nuovo in Ravenna, which the Gothic king Theoderic had finished about a century and a half earlier, the Dome of the Rock loudly and conspicuously proclaims the arrival of a new power to challenge the old. Also like Sant'Apollinare Nuovo, with which its lush interior decorative motifs have been compared, the Dome of the Rock asserts that arrival in the aesthetic idiom of the old power, which in both cases was Byzantium.

The Dome of the Rock perfectly symbolizes Byzantium's influence on the emerging civilization of Islam. Based on Byzantine Christian building traditions—the structure copied the nearby Church of the Anastasis—Islam's first public monument was not imitated by later Muslim builders.

It made no lasting impact on Islamic architecture, which went in other directions. In much the same way, Islamic civilization took the Byzantine imprint in its early stages, but ever since has seemingly struggled to erase all traces of it.

"Say Not 'Three'"

Where Sant'Apollinare Nuovo brashly pleads the Gothic case for assimilation, the Dome of the Rock takes Byzantine art and flings it in the empire's face. The Gothic decorations feel merely saucy; the Arab ones convey a sense of energized superiority. Elaborate Byzantine-inspired mosaics ring the heart of the structure, its interior colonnade. Their patterns incorporate repeated emblems of Byzantine (and to a lesser extent Persian) power that would have been immediately recognizable to all: crowns, bracelets, earrings, necklaces, breastplates. Persia by this time had been completely conquered by the victorious Arabs, but the Byzantines still held out, though much of their former territory was now in Arab hands. The Holy Land had fallen, and even as the Dome went up Abd al-Malik was wresting North Africa from Byzantine control. By displaying their imperial symbols this way, the Dome flouted Islam's older enemies. One of those enemies the Arabs had vanquished. The other, they believed, they were in the process of vanquishing.

The Dome of the Rock also has a number of Koranic inscriptions that drive the same point home in religious terms. These are clearly directed at Christians and (less so) at Jews, the Muslims' monotheistic forebears, both of whom the Koran honors as *ahl al-kitab*, People of the Book.

Despite this limited recognition, the inscriptions' main religious point is that in worshiping Jesus, and in further

introducing the idea of the Trinity, Christians have corrupted
the original monotheistic message of God's unity:

> Say: He is God, the One, God the eternal; He has not begot-
> ten nor was He begotten; and there is none comparable to
> Him. . . . Believe therefore in God and his apostles, and say
> not "Three." It will be better for you. God is only one God.
> Far be it from His glory that He should have a son.

Later Islamic buildings would use many of the same inscriptions, though the Dome of the Rock is unusual in the high
number of them that it features.

The Dome of the Rock is not a mosque. Instead, it is a
mashhad, a shrine for pilgrims, as its location might suggest.
According to Jewish tradition, it was here, on the rock over
which the dome is suspended, that God commanded Abraham to sacrifice Isaac. Later Umayyad propaganda would
build on this association, linking Jerusalem with Muhammad's famous Night Journey and his miraculous ascent to
heaven, which would be located at Moriah as well. Like Abd
al-Malik's construction of the Dome, all this was meant to
buttress the importance of Jerusalem for Muslims. But for
Abd al-Malik, the connection with Abraham was the one that
mattered; the historically spurious connection with Muhammad lay in the future. Claiming common descent with the
Jews from Abraham (through Hagar and Ishmael), the Arabs
in Abd al-Malik's day saw their new faith as the culmination
of the Abrahamic tradition.

Islam, Abd al-Malik was telling the world, was here to
stay.

Up to then the world had good reason to wonder. The
Arab empire had been split almost from its inception by

dissension, factional strife, and assassination. One of Abd al-Malik's main reasons for wishing to enhance Jerusalem's religious prestige was that Mecca and Medina were at that time outside of his control. Jerusalem, by contrast, was close to the Umayyad capital, Damascus.

It was under the Umayyads, who ruled from 661 to 750, that the center of Muslim power had moved from Arabia to Syria, territory the Umayyads had conquered from Byzantium. In making the transfer they had not gone unchallenged. It was also under the Umayyads, and under Abd al-Malik especially, that Islam took the first steps toward becoming a civilization as well as a faith.

Islamic civilization had two parents, and they were the same two older civilizations from which Abd al-Malik took such pains to distinguish his own in the decorations of the Dome of the Rock: Byzantium and Persia. But Byzantium and Persia also influenced Islam *before* it became a civilization, starting with the rise of the new faith during the disparate yet oddly intertwined lives of Islam's founder, the prophet Muhammad, and his near exact contemporary, the Byzantine emperor Heraclius.

HERACLIUS, MUHAMMAD, AND THE FIRST JIHAD

For centuries, Byzantium and Persia had fought each other. The border between them oscillated back and forth within a relatively narrow band that divided the Fertile Crescent in two. Neither could get the upper hand for long, though both enjoyed periods of brief dominance over the other. By the early seventh century, however, this long war was changing its shape. At that point Heraclius and Muhammad both were around forty, and both were about to embark on the ventures that would determine the rest of their lives.

On the Byzantine side, Christianity had soaked into society in a way that had not been the case earlier, as the religious sponge that was Byzantine civilization reached its saturation point. The traumas that attended Justinian's over-ambitious adventurism pushed this process forward: plague, riots, wars, earthquakes, oppressive taxation, and the empire's many looming enemies. Slavs had burst into Greece from the north, and in the Balkans they had allied themselves with the fearsome Avars;* most of Italy was lost to the Lombards; Persia was resurgent against Byzantine armies in the east. People needed reassurance.

They found it in the form of icons, which took on a new importance in public and private worship, and Constantinopolitans found it especially in the image of the Virgin Mary, who now emerged as the city's special patron and protector. In 566, the year after Justinian's death, the poet Corippus first described Constantinople as a city guarded by God. The idea would last as long as Byzantium itself, and the Virgin Mary's powers of intercession were the key to ensuring that divine protection. Byzantine armies began taking the field behind large icons. By the time Heraclius came to the throne in 610, Byzantines commonly compared their threatened nation with that of the ancient Israelites.

The Persians, too, had a state monotheism, Zoroastrianism, that had gradually been assuming a more and more central role over the past few centuries. The Sassanid dynasty, which had come to power in the early third century,

---

* The Avars were a group of Turkic nomads who dominated the Balkans in the sixth and early seventh centuries.

portrayed itself as reviving the glory days of Achaemenid rule, and the promulgation of state Zoroastrianism was part of this effort.* As in Byzantium, church and state grew closely linked under Sassanid rule, with increasing centralization, intolerance, and persecution of heresies marking the alliance of religion and government.

Struck over centuries, the sparks from these two increasingly flinty monotheisms eventually ignited holy war. In 614, the Persian sack of Jerusalem brought the war's new religious aspect into sharp relief. Since the time of Constantine, the holy city had been growing in importance as a destination for Christian pilgrims. Jews there had been expelled or persecuted as part of a general rise in state-supported anti-Semitism since the time of Justinian. Now, in addition to slaughtering untold numbers of Jerusalem's defenders, the Persians destroyed churches and exultantly seized or destroyed precious Christian relics. Adding insult to injury, the Persians opened the city to Jewish settlers and left them in charge of it. By the end of the decade, Byzantium had lost nearly half its territory to the Persian onslaught, and it was the wealthier half. Byzantium was broken, finished, and everyone knew it.

Except Heraclius, who marched with his army deep into Persia, gambling that his capital would hold out. He was right, but only just. In 626, the Persians allied themselves with the Avars and the Slavs to lay siege to Constantinople by both land and sea, which was the only hope an attacker had of taking the city. At Byzantium's moment of maximum peril, the Byzantine navy saved the day, breaking the siege by

---

* Founded by Cyrus the Great in the sixth century BC, the Achaemenid dynasty ruled the first Persian empire until it was conquered by Alexander the Great in the fourth century BC.

defeating the Avars and Slavs at sea and preventing the Persians from crossing the Bosporus.

From the Byzantine point of view, the real work was done by the Virgin Mary, and by the staunch patriarch Sergius, whom Heraclius had left in command. At the worst moments, Sergius could be seen parading along the city walls holding up the famous icon of the Blessed Virgin. It was clear to all that victory was owed to her intercession. Hadn't she herself appeared sword in hand over the waters of the Golden Horn—close by her church at Blachernai—encouraging her people to slay the enemy? Hadn't even the Avar Khan glimpsed her stalking the battlements?

It was Byzantium's finest hour, and the turning point of the war. Heraclius went on to win a series of battles in the East. Soon enough, the Persian king was overthrown and a Byzantine puppet installed in his place. In 630, Heraclius celebrated with a magnificent ceremony in which he restored the fragments of the True Cross to their place at the Church of the Holy Sepulcher in Jerusalem.

With Heraclius as his instrument, and through the Virgin Mary's intercession, God had miraculously saved the Byzantine empire and His chosen people. Everyone breathed a big sigh of relief. But like a horror flick in which the monster keeps coming back to life, the show wasn't over yet.

In 622, just when Byzantine morale had reached its lowest ebb, far to the south another chosen people had also come under threat of extinction. This was the *hijra*, the sojourn that Muhammad and his small band of followers spent in nearby Medina after being driven out of Mecca by the hostile Meccans.

At that point Islam was about a decade old. The newfound religious vibrancy of the two great clashing monotheistic empires to the north had set off resonating vibrations among the disorganized and feuding Arabs. Muhammad brilliantly focused these chaotic impulses. His basic message was one of religious and political unity under his personal leadership, unity along the lines aspired to, if never achieved, by the Byzantines and the Persians. Looking at the failed unity especially of the Christians, Muhammad thought he could get it right by dwelling on God's unity, which both reflected and would be reflected in the oneness of the Muslim community, the *ummah*.

Over the next several years in Medina, Muhammad's unity movement steadily gained in force. In 630, the same year that Heraclius returned the fragments of the True Cross to Jerusalem, Muhammad led an army of ten thousand against Mecca. The city surrendered peacefully, and many Meccans now embraced Islam, "submission" to the will of the one God. A flood of new warriors bolstered Muhammad's growing army. Now the strongest leader in Arabia, Muhammad imposed the condition of conversion to Islam upon those seeking his protection. Muslim ("one who submits") could not attack Muslim, so conversion meant security. Once a certain threshold was reached, it also meant that the Muslims had to go farther and farther afield to find conquests. "Believers, make war on the infidels who dwell around you," the Koran orders Muslims. "Deal firmly with them. Know that Allah is with the righteous."

In 632 Muhammad died after a brief illness. He was somewhere in his early sixties. He and his Muslims controlled virtually the entire Arabian peninsula, and he had begun leading exploratory raids in Byzantine Syria, where he planned the next stage of conquest. Having mastered the new art of holy war, the student had decided to test it against the teachers. It would be up to his successors to carry out the mission.

The Road to Damascus

First stop, Byzantium. Or more precisely, Byzantine Syria and Palestine, where disturbing omens would later be recalled: "There was an earthquake in Palestine, and a sign called an apparition appeared in the heavens to the south, predicting the Arab conquest. It remained thirty days stretching from south to north, and it was sword-shaped."

Victorious Byzantium was also exhausted and off guard. The Arabs engaged and destroyed the main Byzantine army of Syria at a spot of the Arabs' choosing on the Yarmuk River. A decisive turning point, the victory of the Yarmuk cracked Byzantine Palestine, Syria, and Mesopotamia wide open, leaving the cities there totally exposed. Those that tried to hold out were conquered and sacked; to avoid that fate, most capitulated voluntarily. The great Byzantine cities of Damascus, Antioch, and Jerusalem all fell to the Arab armies only a few short years after the Byzantines had so exultantly regained them from the Persians. Damascus would remain in Muslim hands forever after, while Antioch and Jerusalem would be temporarily recaptured by Christian forces much later, the former falling to the revived Byzantines in the late tenth century and the latter to Western European Crusaders in the early twelfth. By 640, Byzantine power in Syria, Palestine, and Mesopotamia was shattered. By the mid-640s, Byzantine Egypt too had fallen, with its glorious city of Alexandria, a vital center of ancient Greek learning. In all these places, many people were Monophysite Christians, whom the Byzantines persecuted as heretics. Often they welcomed the Arabs as liberators.

The Arabs had also begun looking westward to the Maghrib, "the West," as they called coastal North Africa. But at that point Heraclius, who had lived just long enough to feel his miraculous triumph over Persia turn to ashes in his mouth, was dead. Reportedly driven mad by the harsh turn of fate, he succumbed to dropsy in 641, a broken and pathetic figure.

The beleaguered Byzantines held the Arabs off at the border of Syria and Asia Minor, just north of Antioch, turning back numerous raids into the peninsula's mountainous interior, where the Arabs, desert fighters unused to the high country, never really got a foothold. It would be up to the migrating Turks, whose origins lay in the mountain uplands of Central Asia, to claim Asia Minor for Islam, but that big step lay centuries in the future. For now, though deprived once again (and permanently, this time) of its richest provinces, and still facing real peril, Byzantium would survive.

Soon after the first victories had been won in Palestine and Syria, the Arabs had also begun simultaneous incursions into Persian territory, starting with today's southern Iraq. Around the same time as the victory on the Yarmuk opened the Byzantine north and west to them, they had struck a similarly decisive blow against the Persians at Qadisiyah in Iraq, opening up the Persian East.

The Persian capital of Ctesiphon lay just over the border from Arabia. Near the site of the future Baghdad, it was within easy striking distance of the Arab raiders and fell rapidly. Once Ctesiphon fell, the already shaky Sassanid state crumbled, unable to mount an effective defense from its provincial centers, where ties to the capital had not yet been firmly reestablished after the war. The Persian strategic situation was the opposite of the Byzantine one: Byzantium was exposed in its provinces, perhaps, but relatively secure in its distant, well-fortified capital.

By about 650, the Arabs had conquered nearly all of the Fertile Crescent, as well as Egypt and most of Persia, where some mopping-up operations remained. These lands, a huge area that the British began calling the "Middle East" in the early twentieth century, would constitute the heart of the Arab Islamic empire. Muslim Arab settlers immediately began pouring into them from Arabia, many of them at first living in newly founded garrison towns (such as Basrah or Kufah in southern Iraq) and only later blending with the local populations.

But Muhammad's beautiful dream of unity now fell apart. Uthman, the fourth and last of Muhammad's elderly companions to hold power as caliph, and a member of the Umayyad clan, was assassinated by mutinous soldiers. Followers of the prophet's nephew Ali pushed him forward as caliph, but opposition to Ali coalesced around Ayesha, the prophet's favorite wife. It included Muawiyah, the governor of Syria, who was an Umayyad cousin of the murdered Uthman.

Muawiyah had conquered Syria for Islam, and he now refused to recognize Ali as caliph. When Ali was assassinated by an embittered former supporter, Muawiyah was confirmed as caliph. In these events, though, were the seeds of further dissension, because they gave rise to the Shiite movement, creating Islam's bitterest division. Alienated from the Sunni mainstream, Shiites would cling to the memory of Ali's assassination.

Muawiyah moved the Muslims' capital from Medina to Damascus, a logical choice for him, since it was from there that he had governed Syria. Thus the Umayyad dynasty was founded, with the former Byzantine city of Damascus serving as what amounted to the Arabs' first imperial capital. And, for the moment anyway, a semblance of unity was restored.

THE "NEO-BYZANTINE EMPIRE" OF THE UMAYYADS

"The first to use a throne in Islam was Muawiyah," writes the great fourteenth-century Muslim historian Ibn Khaldun, picking out a key moment as the caliphate evolved from its original Bedouin simplicity toward the majesty familiar to Westerners from sources such as the *Arabian Nights*. Earlier, Ibn Khaldun explains, the Muslims had "despised pomp, which has nothing whatever to do with the truth. The caliphate then came to be royal authority, and the Muslims learned to esteem the splendour and luxury of this world."

The move to Damascus that established royal authority also put the center of that authority firmly in a Byzantine milieu: the Arabs' first teachers in pomp and circumstance were the Byzantines. The Arabs could scarcely have done better, unless perhaps they had chosen the Persians—who would become their second teachers.

That second stage, the Persian-inspired Abbasid caliphate of Baghdad that we associate with the *Arabian Nights*, was nearly a century off when Muawiyah assumed the first caliphal throne in Damascus.* Long before Baghdad was founded, the splendor of Byzantine court ritual first seduced the Arabs into imitating it in their own ceremonials. Not that Muawiyah wasn't criticized for putting on royal airs. In defense he explained "that Damascus was full of Greeks, and that none would believe in his power if he did not behave and look like an emperor."

But Byzantine influence on the emerging Islamic civilization, a tidal pull that now reached its high-water mark,

---

* The Abbasids were the second imperial Arab dynasty, founded in 750 and extinguished by the invading Mongols in 1258.

went far beyond the caliph's assumption of royal ways. It covered virtually all areas of life.

On the official side of things, from the first conquests of Byzantine and Persian lands in the 630s, the Arab conquerors had maintained the civic institutions that already existed in those lands. As newcomers to the challenges of ruling such vast territories, the Arabs had no time-tested institutions of their own to impose. Wisely, they let things go on pretty much as before, relying on their new subjects to keep the wheels turning. "The Muslims were illiterate Arabs who did not know how to write and keep books," writes Ibn Khaldun of this early period. "For bookkeeping they employed Jews, Christians, or certain non-Arab clients versed in it."

Tax structure, currency, civic administration—from Egypt to Antioch the rhythms of official life generally kept the same or a similar flavor, except that Arab Muslim commanders replaced the old imperial officials at the top. Numerous Arab loanwords from Greek reflect the wholesale continuation of the old institutions under the new overlords, as the Arabs simply transliterated words from Greek that had no Arabic equivalent. The Byzantine poll tax called the *demosia* became *al-haraj ad-dimusi;* taxable farmland or *pakton* became *baqt;* the officials who collected the taxes, the *grapheis* and the *meizon,* became the *garafisis* and *mazun,* respectively; and the currency, the Byzantine *denarius,* became the *dinar.* Similar phenomena can be traced in former Persian lands, though again the fact that the Umayyad power center lay in former Byzantine territory weighted things in Byzantium's favor in these early days.

Another sort of impact took place on the levels of folk culture and artistic expression, where oversight gave way to apprenticeship. As nomadic Arab tribesmen arrived to garrison their outposts in the wake of conquest, Ibn Khaldun says, they exchanged settled ways for their old Bedouin life. Though at first they acted as overlords to the former Byzantines and Persians, eventually the Arabs were tutored by their civilized subjects in the skills necessary for the sedentary existence.

As with administrative matters, this process left its traces in Greek loanwords that found their way into Arabic in areas from domestic life (household items, furniture, cooking, clothing, cleaning, jewelry) to agriculture (animals, crops, other plants, containers), commerce (measures, ships, other nautical matters), literature (writing tools and methods), arts and crafts, and religion.

Scholars have also traced Byzantine and Persian influences in Arab music and painting, both of which Ibn Khaldun says the Arabs learned from their new subjects.* And Byzantine law was taken up by early Islamic *qadi*s or judges, contributing toward the body of jurisprudence that would become the *sharia*, or Islamic law. Byzantine continuity and Arab imitation were so pervasive that modern historians have called the Umayyad caliphate of Damascus a "Neo-Byzantine empire."

Constantinople: The Arabs' Unfulfilled Dream of Conquest

When Muawiyah was still governor of Syria, having found himself checked in Asia Minor by land, he had begun building up the Arabs' naval fleet, aggressively challenging Byzantine

---

* According to Ibn Khaldun, before the conquests the Arabs had not known singing, which they now discovered. Pre-Islamic Arabs had cultivated only oral poetry, which was carried over into the Islamic period through recitation of the Koran.

mastery of the sea. With a fleet in place, and with Byzantine naval dominance a thing of the past by the 670s, the Arabs could raid coastal Asia Minor, establishing garrisons as they went, and work their way closer to the Byzantine capital by that route. By this time, too, Muawiyah was attacking Byzantine forces in North Africa and Sicily by sea. In 674, the Arab fleet entered the Bosporus, blockading Constantinople and raiding right up to the walls. The blockade and the raids lasted four years, with the Byzantine navy penned into the Golden Horn lest it be destroyed by the stronger Arab fleet.

Finally the Byzantines risked battle, sending out ships armed with their secret weapon, a napalm-like substance called Greek Fire, which scorched some Arab ships, probably frightening more than it harmed. But the Arabs were demoralized by now, and they headed for home. The fleet was wrecked in a storm on its way, and most of the ships and men were lost. At the same time, the Byzantines badly defeated the Arabs in several land battles. Forced to negotiate for a truce—according to which the Arabs agreed to pay tribute to the Byzantines, an indignity that must have rankled—Muawiyah died the following year, in 680.

Before his death, Muawiyah had publicly designated his son Yazid as his successor, thus breaking with earlier practice and adopting the principle of dynastic succession. Yazid faced big trouble from the beginning. The Byzantines were counterattacking, backed by Christian guerrillas in Syria, and the Berbers of North Africa soon also rebelled against the governor that Yazid appointed there. The old Muslim families in Medina let it be known that they opposed Yazid, encouraging Ali's son Husayn to rebel in Kufah. Yazid's forces easily crushed Husayn and his small band of supporters, surrounding them in the desert at Karbala and, when they refused to surrender, killing them all.*

Yazid died unexpectedly in 683. Further chaos ensued, but eventually another branch of the Umayyad family arose under Muawiyah's cousin Marwan, who claimed the caliphate, and Marwan's son Abd al-Malik, who succeeded his father in 685. It took still more bloodshed, but by 692—the year after he completed construction on the Dome of the Rock—Abd al-Malik had vanquished his rivals, subdued the Shiites and other rebels, gone back on the offensive against the Byzantines, and won general recognition as the rightful caliph, restoring the Umayyad dynasty to full glory. If the Dome of the Rock said that Islam was here to stay, it also said the same thing about the Umayyads, and about Abd al-Malik himself, who had fought so hard to reestablish their power.

With Abd al-Malik begins the High Caliphate, a period of some two and a half centuries during which Arab imperial might reached its zenith. Abd al-Malik's assertive Dome of the Rock notwithstanding, the Umayyads would preside only over the first half century or so of this imperial and cultural flowering. The real florescence of Islamic civilization would occur under their successors, the Abbasids, and it would be centered not in Byzantine-flavored Damascus but in the new Arab-built capital of Baghdad, far to the east in former Persian territory. From a Neo-Byzantine empire, the High Caliphate would evolve into a Neo-Sassanid empire, as Persian cultural influences rose to shape the larger outlines of Islamic civilization and the earlier Byzantine framework fell away.

Yet, it was still within the Byzantine context that the first

---

* Even more than the assassination of Ali, Husayn's martyrdom fixed in place the Shiites' resentment and sense of guilt (Shiites still ritually flog themselves for not having come to Husayn's rescue).

scaffolding was put in place. The Dome of the Rock was not an isolated projection of Islamic and Arab pride but part of a larger, coherent program by which Abd al-Malik proposed to declare Islam's and the Arabs' arrival, to differentiate Islamic civilization from its Byzantine sources even while continuing to draw on them.

Other aspects of Abd al-Malik's program included the replacement of Greek by Arabic as the language of government, and the minting of coins that, for the first time, broke away from their Byzantine models and took on an Islamic look and feel. Up to then, the Umayyads had struck coins that copied the Byzantine ones right down to the portraits of Christ or the emperor on one side, the only concession to Islam being the removal of the arm of the Christian cross on the other side (leaving just the upright). Now Abd al-Malik replaced such emblems with Koranic inscriptions, though the basic denominations remained the same.

One reason that the earlier coins had had to look Byzantine was so that they would be accepted by the Byzantines themselves, whether in tribute payments or in commercial transactions. As it became clear that the Arab conquests were not going to be reversed, the Byzantines would increasingly be forced to accommodate the Arabs, even copying their coins in turn, while the Arabs would realize that they were the ones who could throw their weight around. Byzantium was entering its Dark Age, shorn of its wealthiest provinces and pushed onto the defensive not just by the Arabs but by other new enemies as well. Its relative poverty would stand in stark contrast to the vigorous prosperity of the rising Arab empire, which now controlled many times more manpower, resources, and land.

In Byzantium, the destabilizing shock of such realities was reflected in a series of coups and countercoups that rocked the Byzantine empire starting during Abd al-Malik's reign. And at the height of this instability, as the Byzantines fought out a devastating civil war between rival claimants to the throne, the Umayyads once again sought the goal that had so frustratingly eluded the great Muawiyah.

After all, the Prophet himself had predicted that Muslim armies would one day occupy Rum (Rome), as the Arabs called both Constantinople and its empire. Though alarming, the earlier attempt had amounted to little more than an extended series of raids, backed by a naval blockade, during which simultaneous efforts were undertaken against the Byzantines and other enemies in other theaters of war. This time it would be different. This time, the Arabs' full strength would be brought to bear in a concerted and sustained effort to capture the Byzantines' capital and put an end to their empire altogether.

The Umayyads' second siege of Constantinople was planned by Abd al-Malik's son and successor al-Walid, begun in 717 by al-Walid's brother Sulayman, and continued by their cousin Umar II, who succeeded Sulayman after the latter's death that same year. The invading force reportedly comprised 120,000 men and 1,800 ships.

From the start, however, things went badly for the Arabs. By the time the planning was over, so was the Byzantine civil war, and the new emperor who emerged as victor, Leo III, was a gifted, experienced, and resolute commander who had bested the Arabs a number of times in the past. In addition, the winter of 717–18 was unusually cold and harsh, catching the Arabs by surprise and decimating them through illness and exposure. The Arabs were also hampered by the fact that many of the sailors on the ships sent to relieve the besieging forces in the spring of 718 were Christians from Egypt and North Africa. Having tasted Arab rule for nearly a century, they were no longer so well disposed toward the

Arabs as their ancestors had been at the time of the conquests, and many came over to the Byzantine side. Finally, the Byzantines were assisted by their sometime enemies the Bulgars, who swept down upon the Arab forces investing the city by land, killing thousands. In August 718, just over a year after the siege began, Umar called for the Arabs to retreat. Once again, on its homeward voyage the Arab fleet was wrecked in a storm.

The Umayyads' Syrian power base and its nearness to Byzantium had worked to the advantage of the early Umayyad caliphs such as Muawiyah and Abd al-Malik. Muawiyah had risen to the caliphate in the first place largely because he was governor of the province that was on the front line of the struggle with Byzantium—he himself had conquered the lands he ruled as governor. This early success, however, held the Umayyads hostage with a logic that pointed inexorably to a single outcome. They had to vanquish the Byzantines and replace them as overlords of Constantinople, which was clearly their only real choice of imperial capital.

The failure of the second siege made it clear that this was not going to happen. As a consequence, the Umayyads' forward momentum ground to a halt. They were left to chill slowly in the long shadow of a great capital city that would never be theirs.

Byzantium's stubborn survival has another set of implications. In the West, too, the Arab advance posed a grave threat. Having occupied North Africa and Spain, invading Muslim armies were turned back only in central France, at the battle of Poitiers in 732.* But had Byzantium fallen a

---

* By the Franks under Charles, called Charles Martel ("Charles the Hammer") for the victory. Charles, not a king but an official of the crumbling Merovingian dynasty, used the prestige from this victory to found a new dynasty, the Carolingian. His grandson Charlemagne would expand its dominions to rival Byzantium as a "Roman" empire.

decade and half earlier, the Arabs might have been able to mount a simultaneous invasion from the East, catching Europe in a pincer. The outcome might just possibly have been a Muslim Europe. Constantinople's great walls protected more than just a city, more even than just an empire. Although this card can be overplayed, Byzantium was a bulwark for Europe in the East.

By the 740s the Umayyads' nearness to Byzantium had turned from an advantage to a liability, from a harbinger of victory to a nagging reminder of unfulfilled promise. The failure to take Constantinople helped push the Islamic world's center of gravity eastward, into Persian territory. Paradoxically, however, only after such a move could the Arabs open themselves to a whole new influence from Byzantium: the legacy of ancient Greece.

CHAPTER SEVEN

THE HOUSE OF WISDOM

During the High Caliphate, Islam claimed a place as the world's most vital, expansive civilization. No longer were the Arab settlers in the conquered lands isolated in their garrisons, an alien presence imposing an alien rule, aloof from the local population and seeking to cultivate Islam apart from the peoples they ruled. Over a vast and prosperous area extending from Afghanistan, Iran, and Iraq through Syria, Egypt, North Africa, and Spain, Arabs now began blending with local populations. At the same time, the local people—Christians, Zoroastrians, Jews, pagans—began converting to Islam in greater numbers.

As the weight of the Islamic world shifted eastward, Umayyad leadership was challenged by the Abbasids, a powerful clan in the former Persian territory of Iraq. In February 750, Abbasid and Umayyad forces met in battle at the river Zab, a tributary of the Tigris in northern Iraq, and the Abbasids won decisively. The Umayyad caliph Marwan II fled, dying soon after, and the Abbasid leader al-Saffah—who had

already been proclaimed as caliph by his followers the previous year—was confirmed in power.

Al-Saffah founded the Abbasid state, but he died after
ruling only four years. He was succeeded by his younger
brother al-Mansur, who immediately faced a rash of rebellions and challengers.

An experienced commander, still vigorous in his forties
when he became caliph, al-Mansur had little real difficulty
putting down the rebellions as they arose, but he couldn't
keep new ones from erupting. He needed a capital, a center
of gravity for the turbulent cities of the Abbasid heartland
from which he drew his power. As its location, he chose a
place on the Tigris River where it approaches close to the
Euphrates, not far from the old Persian capital of Ctesiphon.
Al-Mansur called his new capital Madinat as-Salam, "city of
peace"; it soon became better known by its Persian name of
Baghdad.

"The Most Prosperous City in the World"

Al-Mansur chose his site for the same two reasons that had
led Constantine to choose Byzantium: it lay at the junction of
rich trade routes, and it was, so he thought, highly defensible,
nestled as it was between two wide rivers. Unlike Constantine, al-Mansur was only half right.

It certainly was a superb site for trade. Ships came up
the Tigris by way of the Persian Gulf from Arabia, East
Africa, and India, or downriver from Kurdistan with goods
from Azerbaijan and Armenia. The nearby Euphrates brought
merchandise and travelers from the west: Syria, Egypt, North
Africa, Byzantium. Baghdad also lay athwart the Silk Road to

China, which ran eastward through the Persian heartlands of Isfahan and Khorasan. Declaring his intention to build "the most prosperous city in the world," al-Mansur predicted that his new capital would long reign supreme as a glittering diadem for the Arabs' new far-flung dominions.

But rivers can be bridged and crossed. Because of al-Mansur's misjudgment on this score not a trace of his unique original plan remains today: the Round City, a perfect circle over a mile across, circumscribed by thick, high walls that have long since vanished, with a domed central palace complex that was ignored by al-Mansur's successors well before it fell to ruin in the thirteenth century, when the city was sacked by the Mongols. The famous green dome was crowned by a statue of a horseman carrying a spear, which was said to face in the direction of the next threat to the caliph's rule. The legend is a giveaway. For all their fabulous wealth and glorious cultural patronage, the Abbasid caliphs forever faced challenges to their legitimacy and power. The Round City was to be Baghdad's heart, the home of the caliph, his administrators, his slaves, his soldiers. It cannot even be located with confidence within modern Baghdad.

Outside it lay the rest of the city, spreading out on both sides of the winding Tigris, which was spanned by a series of pontoon bridges. At first al-Mansur wanted to put the markets inside the Round City. He was advised against it by a visiting Byzantine ambassador, who warned the caliph that his enemies would use the pretext of commerce to enter the walls and spy out his secrets. No one could know the ins and outs of espionage better than a Byzantine ambassador; the markets were moved. The biggest was in the southern district of Karkh, a bewildering but tightly organized maze of stalls and stands on the west bank of the Tigris, where each specialty was firmly staked out in its own separate domain.

(Al-Mansur ordered the butchers' market placed farthest from the palace, averring that butchers have dull wits and sharp knives.) Between Karkh and the Round City lay another bustling market district, Karkh's rival Sharqiya, which was said to have had a hundred bookshops.

The Arab histories of Baghdad are full of accounts of overawed Byzantine ambassadors to the caliphal court. Cataloguing the wonders that the Byzantines encountered on their entry into the city and rehearsing their predictable amazement became a standard way of dramatizing Baghdad's splendor. One ambassador in the early tenth century was held up for months as the caliph finished redecorating. He was then conducted between endless ranks of assembled troops and taken through a long underground passage into the palace, where he was paraded in front of the thousands of eunuchs, chamberlains, and African slaves who staffed it. In the treasury he saw the caliph's gold and jewels all arranged specially for display. And several decades before Liudprand of Cremona was awed in Constantinople by the emperor's golden tree and mechanical birds, this Byzantine ambassador to Baghdad had the same experience in the caliph's throne room, right down to the twittering birds. It has been suggested that the unnamed ambassador brought the idea back with him. But similar devices (which are called automata) had been known in the ancient world, and modern historians aren't sure who got the idea from whom.

Baghdad's foundation coincides with the low point of Byzantine morale during the Dark Age. Classical learning had all but disappeared, and even religious literature virtually dried up as the empire went onto a permanent war footing. Not an inch less devout but stripped down now for action, the Byzantines went so far as to give up their beloved icons. Leo III, the emperor who successfully brought Constantinople through the Arab siege of 717–18, was the first to impose Iconoclasm on his reluctant subjects, tearing down icons from churches and other public places, and discouraging their use in private worship.

His son Constantine V, an even more ardent Iconoclast, went further and actually destroyed the religious pictures. As a consequence, nearly all surviving Byzantine icons are from later periods, when the icons were restored, and when Constantine V himself was given the disrespectful epithet Copronymus, "shit-named," which supposedly arose from an unexpected incident during his baptism. Though he was one of Byzantium's greatest warrior-emperors, Constantine V Copronymus would be reviled by generations of outraged Orthodox icon venerators.

The Judaic scriptural ban on graven images had always provided ammunition for Christians who objected to religious pictures. Such objections aside, Iconoclasm's real justification was that icons had failed to bring victory against the Muslims, who themselves were known for banning human images in religious art. It seemed God was punishing the empire for having wandered into the error of idolatry in the age before the Arabs, when icons had jumped into public prominence. In place of the discredited icon, Byzantine armies now began marching under the stark, simple cross, an austere symbol for an austere time.

Iconoclasm was agonizing for the empire, but the problem was that it seemed to work. Throughout the Iconoclast period, with uncanny consistency emperors who supported it (like Constantine V) won battles, while those who temporarily restored the icons immediately started losing.*

---

* Iconoclasm was officially in force in Byzantium from 726 to 787, and again from 815 to 843.

The most impassioned and eloquent defense of icons came not from within the empire but from Umayyad Syria, where John of Damascus, son of a Greek tax collector, wrote tracts justifying icon veneration; his main theological point was to distinguish between venerating the icon for what it represented and actually worshipping the image itself. Later, John of Damascus would himself be venerated as one of Orthodoxy's great hero-saints. But at the time icons had acquired a suspicious air of weakness, softness, femininity. The two rulers who most conspicuously championed the icons during this era were both empresses, neither of whom enjoyed much military success against the Arabs.

Despite the imbalance in power and wealth between them, the Byzantines remained dug in, always the Arabs' stubborn opponents and the chief object of their competitive hostility. Almost every year, the Arabs would send out spring and summer raids from Syria or Armenia over the border into Byzantine Asia Minor. Yet, high-level embassies constantly traveled between Baghdad and Constantinople, and for some time a lurching cooperation brought Arabs and Byzantines together in joint rule over the island of Cyprus.

Constant skirmishing along the frontier bred a tough warrior aristocracy in the borderlands, where Byzantine and Arab culture blended, and where opposing warlords had more in common with each other than with their rulers back in Baghdad or Constantinople. One such was Diogenes, a local Byzantine commander famous for his valor, who perished in battle against the raiding army of the caliph Harun ar-Rashid, al-Mansur's grandson, just north of the Cilician Gates in the year 786.* It is thought that this Diogenes inspired

---

* The Cilician Gates, a narrow pass in the rugged Taurus Mountains, offered the only easy route between Arab-controlled Cilicia and Byzantine-controlled Asia Minor.

oral poets to celebrate his feats, and that the resulting verses gave rise to what has been described as the Byzantine national epic, a long two-part poem called *Digenes Akritas*.

In the first part, a dashing Arab emir kidnaps the beautiful daughter of a Byzantine general, then falls in love with her and converts to Christianity. Their son is Basil, a half-Arab, half-Byzantine also known as Digenes Akritas, which means "two-blooded border guard." His exploits are told in the second part:

> And when the well-born Digenes the fair
> Himself came to the measure of his prime
> And among men was counted a right man;
> Then on a day he sprang to horse and rode,
> Took up the club and spear he had,
> Gathered his company and took them with him.

Later Digenes meets the emperor himself in the borderlands near the northern Euphrates. The emperor praises the young man's prowess and offers him whatever he would like as a reward. The pious hero replies, as all such do, that the emperor's love is enough for him, and besides, he knows that the emperor has an expensive army to maintain:

> So I beseech your glorious majesty:
> Love him who is obedient, pity the poor,
> Deliver the oppressed from malefactors,
> Forgive those who unwittingly make blunders,
> And heed no slanders, nor accept injustice,
> Sweep heretics out, confirm the orthodox.

At almost exactly the same time on the other side of the Arab empire, skirmishing between Arabs and Franks resulted in a very similar poem, the *Song of Roland*, about a faithful knight of Charlemagne's who dies saving the army from the Arabs.

Such rugged but pious chivalry contrasts sharply with the dangerous, decadent sensuality of Harun's Baghdad, at least as described so memorably in works such as the *Arabian Nights*, which is actually thought to give a fairly accurate picture. By about 800, when the celebrated Harun was nearing the end of his life, Baghdad had grown into a thriving metropolis of around one million people. It gave every indication of having fulfilled al-Mansur's highest expectations.

Meanwhile, in monochrome, iconless Constantinople, the only major construction that had occurred in the past century was the repair of buildings and churches after a severe earthquake in 740. As for classical scholarship, we have little evidence but one or two shadowy names—dry skeletons that cannot be fleshed out with any confidence. Jerusalem had paled and Athens, to all appearances, had given up the ghost entirely.

THE CALIPH'S DREAM OF REASON

According to tradition, the Arabs' interest in ancient Greek learning began in the early ninth century, when the caliph al-Mamun, the son of Harun ar-Rashid, dreamed that he met a ruddy, handsome, blue-eyed man who identified himself as Aristotle. In his dream, the story goes, al-Mamun asked the famous philosopher to answer a question: "What is good?"

"Whatever is good according to reason," Aristotle replied.

"What else?" asked the caliph.

"Whatever is good according to religious law," came the answer.

"And what else?"

"Nothing else," said Aristotle.

The tenth-century Baghdad bookseller and author Ibn an-Nadim describes the dream in his *Fihrist,* or "Index," a compilation of Arab literature up to that point. An-Nadim goes on to say that the dream prompted al-Mamun to write to the Byzantine emperor, whom he had just defeated in battle but whom he now asked for help. The caliph wondered if he might "send people to select books on the ancient sciences from those preserved in the libraries of Byzantine territory." At first the emperor refused the request, but then he consented. The caliph immediately sent a group of learned scholars to Byzantium, who "made their choice among the material which they found there and took it along to al-Mamun. He ordered them to translate it, and this was done."

The scholars, an-Nadim tells us, belonged to the "House of Wisdom," which modern historians have long taken as an organized research institution that al-Mamun established especially for the task of translating Greek texts into Arabic. Recent research has cast some doubt on this picture—the fabled "House of Wisdom" may have been conjured up by later writers such as an-Nadim as they tried to explain a translation movement that went back much further than al-Mamun. Al-Mamun traditionally gets the lion's share of the credit, but this research suggests that it was al-Mansur who inaugurated the first systematic attempts to make ancient Greek learning available to the Arabs. And the translators themselves were part of a movement to translate Greek literature that was already well established under the Sassanid Persians, long before the Arabs arrived.*

---

* This reinterpretation of the evidence is presented by Professor Dimitri Gutas in his 1998 book *Greek Thought, Arabic Culture.*

An-Nadim's and other similar accounts probably tell us more about how later generations looked back on the origins of the translation movement, which played a central role in early Abbasid society, than they do about those origins themselves. One thing that stands out in them is the idea of Byzantium as the repository of reason's ancient secrets. Whether or not these accounts are historically accurate in their portrayal of the House of Wisdom, in a larger sense they idealized Byzantium itself as a House of Wisdom for the questing and curious civilization that had, by their own era, clearly emerged in Islamic lands.

THE SYRIAN SCHOOLS AND HUNAYN IBN ISHAQ

The translators who did this work were not Byzantines, but they came from a culture whose roots went back to Byzantium. They were Syrians, members of Christian traditions that had been excluded or suppressed by the Byzantines' increasingly narrow, intolerant piety. The schools in which these translators learned Greek also owed their origins to Byzantium, since most of them were based on the school of Alexandria in Egypt, which before the Arab conquest was the capital of secular learning in the Roman and Byzantine world. Much of the translation work took place in Baghdad, but the translators received their training in this network of schools.

The greatest of them was Hunayn ibn Ishaq, born near Baghdad in 808 and known to the West as Johannitius. His name would become linked in the *Fihrist* and other later sources with the House of Wisdom, and most modern accounts follow these sources in portraying Hunayn as taking daring field trips to Byzantium from the House of Wisdom in order to acquire precious Greek manuscripts.

But in fact he himself never mentions going to any specific Byzantine territory by name, though later sources have him going at one point "to the land of the Greeks." This could mean Byzantium, or it could mean a city such as Alexandria. He does write about wide-ranging journeys to lands the Arabs had conquered from the Byzantines, such as a trip he took in order to find a good manuscript of Galen's *On Demonstration*: "I traveled in its search in northern Mesopotamia, all of Syria, Palestine and Egypt until I reached Alexandria. I found nothing except about half of it, in disorder and incomplete, in Damascus."* Nor does he ever mention the House of Wisdom, as he almost surely would have done had he worked there.

Hunayn's family were Nestorians, Christians whose distinctive religious outlook had originated in Byzantium with a fifth-century bishop named Nestorius. Nestorius had been embroiled in the controversies over the nature of Christ that were raging through the church at the time, and had settled on a position that, like that of the Arians, emphasized Christ's humanity, and that was eventually rejected by the Orthodox as heretical. It stood in distinction to the position of the Monophysites, who emphasized Christ's divinity. Nestorian beliefs, like Monophysite ones, were popular in eastern parts of the empire, especially among Syrians and Egyptians. Orthodox authorities persecuted Nestorians along with Monophysites in Syria, as well as in Egypt and elsewhere.

Most of the Nestorian Syrians ended up leaving Byzantium for Persia. There these religious refugees found a warm

---

* Galen, a Greek who lived in the second century, was the greatest medical authority of the ancient world. In *On Demonstration*, he emphasizes the importance of logic in "demonstrating" medical truths.

welcome from the Sassanids, who were happy to have an alternative and rival version of Christianity to throw up against the Byzantines. In time Nestorian missionaries spread their version of Christianity far into Central Asia and even China, where Nestorian communities existed into the eleventh century. In contrast to the Nestorians, most Syrian Monophysites stayed within Byzantine borders, though their homelands, too, eventually fell to the Arab conquest.

The Nestorians, then, were descended from Byzantine Syrians who had settled in Persian Iraq before it was conquered by the Arabs. Up to the conquest, the Syrians had been one of Byzantium's dominant ethnic groups, and they remained important after it, though the bulk of the Syrian population now lived in the conquered areas. By Hunayn's day most spoke Persian as a first language, but like Hunayn many would have grown up comfortable also in Syriac and perhaps also Greek, both of which were used in liturgy, and in Arabic, the language of the governing class with which they were so closely associated.

In Hunayn's time, learned Syrians—and there were many of them—considered themselves descended from the ancient Babylonians or, alternatively, from the Assyrians, both of whose empires had contested over the Fertile Crescent before the rise of Persia. But Syrians were related to the Arabs, and their native language, Syriac, was a Semitic language (like Arabic and Hebrew) that had evolved from Aramaic, the language of Jesus. Syriac's similarity to Arabic would play a key role in the translations, since it meant that relatively little effort was needed to render into Arabic a Greek work that already existed in Syriac. It took much more effort to sit down and make an original translation directly from Greek into Arabic, with the result that the majority of

Greek works that made it into Arabic went through the middle stage of Syriac.

Starting in the fifth and sixth centuries, the religious controversies and later the missions to the East spurred demand among Syrians for religious texts in their own language. The early translators focused mostly on biblical and patristic writings. Long before the Arab conquests, as they developed a stronger tradition of translation from Greek into Syriac, they branched into secular learning as well, and Greek literary forms deeply shaped their own emerging literature.

Hunayn may have been the star translator, but he was certainly not alone. Moving back in time, a sampling of his illustrious predecessors might include the eighth-century Nestorian patriarch Timothy I, a learned bibliophile who translated Aristotle's *Topics* and other works for the Abbasids, reinvigorated the Nestorian clergy, and brought the missionary effort to its high point; Jacob of Edessa, a seventh-century Nestorian bishop who (like many of these figures) studied Greek in Alexandria; and Jacob's teacher Severus of Nisibis, the leading Syrian intellectual of the seventh century, another polymath Nestorian bishop, translator, astronomer, and logician, fluent in Greek and Persian but proud of his Syrian culture to the point of chauvinism.

The Syrians had an abiding sense of their own place at the center of the universe. In late antiquity the stereotypical holy man was a Syrian, such as the fifth-century Symeon the Stylite, who lived in contemplative seclusion outside the Syrian city of Antioch—first in a dry cistern, then chained to a rock in a little cell, and finally on a tiny platform at the top of a fifty-foot-high column or *stylos*. This famous Christian ascetic attracted pilgrims from as far away as Britain, Gaul, and Spain in the West to Armenia and Persia in the East.

They wanted to touch him, which was partly why he kept adding to the height of the column, which had originally been much shorter, erected to remove him first from the world of sin and only later from his fans as well. Symeon set a fashion in asceticism. Monk-capped columns began popping up like toadstools, which they resembled.

This was the world of the Hellenized Syrians—brilliant, polyglot, devout, and assuming more than its share of cosmic entitlement. For the Abbasids, the Syrians made up a preexisting, accessible pool of talent and knowledge in Greek studies. They would always constitute the core group of translators in the translation movement.

By the time of the Arab conquests, the Hellenized Syrians enjoyed an extensive network of monasteries and schools in the conquered areas, and these schools would make up the most important institutional framework for the transmission of secular Greek learning to the Arabs. In contrast with broke and battered Byzantium, the Fertile Crescent under the Arabs was dotted with prosperous, well-established Syrian schools that offered Greek studies. The heirs of Alexandria itself, they constituted the leading centers of Hellenism in the world. Each had its own specialties and traditions, from Antioch, Edessa, and Qinnasrin in the west, to Nisibis and Mosul in Iraq, to the famous school at Jundi-Shapur to the east, deep in Iran. Though ultimately originating in the Byzantine cultural milieu, by the time of the conquest these schools were much more sophisticated than anything Constantinople could offer.

Most were Nestorian, and they had been strongly supported by the Sassanids. Nisibis, which had inherited leadership from Edessa in the fifth century, was the largest, and was considered the center of Nestorian culture. While theology took pride of place in all of them, the Nestorians also gravitated to science and medicine, and it was these areas that drew the Sassanids' and later the Abbasids' support.

Under both regimes, the Nestorians held what amounted to a near monopoly on medicine. Hunayn's father, Ishaq, was a pharmacist, and Hunayn himself is reported to have studied medicine as a young man at Baghdad and Jundi-Shapur, where a renowned practicing hospital supplemented the coursework. Like Hunayn, whose own son Ishaq ibn Hunayn* also became a famous translator, many of the leading translators belonged to families whose activities were passed on through generations. The leading Nestorian medical dynasty was that of the Bukhtishu, but others included the Masawayh, the al-Tayfuri, and the Serapion, tightly knit clans that were prominently associated with the school at Jundi-Shapur.

Since all the important medical writings were Greek, there was a logical connection between medicine and translation. But the same held true for other areas. In addition to medicine, students at the Nestorian schools could also take up philosophy, music, mathematics, geography, zoology, botany, meteorology, and astronomy, as well as basic grammar and rhetoric.

Hunayn's teacher in Baghdad was none other than al-Mamun's personal physician, a severe and sharp-tongued Nestorian named Yuhanna ibn Masawayh, scion of one of the leading dynasties. Yuhanna, who possessed what one can only hope was an unusually macabre and ironic sense of humor, glowers from the sources with the bedside manner of a peckish condor. He not only protested against the caliphal ban on dissection for medical purposes, but nominated his

---

* *Ibn* means "son of," so that Hunayn ibn Ishaq amounts to the Arabic version of "John, son of Isaac," while Ishaq ibn Hunayn means "Isaac, son of John." Sons were often named for their grandfathers.

own son, whose intellectual prowess apparently fell short of Yuhanna's desires, as a candidate for vivisection:

> Had it not been for the meddling of the ruler and his inter-ference in what does not concern him, I would have dissected alive this son of mine, just as Galen used to dissect men and monkeys. As a result of dissecting him I would thus come to know the reasons for his stupidity, rid the world of his kind, and produce knowledge for people by means of what I would write in a book: the way in which his body is composed, and the course of his arteries, veins, and nerves. But the ruler pro-hibits this.

Offering scarcely more tolerance to the young Hunayn, whose endless questions irked him, Yuhanna in fact soon ended up angrily dismissing Hunayn from the medical school.

Hunayn is depicted in the sources as having spent the next few years traveling and studying Greek. His exact whereabouts during this sojourn are uncertain (this is when he is reported to have gone "to the land of the Greeks"), but when he reappeared in Baghdad, he'd got a good start in gaining the mastery of Greek that would eventually make him famous, to the point where he could supposedly recite passages of Homer from memory.

He was soon reconciled with his former teacher Yuhanna, who demonstrated the sincerity of both his change of heart and his anatomical curiosity by commissioning Hunayn to translate Galen's *On the Anatomy of Veins and Ar-teries* and *On the Anatomy of Nerves,* plus seven other Galenic works. Still, just to be on the safe side (and to avoid potential vivisection), Hunayn records that with these translations es-pecially he "took pains to express the meaning as clearly as

possible; for this man likes plain expression and urges constantly in that direction."

After studying Arabic in Basra and finishing his medical
education at Jundi-Shapur, Hunayn returned to Baghdad,
where he eventually won appointment to Yuhanna's old position, that of court physician, under one of al-Mamun's successors, al-Mutawakkil. All the time he continued with the
translations, which were in high enough demand that professional translators like Hunayn could charge very handsome
fees for their work. The demand came from the Abbasid
court and its courtiers, from state and military officials, and
from doctors, scientists, philosophers, and scholars. Like the
translators themselves, many of the wealthiest patrons were
members of dynasties whose patronage spanned generations. One such clan, the well-known Banu Musa or "sons of
Musa," is recorded as paying 500 dinars a month "for full-
time translation," which one scholar has worked out to about
$24,000 in today's American dollars. At such rates the trans-
lation movement could and did attract the best talent, and
the Banu Musa reportedly favored Hunayn, introducing him
to al-Mamun and helping advance his career.

Hunayn is credited with literally hundreds of translations, from disciplines that included medicine, philosophy,
astronomy, mathematics, magic, and dream interpretation,
and even a highly praised version of the Old Testament. He
also wrote around a hundred works of his own, many
summarizing his translations. Modern philologists have
found Hunayn's techniques almost unbelievably advanced—
essentially the same as those used today, though reinvented
in the West nearly eight hundred years later by Lorenzo Valla
and his successors. Textual critics have used many of
Hunayn's translations to help restore the original Greek text
in cases where no Greek manuscript survives.

The author best represented in Hunayn's translation work was Galen, and Hunayn kept a record, the *Risala*, of his Galenic translations that records 129 of them, and is thought to be incomplete at that. Some three-quarters of the translations were from Greek into Syriac, often with a student such as Ishaq or Hubaish later performing the easier task of rendering the Syriac into Arabic. The *Risala* shows that the Syriac versions were made for Christian patrons and the Arabic versions for Muslim ones, which gives an idea of how Nestorians dominated the medical profession. All but a few of the Syriac versions have been lost.

The *Risala* constitutes an invaluable resource for modern scholars, since Hunayn's notes on each Galenic work include insights and information on topics such as the quality of earlier translations, the availability of manuscripts, the desires of patrons, and much else besides. In particular, many of the entries illuminate Hunayn's methods with richness and immediacy. Here he records his work on one text, Galen's *On Dissection,* over a span of many years:

> I translated it [into Syriac] when I was a young man . . . from a very defective Greek manuscript. Later on, when I was about forty years old, my pupil Hubaish asked me to correct it after having collected a certain number of [Greek] manuscripts. Thereon I collated these so as to produce one correct manuscript, and compared this manuscript with the Syriac text and corrected it. I am in the habit of proceeding thus in all my translation work. Some years later I translated it into Arabic for Abu Jafar Muhammad ibn Musa.

The biggest problem the translators faced was generally not the difficulty of the Greek itself but the scarcity of good, accurate Greek manuscripts. Perhaps this helped give rise to the later myth of Hunayn's supposed journeys to Byzantium in search of texts.

Altogether, Hunayn and his group produced the most significant body of work in the translation movement. In addition to the medical books of Galen and others, they also accounted for the vast majority of important philosophical works, including those of Plato (*Sophist, Timaeus, Parmenides, Crito, Laws, Cratylus, Republic, Phaedo,* and *Euthydemus*) and Aristotle (*Categories, Hermeneutica, Analytica Priora, Analytica Posteriora, Sophistics, Topics, Rhetoric, Physics, On the Heavens, On Generation and Corruption, Meteorologica, Book of Animals, On the Soul, On the Plants, Metaphysics,* and *Nicomachean Ethics*).

Hunayn's spectacular success as a translator may actually have lain partly behind the major setback in his career. This occurred during the reign of al-Mutawakkil, and it has traditionally been chalked up to the jealousy of Hunayn's Nestorian colleagues. Apparently Hunayn held views that were sympathetic toward the Iconoclast movement, which was just coming to a close after more than a century of dominating the Byzantine Orthodox Church. In this, he would have differed from the official Nestorian line, which supported the veneration of icons. The story goes that a few of Hunayn's fellow Nestorians somehow persuaded him to spit on an icon, which, as they no doubt anticipated, outraged the Nestorian patriarch when he heard about it, which of course they made sure he did. With the caliph's approval, the indignant patriarch had Hunayn flogged and imprisoned for six months, with the added punishment of confiscating both his fortune and—worse—his precious library.

After his release, the loss of his books hindered Hunayn's work to some degree. He refers to it repeatedly in the *Risala*. In the entry for the year 856 he explains to his patron Ali ibn

Yahya, who commissioned the *Risala* and who had asked him for a list of Galen's translated works, why he had been unable to comply with the request:

> I continued to refuse your demand (viz. to write a list of all the translations of Galen's books) and put you off till a later time, because I had lost all the books which I had gradually collected during the course of the whole of my adult life in all the lands in which I had travelled, all of which books I lost at one blow, so that not even the . . . book in which Galen enumerates his works remained to me.

Hunayn got back into al-Mutawakkil's good graces by curing one of his courtiers of an illness. He records that the grateful caliph bestowed three houses upon him, "completely furnished and containing books," although it's unclear whether this refers to the confiscated library. Nor is it known for certain whether Hunayn ever got his books back, though he seems to have escaped further unpleasant brushes with authority, carrying his translations on as best he could with or without his library. Reinstated to his old position of court physician after his release, he held the job until his death in 873. His lifetime bridged the reigns of ten caliphs, nine of whom he served with rare dedication and distinction.

Chapter Eight

The Arabic Enlightenment

I n one of his Galenic translations, Hunayn ibn Ishaq makes an omission that perfectly captures the spirit in which the translators and their patrons approached the Greek legacy. The text he's translating, fittingly, is *On Medical Names,* and the omission is a brief quotation that Galen has made from the Athenian comic playwright Aristophanes, whose satirical observation of politics and social life in classical Athens has done much to round out (and enliven) our picture of the ancient Greeks.

As Hunayn explains in a note, he has two reasons for omitting the quotation:

> I am not familiar with the language of Aristophanes, nor am I accustomed to it. Hence, it was not easy for me to understand the quotation, and I have, therefore, omitted it. I had an additional reason for omitting it. After I had read it, I found no more in it than what Galen had already said elsewhere. Hence, I thought that I should not occupy myself with it any further, but rather proceed to more useful matters.

Leaving aside the internal inconsistencies in Hunayn's explanation (if he could translate the quotation, what makes its difficulty per se a good reason to leave it out? Alternatively, if he couldn't translate it, how could he be sure that it held nothing useful?), his reasons are revealing in themselves.

The first one shows us that however competently Hunayn could handle medical and scientific Greek, his knowledge reflected a narrow slice of what was in reality a large linguistic pie. This won't be surprising to any student of the language, who will be used to the challenges that come with shifting authors within a genre, not to mention shifting from one genre to another. One can be getting along quite well in Herodotus yet be flummoxed when first turning to Thucydides, much less be able to glide effortlessly from either of these historians to, say, Aeschylus or Euripides. In addition to these challenges of newness to which Hunayn alludes, some writers are just plain harder than others. Thucydides, for example, is simply more difficult than Herodotus. Aristophanes is harder than Herodotus, too, but not as hard as Aeschylus or Euripides.

Compared with such belletristic works, scientific writing tends to be linguistically and stylistically more straightforward, which would have put Hunayn at a further disadvantage. Even Plato, renowned as a graceful and subtle Greek prose stylist, holds few linguistic obstacles if one is concerned with essence more than nuance. This goes double for scientific texts. Because they're aimed primarily at conveying practical information, the main challenge in reading them is their technical vocabulary, and the reader who has mastered that enjoys relatively smooth sailing. (That's why it's appropriate that the tract from which Hunayn omitted the Aristophanes quotation was one concerning medical terminology.) Such considerations help to explain how the great Hunayn could be stumped by a quotation that, more than likely, any moderately gifted British schoolboy of the nineteenth century would have been able to get through in fairly short order.

Hunayn's second reason underscores the practical applications of scientific writing, and shows that the translators and their patrons magnified those aims to the virtual exclusion of all others. Why else leave out a quotation that doesn't contribute anything "useful" to the discussion?

The idea, in other words, wasn't to provide a faithful rendition of the original text as the author wrote it, which is how we conceive of the enterprise of translation. Instead, Hunayn and the others wished above all to provide access to the hard information that the text contained. Nothing else mattered, certainly not an intrusion by a comic voice whose sexual punning and profane satire would have been offensive and irrelevant to the Syrian Christians even had the language not been impenetrable.

This approach cut out huge swaths of what we think of as Greek literature, including (to take just two conspicuous examples) poetry and history, the types of writing that comprised the earliest interests of the Italian humanists. The Greco-Arabic translation movement of Baghdad stands about as far as it's possible to get from the obsessive, all-consuming classicism of quattrocento Florentines like Niccolò Niccoli.

The movement lasted well over two centuries, a convenient date for its end being the year 1000. By that time, most of the "useful" texts had been translated.

The translation movement confronted Islam with the imposing presence of Greek philosophy, which was part and parcel of the "useful" body of knowledge that the Syrians made available to the Arabs. Jews and Christians, of course, had also had to face this legacy of free inquiry. But the Arabic philosophers were more successful in building on the rationalistic tradition that Greek philosophy embodied. Where others had stagnated, they moved forward.

Western scholars have often assumed that the translation movement ended because the Arabs lost interest in the subject matter, but clearly that's far from the case, since Arabic science and philosophy continued to break new ground long afterward. It seems quite apparent that the translation movement ended precisely *because* Arabic scientists and philosophers were breaking new ground: they had moved on, and the Greeks had nothing left to teach them. All the relevant works had been translated long since, and the Greek material that had sparked the Arabic Enlightenment was no longer on the cutting edge.

Falsafa

This movement is known in Arabic as *falsafa*—the Greek word *philosophia* transliterated into Arabic—and its practitioner was the *faylasuf,* another transliteration, this time of the Greek *philosophos,* philosopher. The *faylasuf* was devoted to living according to reason, which was held to be the ordering principle of the universe. As proponents of reason, and of understanding the rational cosmos, the *faylasufs* held themselves apart from the other two influential groups in Abbasid culture, the religious scholars, or *ulama,* and the pleasure-loving poetic dabblers who surrounded the court, the *adibs.**

---

* The *adibs* were those who cultivated *adab,* a sophisticated and self-consciously "aesthetic" lifestyle—Bloomsbury in Baghdad—that is sometimes rendered in English as "humanism." However, *adab* has nothing to do with the classical revivalism that defined Western humanism.

Unlike modern philosophy, *falsafa* was considered very much a practical pursuit. The professions that the *faylasufs* typically specialized in were the two leading "applied sciences" of medicine and astrology, the second of which incorporated both mathematics and astronomy.

In a rational cosmos, it was thought, the actions of the stars and planets clearly must have measurable consequences in our human lives here on earth, and the aim of astrology was to quantify and predict those consequences. *Faylasufs* also energetically pursued alchemy, another area of Greek wisdom literature that our modern outlook hardly associates with reason, though a figure such as Isaac Newton, viewed today as a paragon of Western reason, was deeply interested in both. It was partly for such wizardry and black arts, as well as for their other pursuits that we would recognize as rationalistic, that the *faylasufs* eventually incurred the *ulama*'s opposition.

The first Arab *faylasuf* was the venerable al-Kindi, often called the "Philosopher of the Arabs." He was a contemporary of Hunayn's, born into the Arab aristocracy at Kufa, where his father was governor, and educated at Basra and Baghdad, where he enjoyed the patronage of three caliphs. Al-Kindi idolized Aristotle, and his prodigious literary output reflects an Aristotelian breadth of interest: he wrote on logic, metaphysics, geometry, mathematics, music, astronomy, astrology, theology, meteorology, alchemy, and the soul, among other topics. His approach was encyclopedic, attempting to summarize known information in each of these fields, and incorporating learning not only from Greek sources but also from Indian and Chaldean ones. In his theological writings he championed the theme of God's unity. He upheld the validity of the Koranic revelation, using Aristotelian syllogistic logic in an attempt to demonstrate its truth, but insisting that revelation trumps reason.

This could hardly be said of the next major figure in Arabic philosophy, the radical freethinking Persian Platonist Abu Bakr al-Razi, known to the West as Rhazes. Born in Rayy, Persia (hence al-Razi, "the Rayyan"), Rhazes studied medicine there and in Merv before coming to Baghdad. He became a celebrated physician as well as a philosopher, styling himself another Hippocrates in medicine and another Socrates in philosophy. His rugged Platonism recalls no one so much as George Gemistos Pletho: Rhazes took a hard-line rationalist position that utterly rejected revelation as a path to truth.

The cause of reason was taken up in the generation after Rhazes by the imposing figure of Muhammad al-Farabi, called Alpharabius in Latin. Reportedly a Turk whose father served in the caliph's bodyguard, al-Farabi studied with leading *faylasuf*s in Baghdad before moving to Aleppo, Syria. There he served in the court of the warrior-poet-prince Sayf al-Dawla, a leading patron of Greek philosophy and a military scourge of the Byzantines. Al-Farabi, too, upheld the supremacy of reason, but left room for revelation, which, al-Farabi suggested, offered a digestible version, in symbolic form, of truths that were more meaningfully if less easily explored by the pursuit of reason. He attempted to prove the existence of God, adumbrating the famous ontological proof later articulated in the West by St. Anselm.* If, like Rhazes, al-Farabi put reason first, he had less confidence than Rhazes in the ability of the masses to deploy it, and so he found revelation more suitable for everyday consumption.

Most modern scholars have characterized al-Farabi's ultimate interests as social and political. Whereas al-Kindi

---

* Anselm, an eleventh-century founder of Scholasticism, proposed that a perfect God must exist, since if He didn't exist He wouldn't be perfect. Clearly, logic had a ways to go from here.

had summarized an eclectic but largely Aristotelian body of scientific knowledge, and Rhazes had based his individualistic (and virtually atheistic) thought mostly on the writings of Plato, al-Farabi brought the full power of the Neoplatonic synthesis to bear on the question of what would constitute the ideal Islamic society, which he described as "the virtuous city." Al-Farabi essentially took Plato's famous ideal of the "philosopher king" and equated it with the monotheistic ideal of the prophet. The prophet (or caliph, or imam), at once the receiver of divine revelation and the possessor of the highest reason, is also the ideal ruler—a pat blend of Neoplatonic utopianism and Islamic theocracy.

The most influential *faylasuf* of all, Abu Ali ibn Sina, known to the West as Avicenna, built on al-Farabi's comprehensive working out of Neoplatonism, but was less interested in envisioning an ideal Islamic society based on it. Instead, he concerned himself more with how al-Farabi's Neoplatonism could relate to the particulars of Islamic society as it had actually developed, and especially with the *sharia*, Islamic law. Avicenna lived in the late tenth and eleventh centuries. He wrote close to three hundred works, yet it's not his productivity that sets him apart from the others. All of these *faylasuf*s were awesomely prolific by modern standards. Avicenna's clear and elegant style gave his writings a literary appeal that transcended the narrow world of *falsafa,* and this wider readership meant that more of his work survived. It also meant that he became identified with Neoplatonism in a way that al-Farabi did not, even though Avicenna himself acknowledged his debt to his great predecessor.

In contrast with al-Farabi, about whose life only the bare bones are known, Avicenna left an autobiography that gives us a fairly full picture of the man. A Persian, Avicenna was born near Bukhara in Central Asia (today's Uzbekistan), and by his own account he was recognized early on as something of a prodigy. His family moved to Bukhara when he was very young, and he studied religion, Arabic poetry, medicine, science, and mathematics there with a number of well-known teachers. He memorized the Koran by age ten, and by the age of sixteen, he tells us, he was being sought out for advice by older, established physicians.

Avicenna came of age in the twilight of the Persian Samanid dynasty, one of the many regional powers that sprang up across the Islamic world as Abbasid power declined over the course of the ninth century. The Samanids, munificent patrons of learning and the arts, made their capital at Bukhara, and Avicenna tells us that he took advantage of their superb libraries, reading everything he could get his hands on. Despite his brilliance, however, the one area that remained a blank to him was metaphysical philosophy, and he reports that he read a translation of Aristotle's *Metaphysics* forty times without making any headway. Only when he discovered al-Farabi's commentary on the book did its meaning suddenly fall into place. Al-Farabi would remain Avicenna's model, and by some assessments anyway Avicenna's most significant achievement was to refine and disseminate al-Farabi's ideas.

Avicenna had won the patronage of the Samanid ruler Nuh ibn Mansur by successfully curing him of an illness. However, when Avicenna was still under twenty, the Samanids fell to the rising power of the Ghaznavids, a group of Turkish slave-soldiers who rose and claimed power in their own right. After a period of wandering, Avicenna found a place in the court of a Buyid prince at Hamadan in western Persia. He remained there, churning out a huge body of work over a career that amounted to a roller-coaster ride of palace intrigue, becoming vizier (prime minister) twice between periods of disfavor and even, once, prison. He worked out the tensions of this precarious existence by overindulging in drink and sex, dying at age fifty-eight after attempting an unconventional self-cure for stomach trouble.

Avicenna's magnum opus was the *Kitab al-Shifa*, or *Book of Healing*, a massive fifteen-volume summary of Greek learning and its Arabic augmentation that would become known in Latin as the *Sufficientia*, and that Avicenna himself helpfully abridged under the title *Kitab al-Najat* or *Book of Salvation*. His introduction to the *Book of Healing* describes the work as expository in nature, an attempt to lay out the most important aspects of the philosophic and scientific tradition to date.

AL-GHAZALI AND AVERROËS

Western commentators have often blamed a leading writer of the next generation, Abu Hamid al-Ghazali, for exalting mysticism and discrediting reason in the Islamic world, thereby bringing about the end of *falsafa* and the Greek legacy in Islam. Those same commentators have portrayed the twelfth-century *faylasuf* Abu al-Walid ibn Rushd, Averroës to the West, as opposing al-Ghazali and fighting a rearguard action for reason. Though it failed in the Islamic world, that effort had momentous consequences for Western civilization. Averroës' thought—and the Aristotelian vision enfolded within it—was later taken up by Scholastics such as St. Thomas Aquinas.

Al-Ghazali was born in Khorasan near the town of Tus, where he received a strong education in Islamic jurisprudence and theology (*kalam*). By his early thirties, he had won a coveted position as head of an important *madrasah*, or religious school, in Baghdad. He relates in his autobiography, *The Deliverer from Evil,* that while teaching upward of three hundred students he also spent three years mastering *falsafa.* But by the end he had descended into a desperate crisis of faith and found himself unable even to teach. His depression led him to leave his job at the *madrasah* and join a group of Sufis, the Muslim mystics whose traditions of contemplative communion with God make them the Islamic equivalents of Byzantium's Hesychasts. Al-Ghazali came out of his retreat with the Sufis a convert to the mystic path, essentially giving up on both theology and philosophy as inadequate, and settling on direct experience of the divine as the only viable way to approach God.

Like Gregory Palamas nearly three hundred years later, al-Ghazali rejected the idea that reason can say anything meaningful about God at all; also like Palamas (and other Byzantine theologians) he suspected that the same was true of theology, which after all was influenced—contaminated, one might say—by rationalistic Greek strands in both religions. Al-Ghazali believed that mystical ability was like any other talent in that not everyone possessed it, and that anyone who didn't possess it could have little or no grasp of the divine. For those people, he allowed, theology might be of some limited use, as a pale substitute for the real thing, but only if handled with caution.

Al-Ghazali's great attack on *falsafa,* especially *falsafa* as represented by al-Farabi and Avicenna, is called *The Incoherence of the Philosophers.* His critique, while devastating in exactly the way the title suggests, did not attempt to tear up *falsafa* root and branch. On the contrary, al-Ghazali conceded the *limited* usefulness of reason in areas where certainty can be achieved (such as logic and mathematics) or that have to do with understanding the material world (such as science and medicine). In the end, though, he insisted that it was best simply to accept the world as God's creation without trying to understand it.

The *faylasufs'* metaphysical claims especially irked al-Ghazali, since their attempts at such rationalistic speculation trespassed, as he saw it, on territory that properly belonged to religion. He leveled three main charges against the emanationist philosophers, errors that, he said, led them into heresy: first, they upheld the eternity of the world (which didn't leave room for a creator); second, they asserted God's knowledge of universals but not of particulars (which made God less than all-knowing); and third, they denied the resurrection of the body (which religious authorities said would occur for everyone at the Last Judgment). Such errors made *falsafa* dangerous, especially for the weak-minded masses. If hardly constituting a "deathblow" to *falsafa*, Al-Ghazali's widely read book soon became a classic, and did undercut the *faylasufs'* prestige and enhance that of the Sufis throughout the Islamic world.

A generation after al-Ghazali's death and almost exactly 3,000 miles away from Tus, on the far western edge of the Islamic world, the religious scholar and *faylasuf* known to the West as Averroës was born in Córdoba, the spectacular capital city of al-Andalus (Moorish Spain). His family was a prominent one in Córdoba's religious leadership, and his grandfather had been a leading *qadi* or religious judge. In keeping with the family tradition, Averroës studied *kalam* and Islamic jurisprudence extensively as a boy, along with medicine and Arabic literature. By his early forties he had won appointment as *qadi* of the nearby city of Seville, and a couple of years later he was named grand *qadi* in Córdoba.

Averroës lived and worked in a cultural environment

that was very different from that of the eastern Islamic lands. At first, as Baghdad and the wealthy eastern lands witnessed the translation movement and the rise of *falsafa*, al-Andalus remained an intellectual backwater under a surviving off-shoot of the Umayyad dynasty. By the tenth century, how-ever, Córdoba had grown into Western Europe's most vital city, studded with palaces and mosques (the Great Mosque of Córdoba was finished in 976) and famed for its luxury textiles, leatherwork, and jewelry. But the Umayyad dynasty dissolved by the twelfth century, and in Averroës' time al-Andalus was ruled by puritanical Muslims called the Almo-hads, who called for a return to strict Islamic practices such as the veiling of women and abstinence from alcohol.

Falsafa had finally established itself in al-Andalus by the time the Almohads came to power. Averroës' teacher and pa-tron, Ibn Tufayl, was the second major figure in the *falsafa* movement of al-Andalus, and served as court physician to the Almohad caliph. He struggled to reconcile al-Ghazali with Avicenna, accepting al-Ghazali's elevation of mystical enlightenment over reason, but defending Avicenna's thought against al-Ghazali's attack. Ibn Tufayl introduced Averroës at court, where Averroës would succeed him as physician after Ibn Tufayl's death. Averroës had already begun his study of Aristotle, and had also spent time as an amateur astronomer observing the heavens (he's credited with discovering a new star). His first Aristotelian commentary was on Aristotle's as-tronomy book *On the Heavens*.

It was probably in 1159, the year Averroës wrote this work, that Ibn Tufayl brought Averroës to meet the future Al-mohad caliph Abu Yusuf, then governor of Seville. An ap-pealing story depicts the young but already erudite Averroës as tongue-tied in the future ruler's presence, until the Almohad prince, himself knowledgeable on astronomical matters, broke the ice by launching into a lively discussion with Ibn Tufayl, whereupon Averroës relaxed and joined in.

Later on, Ibn Tufayl is said to have persuaded Averroës to continue what would turn out to be his life's work, urging him that Aristotle's works badly needed someone who could "explain their meaning clearly so as to render them accessible to men!" The voluminous commentaries on Aristotle's works that resulted were essentially conservative, aiming to jettison the recent accretions to the tradition represented by *faylasufs* such as Avicenna and to recover the "purity" of Aristotle's actual thought. This approach allowed Averroës to deflect al-Ghazali's charges, which he did in a book whose title, *The Incoherence of the Incoherence,* made joking reference to al-Ghazali's earlier work. Where al-Ghazali insisted on the primacy of faith over reason, Averroës argued that reason and faith were two different ways of perceiving the same truth of God's creation, and that therefore they could never conflict with each other. There was no incompatibility.

Averroës upheld the elitism implicit in the work of the earlier *faylasufs,* even extending it. Not only was *falsafa* difficult to understand, and thus too dangerous for the masses, but so were *kalam* (theology) and mysticism. Instead of searching out profound truths, he argued, most people were better off accepting certain points of dogma that Averroës maintained would secure their salvation. Formulating such dogma was the role of the *faylasuf,* who was the only person properly equipped to do so, based on a strict reading of the Koran.

The way to salvation, in other words, was through dogma, a basic approach that was way out of step with the rest of Islamic thinking, but which would help make Averroës sympathetic to thinkers in the West. Within decades,

Averroës and his commentaries, conveniently accessible in nearby Spain, had sparked the rise of Scholasticism; for Thomas Aquinas, who built his thought squarely on Averroës' Aristotelian commentaries, Averroës was simply "the Commentator." This marked the West's first rediscovery of the Greek legacy, before the broader access that came with the Renaissance.

THE ECLIPSE OF REASON

The expansive and confident outlook that at first characterized the High Caliphate eventually curled around the edges. Even in the time of al-Mamun, the Abbasids' endemic political instability began to take its toll. Al-Mamun himself came to power only after a terrible civil war against his brother in which much of the Round City was destroyed.

After al-Mamun, Baghdad fell into gradual decline. For much of the ninth century, the Abbasid caliphs ruled—or attempted to—from Samarra, in the north. Even after the caliphs returned, they left the Round City and set up their palaces on the east bank of the Tigris. Outside forces—the Buyids in the tenth century, the Turks in the eleventh—found it all too easy to take over the city and control the Abbasid caliphs, who became no more than figureheads. The careers of *faylasufs* such as Avicenna reveal how political power shifted more and more to regional princes. Al-Mansur's miscalculation caught up with his city and his dynasty.

Although it took a bit longer, it also caught up with *falsafa*. As among the Christians, from the start there were voices among the Muslims that objected to the rationalism of the Greek heritage. Long before the translation movement ended, Islamic zealots had begun to attack it, foreshadowing later attacks they would make on the Arabic scientists and philosophers who built on the movement. As early as the ninth century, the religious scholars condemned the "rational sciences" (*ulum aqliyya*) as a deadly threat to their own "religious sciences" (*ulum naqliyya*).

In an attempt to hang on to power and legitimacy in slippery Baghdad, al-Mamun tried to silence these critics by force, with disastrous consequences for the fate of reason in the Islamic world. Co-opting a rationalist version of Islam called Mutazilism, which was based on an infusion of Greek philosophy into Islam that in some ways resembled the same process in early Christianity, al-Mamun attempted to impose it on all Muslims. He undertook a rationalist inquisition called the Mihna, in which religious scholars were rounded up and forced to pledge their acceptance of Mutazilite doctrine. If not, they were tortured. He had the support of *faylasuf*s such as al-Kindi, but ultimately he failed, and after his death his successors were eventually compelled to abandon the Mihna.

Al-Mamun's rationalist inquisition made it easier for the Islamic hard-liners to make their case against reason. In the coming struggle, they would repeatedly invoke the memory of the outrageous Mihna. Over the long term, their most powerful rallying point has been the martyrdom of their greatest hero, the jurist Ahmad ibn Hanbal, the Mutazilites' main opponent, who was imprisoned and tortured by al-Mamun and his successor al-Mutasim after refusing to recant his beliefs.

Ibn Hanbal died in 855, several years after the Mihna was abandoned. But before he died he founded the severest branch of *sharia* law, the Hanbali school, which today is observed only in Saudi Arabia, and his thought has constituted a main source of the Saudis' harsh Wahhabi brand of

Islam. This xenophobic, hate-filled belief system in turn provided the "Islamic" ideological underpinning for Osama bin Laden and al-Qaeda. Thus have the ripples of the Mihna spread.*

Circumstances that favor the agendas of reason are relatively rare in history. As Baghdad declined, the Turks arrived and wrested leadership of the Islamic world from Arab hands. In the thirteenth century the Mongols shattered that world, destroying Baghdad and leaving a mountain of skulls behind them. Christian Europe finally rallied and went on the offensive, starting with the Crusades and the Reconquest of Spain. Prosperity and expansion swung to the West, which through these contacts with the Islamic world slowly realized the technological and scientific wealth to be found there.

Constriction, adversity, and a loss of cultural confidence favor the appeal to religious zealotry, nativist paranoia, and patriarchal authoritarianism. There are always those ready to promote themselves by making that appeal. After Averroës, throughout the patchwork of smaller worlds that made up the larger Islamic world, the enemies of *falsafa* gradually won the upper hand, successfully stigmatizing it as foreign and un-Islamic. Though *falsafa* carried on, it did so more and more on the edges of society, not at the center. As reason was marginalized, Arabic science fell into stagnation. Even today the Arab world has produced no large-scale history of its own creative contributions to science, once the glory of the Arabic Enlightenment.

---

* Wahhabism draws directly on the writings of ibn Hanbal and his fourteenth-century disciple Taqi ibn Taymiyya, who lived when the Abbasid decline had allowed a profusion of petty local rulers to spring up throughout the Islamic world. Ibn Taymiyya reacted to what he saw as their religious laxity by arguing that only strict adherence to Islamic teachings could give a ruler legitimacy. This point resonates mightily in the Arab world today, beset as it is by corrupt, self-aggrandizing dictators and monarchs.

The Arabs had occupied Jerusalem and made it their own, but straitened circumstances led them, metaphorically, to abandon Athens. This was the same choice that the Byzantines themselves had already made once in the Dark Age, and would ultimately make again in the age of Hesychasm. In between these times, as the Abbasids waned, the Byzantines enjoyed their own era of expansion, in which they, too, had a reach that was once more broad enough to embrace both.

PART III

Byzantium
and the
Slavic
World

CHAPTER Nine

A THREAT FROM THE NORTH

On an early summer afternoon in the year 860—June 18, to be precise—the inhabitants of Constantinople began the most terrifying ordeal that most of them would ever live through. The city had been quiet enough that morning. The emperor, Michael III, was off with the army campaigning against the Arabs in Asia Minor, making the most of the decline that had weakened the Abbasids after the death of al-Mamun nearly three decades earlier. The fleet was also off fighting the Arabs somewhere in the Mediterranean. The empire had begun its long, slow recovery from the disasters of the seventh and eighth centuries, and was again taking the initiative against its enemies. The capital itself hadn't suffered a direct attack in a quarter century, and since then the empire had gone from strength to strength. An air of general confidence prevailed.

The Byzantines' complacency was harshly shattered that afternoon, when without warning some two hundred ships materialized offshore and attacked the capital. In a sermon to the fearful citizens gathered under the huge dome of Hagia Sophia, the learned Photius, patriarch of Constantinople, described the unforeseen and mysterious assault. "Nay, nor did it resemble other raids of barbarians, but the unexpectedness of the attack, its strange swiftness, the inhumanity of the barbarous tribe, the harshness of its manners and the savagery of its character proclaim the blow to have been discharged like a thunderbolt from God."

Photius, whose sermons are the only contemporary source for these events, went on to recall Byzantines' initial horrified reactions:

> Do you recollect that unbearable and bitter hour when the barbarians' boats came sailing down at you, wafting a breath of cruelty, savagery and murder? When the sea spread out its serene and unruffled surface, granting them gentle and agreeable sailing, while, waxing wild, it stirred up against us the waves of war? When the boats went past the city showing their crews with swords raised, as if threatening the city with death by sword? When all human hope ebbed away from men, and the city was moored only with recourse to the divine?

Adding to the shock of the onslaught was the unexpectedness of the direction from which it came: the attacking ships had slipped undetected into the Bosporus from the north, from somewhere in the Black Sea. For centuries, Byzantium's vigilance had been focused to the east and the south, toward its most threatening enemies, the Arabs. Any leftover attention went to the west and northwest, by land, toward the Slavs who had occupied Greece and the Balkans over the past several hundred years. The Bulgars in particular had besieged the city several times by land earlier in the ninth century, but their thrusts had been easily blunted by the great walls. Never before had Constantinople been attacked by a naval fleet from the north.

"Why has this dreadful bolt fallen on us out of the farthest north?" Photius asked, then suggested that it was in punishment for its inhabitants' sins that God had visited this hardship on the capital.

Though several earlier embassies from these northerners are recorded, little was known about their origins. An "obscure nation," Photius calls them, "a nation of no account, a nation ranked among slaves . . . a nation dwelling somewhere far from our country, barbarous, nomadic, armed with arrogance, unwatched, unchallenged, leaderless," which nonetheless "so suddenly, in the twinkling of an eye . . . as a wild boar has devoured the inhabitants of the land." Alert no doubt to the emperor's possible return, the marauders broke off their well-timed attack after a couple of weeks' worth of plunder. By the time the emperor could march back with the army the attackers had long since evaporated, withdrawing to the northern wastes from which they had emerged.

No one among the capital's traumatized populace that June could ever have guessed what the future held, that one day these "arrogant savages" would become the empire's best and most faithful allies against yet undreamt-of enemies. Nor could anyone have envisioned that, centuries after that, this "nation of no account" would inherit from a vanquished Byzantium the leadership of Orthodox Christian civilization, becoming its great new hope as the Greeks passed into their long Turkish captivity.

They had gone away for the moment, perhaps, but the Russians would be back.

THE SLAVS ARRIVE

The Russian attack on Constantinople in 860 was the Byzantines' first real exposure to this rising northern power, and it would be followed by a decade of remarkable Byzantine achievements aimed largely at coping with the new threat. But the Byzantines already had centuries to get acquainted with the populous groups of South Slavs who had long ago settled in the Balkans, as their immediate neighbors.

That story starts in the fifth century, when the populous and primitive Slavic tribes began a great migration that would transform the cultural landscape of Eastern Europe. The Slavs' original homeland lies to the north of the Black Sea, in the area of today's western Ukraine, roughly between the Bug, the Pripet, and the Dnieper rivers. From this center they moved outward in all directions. Some pushed west, among them the ancestors of the Poles, Czechs, and Slovaks. Some pushed north and east, to become the Russians. And some pushed south, where they would eventually settle in Greece and the Balkans. Small-scale farmers and pastoralists, unlettered pagans who worshiped nature's forces, they moved on foot and slowly in small tribal groups. Within a few centuries they had occupied a wide swath of territory extending from the Elbe River in the west to the Volga in the east.

That much the archeological record has filled in. The Slavs first appear in the historical record in the early sixth century, when the southward-moving group breached the Byzantine frontier at the Danube. For the next half century they conducted constant raids into the Byzantine Balkans, terrorizing the Romanized inhabitants and carrying off crops and booty. Toward the middle of the century these incursions began to get longer, and soon instead of raiders the Slavs became settlers. Preoccupied with his ambitious re-conquest of Europe and North Africa, and with war against Persia, Justinian didn't pay enough attention to his own backyard until it was too late. He was certainly aware of the problem, and built hundreds of fortresses across the Balkans, but he never committed the manpower or money to make them permanent and strong. In the decades after his death, these meager defenses collapsed.

By the end of the sixth century, the Slavs were pouring into the Balkans, penetrating all the way down to the southern Peloponnesus, the bottom of the Greek mainland. Writing in 585, the Syriac historian John of Ephesus reports that "an accursed people, called Slavonians," had made themselves masters of the whole Balkan peninsula, including Greece, Macedonia, and Thrace, right up to the walls of Constantinople itself: "And even to this day . . . they still encamp and dwell there . . . and they have grown rich in gold and silver, and herds of horses, and arms, and have learnt to fight better than the Romans, though at first they were but rude savages, who did not venture to show themselves outside the woods."

As they flooded into the Balkans, the Slavs there also picked up a trick that would be repeated in various forms throughout their early history. This was to apprentice themselves to a smaller but more advanced group of non-Slavs, forming an alliance in which the non-Slavic group acted as a warrior aristocracy and the Slavs were the raw manpower—with the result that, more often than not, the numerous Slavs absorbed their masters, whose know-how had gone toward forming a state that the Slavs now dominated.

The first Slavic apprenticeship was to the Avars, a Turkic people who taught the Slavs the fighting skills that so impressed John of Ephesus. Slavs assisted the Avars in the siege of Constantinople in 626, when the Avar-Slav force co-ordinated its attack with the Persians. The Slavs, who had the crucial assignment of ferrying the Persians across the Bosporus in their small boats, were overwhelmed by the Byzantines' superior fleet, and it was this failure that allowed the siege to be broken. The Avars, formerly fierce but now chastened, backed off to the Hungarian plain, while their Slav subjects remained in the Balkans, ending this apprenticeship before the masters could be absorbed.

THE RISE OF BULGARIA

The Slavs' next apprenticeship arose from the ashes of the first, as another group of Turkic warriors, the Bulgars, moved into the northern Balkans and essentially replaced the Avars as the Slavs' overlords there. Crossing the Danube in the late seventh century, the Bulgars occupied the zone known as the Dobrudja, along the Black Sea coast south of the Danube delta. A halfhearted Byzantine attempt to eject them ended in defeat, and in 681 the Byzantines were forced to sign a treaty ceding the Bulgars these former imperial lands.

Byzantium and Bulgaria were now neighbors, and from this point forward their fates would be intimately intertwined. In much the same way as the Italians did in the West and the Syrians did in the Islamic world, the Bulgarians would eventually act as a pipeline for the Byzantine legacy, a conduit through which Byzantine cultural influences flowed to the rest of the Slavic world.

But for the moment, the relationship was characterized mostly by vicious warfare, which constantly erupted between the sometimes desperate Byzantines and their vigorous new neighbor. It raged back and forth throughout the Dark Age. The fearsome Bulgar khan Krum gained further Byzantine territory and dealt the Byzantines several sharp defeats, culminating in the annihilation of a Byzantine army in a mountain ambush in 811. The emperor Nicephorus I himself perished, the first time in nearly five centuries that a Byzantine ruler had died in battle. Krum reportedly took off the top of the emperor's skull, lined it with silver, and turned it into a drinking cup. The Bulgar khan was readying his forces for a major siege of Constantinople when he died suddenly a few years later.

The Slavs in the northern part of the Balkans kept their Slavic identity, and by the end of the ninth century they had completed the process of absorbing their aristocratic overlords. Modern Bulgarian, a Slavic tongue, has fewer than a dozen words of Turkic origin. The Slavs who moved into Greece encountered a very different fate, and in some ways an opposite one.

Even as Krum was toasting his success, Byzantium had begun to revive. Then Byzantium was weaker and smaller than either the Frankish or the Abbasid states, and in danger of being expelled from the Balkans by Bulgaria. By the mid-eleventh century, the Frankish and Abassid empires had both been shattered into smaller principalities, and Byzantium had conquered and absorbed Bulgaria. During this remarkable period of military expansion, Byzantium almost doubled in size.

This revival also allowed the Byzantines to recolonize the Greek mainland. The success of that effort would prove crucial to the survival of Greek culture in future centuries, after the other lands had fallen away. Having overrun nearly all of the Greek mainland, the cities, and the islands, by the tenth century the Slavs in Greece had been converted to

Orthodox Christianity and thoroughly Hellenized. Today, the only evidence of the Slavs' arrival is the presence of Slavic place names, some five hundred or so of them, scattered charmingly throughout the Greek countryside.

PHOTIUS

The renewed confidence of the ninth century spilled over into Byzantine culture to spark the First Byzantine Renaissance, as the Orthodox church embarked on vigorous expansion and Byzantine literary scholars rediscovered the ancient texts. In both arenas the dominant figure was Photius, the patriarch of Constantinople during the Russian attack of 860. On the religious side, as the empire's highest church authority during much of this period, Photius initiated Byzantium's greatest cultural triumph, the conversion of the Slavs to Orthodox Christianity. Yet, long before becoming patriarch, he was also his century's most accomplished lay scholar of ancient Greek literature, and as such he played the pivotal role in the intellectual revival.

This was the age when the pagan classics again began to be copied, a process that was stimulated by the importation of paper from the Arabs. The translation movement was now in full swing in Baghdad, and it has recently been suggested that the Arab interest helped to jump-start the resurgence of interest in Byzantium.* Another impetus came from the development of cursive or minuscule script. Easier both to write and to read (not least because words were now separated for

---

* By Dimitri Gutas in *Greek Thought, Arabic Culture* (1998). Professor Gutas demonstrates a direct correlation between the earliest manuscripts copied during the First Byzantine Renaissance and the texts being studied by the Arabs.

the first time), minuscule rapidly replaced the capital letters or uncial script employed by earlier copyists. Virtually all of the ancient Greek literature surviving today was copied during this period of intense activity, plus much that has since been lost. And Photius towers over it all.

Photius' early life is largely unknown to us. Born around 810, he was a nephew of the famous patriarch Tarasius, who had helped the empress Irene restore the icons in 787, ending the first period of Iconoclasm. But because the sources for this period are so sparse, we can only speculate about how he attained his phenomenal mastery of ancient Greek language and literature.

Photius may have been taught by the man known variously as Leo the Mathematician and Leo the Wise. Along with other shadowy figures active in the early ninth century (we have names, such as John the Grammarian and Ignatius the Deacon, but little hard information about them), Leo often gets credit for pioneering the resurgence of interest in ancient Greek learning that came with the recovery. All of these men held high office in the church. A proponent of mathematical studies especially, Leo constructed a series of beacon lights to send warning of Arab raids from the border near Syria all the way to Constantinople. Even the caliph al-Mamun, legend had it, tried to hire Leo away from the emperor, though as modern scholars point out, the Arabs were so far ahead of the Byzantines in science at this point that they would have been unlikely to require the services of even a Leo, and so the story is probably false. Yet, possibly because of it, when the emperor Theophilus established a new school of secular studies at the Magnaura Palace, he chose Leo as its head. Leo was also widely reputed to have magical powers.

Photius, too, was linked by rumor with the occult, and

one story held that, Faust-like, he gained his knowledge through a pact with a Jewish magician. Like so many Byzantine humanists, Photius was not at all a modest man, and in spreading such rumors his enemies perhaps felt sorely provoked. But magical forces permeated everything like an electrical field. Demons and other malevolent sprites worked constantly in daily life, and were blamed for small misfortunes from colds to crop failures. Even by Byzantine standards, this was a superstitious age, one in which any and all knowledge was mysterious and potentially suspect. It wasn't just the ignorant but also the erudite who conflated the arcane learning of the ancients with the occult.

Though Photius' literary appetite was wide, he favored history, poetry, rhetoric, and novels. His own writings (the secular ones, at least) are largely compilatory in nature. He's best known for his *Bibliotheca,* a randomly organized collection of notes on nearly three hundred secular works spanning the classical age to his own times that runs to some 1,600 pages in the modern printed edition. Since about half of these works no longer survive, modern scholars have found the *Bibliotheca* invaluable as a guide to what was still available at the time, and what has since been lost.

Photius began his career in the civil service and rose quickly through the ranks. He is known to have taken part in an embassy to the Arabs, perhaps sometime in the mid-850s. If this entailed a journey to Baghdad, as is likely, Photius might have met his contemporary, Hunayn ibn Ishaq. It's intriguing to picture them enjoying a quiet conversation of a Baghdad evening, comparing insights into Greek literature— Photius with his broad encyclopedic interests, Hunayn with his narrow focus on the useful.

A Race to Convert the Slavs

Renowned for both his secular and religious learning, Photius had held no official position in the church, nor was he a monk. Never one to suffer fools gladly, he had incurred the hostility of the patriarch Ignatius by deriding him as an ignoramus. So it was unusual and provocative when, as part of a political and personal dispute, the emperor Michael III deposed Ignatius and nominated Photius to be his replacement. On the emperor's orders, Photius was rushed through the ranks of the church in less than a week.

Ignatius had his own supporters, and they eventually enlisted the pope, Nicholas I, on their side. Nicholas refused to recognize Photius and decreed that Ignatius had been wrongfully deposed; Photius in his turn declared the pope deposed. The resulting Photian Schism was brief, though much has been made of it by Western scholars, who in the nineteenth century portrayed Photius as an archvillain out to ruin the papacy and divide the church.

By the time Photius struck back against the pope, other events had made it clear that more was at issue in the Photian Schism than just the fate of Ignatius. Bulgaria, under its vigorous ruler Boris, was on the brink of converting to Christianity. Boris himself had already converted, and he made it clear that he wished to bring his country along with him. A century and a half earlier, the Iconoclast emperor Leo III, reacting against papal condemnation of Iconoclasm, had removed the Roman province of Illyria from papal jurisdiction. At that time Illyria was strategically insignificant, and the papacy didn't object much. But included in the territory of Illyria were most of the lands that in the late ninth century made up Bulgaria, which had become a powerful state on

Byzantium's very border, and thus one that both parties saw advantages in controlling.

Pope Nicholas now made the return of Illyria to papal jurisdiction a condition for his recognizing Photius, and so the struggle between pope and patriarch escalated into a contest over who would control the strategically important Bulgarian church. Boris, for his part, wishing above all to maintain Bulgaria's independence, proved adept at playing both sides against each other.

Nor was it just Bulgaria that was at stake. The Russian attack on Constantinople in 860 underscored Byzantium's need for a Slavic buffer in the Balkans, and awakened the Byzantines to the desirability of getting an Orthodox foot in the Slavic doorway. As Photius realized, Roman efforts in that direction had already begun.

The resulting race to convert the Slavs would initially play itself out not in Bulgaria but in another Slavic land, Moravia, whose prince had sent a request for a Byzantine mission to his country. Moravia would be the first battle-ground between the Roman and the Byzantine versions of Christianity. And while Moravia is now largely forgotten by history, the two missionaries that Photius sent there are not.

CHAPTER TEN

THE MISSION OF CYRIL AND METHODIUS

The two men that Photius chose for the mission to Moravia were brothers. They had grown up in Thessalonica, the empire's second city, which although still a Greek city had been surrounded by Slavic settlers. Slavic was heard in Thessalonica as often as Byzantine Greek. "You are both Thessalonicans, and all Thessalonicans speak pure Slav," the emperor is reported to have told them in encouraging them to accept the assignment. The dialects that would eventually resolve themselves into the various Slavic languages had not yet done so. Slavs could still understand each other wherever they had settled, and so the brothers would be able to communicate effectively in Moravia.

The younger of the two, whose given name was Constantine but who is known to history by his later monastic name of Cyril, had been born around 825. He had come to Constantinople as a young man, where he became a student and protégé of Photius. Known to his contemporaries as Constantine the Philosopher, he was very much a product of the First Byzantine Renaissance and rapidly became one of its leading lights.

The other brother, whose given name may have been Michael but who took the monastic name of Methodius, was older by about a decade. He would be Cyril's devoted helper and, after Cyril's early death, the faithful executive of his plans. Methodius began his career as a high imperial official in a Slavic area in Macedonia but had abandoned his government career to take monastic vows, joining the important monastery of Mount Olympus in Asia Minor.

The brothers—one a humanist scholar, the other a monk—also established reputations as resourceful and efficient missionary-diplomats. Cyril's biographer states that he participated in an embassy to the Arabs. Michael III and Photius had also tapped both brothers for a mission to the Khazars, a group of Turkic nomads who had settled north of the Caucasus Mountains. Long among the Byzantines' most faithful allies, the Khazars had already adopted Judaism, which helped them stay independent of both the Byzantines and Arabs. Their strategic importance to the Byzantines lay in blocking Arab attempts to thrust through the Caucasus, which would have allowed the Arabs to outflank the Byzantines by circling north of the Black Sea. The mission was counted a diplomatic success, even though the brothers were unable to convert the Khazars. So when the Moravian request came, Cyril and Methodius seemed tailor-made for the job, with their proficiency in both missionary work and Slavic language and culture.

Cyril and Methodius accepted the mission, but they didn't leave for Moravia right away. Cyril spent the winter preparing for the assignment by inventing an alphabet that could be used to spread the Gospels in Slavic. The new alphabet, called Glagolitic, contained forty letters. Many were based loosely on either Greek or Hebrew letters, but many also appear invented from scratch. By the time they left Byzantium in the spring of 863, the brothers had used Cyril's new alphabet to translate a selection from the Gospels for use in a Slavic liturgy. This new written language would be called Old Church Slavonic.

Like the Glagolitic alphabet in which it was first written, Old Church Slavonic is considered to be largely Cyril's work. But to say that he "translated" the Gospels and other Greek Christian works is perhaps a bit misleading. It wasn't a matter of just sitting down for a few hours and rendering a passage from the original Greek into a Slavic tongue that was ready and waiting for it. Cyril faced a problem similar to the one that had faced the translators in Baghdad a few decades earlier with regard to Arabic: the language into which these texts were to be rendered didn't yet possess the vocabulary adequate to the task. The Syrian translators had one advantage, though. Arabic was already a written language, with an established if not quite yet "classical" literary tradition. Slavic had never been written down before, and so in addition to lacking vocabulary it also lacked the syntactic sophistication that comes only when thoughts are recorded in writing.

To appreciate Cyril's achievement it's necessary to grasp that oral languages have simpler sentence structures than languages that are both written and spoken, which goes beyond the relatively straightforward recognition that even with languages of the latter kind, no one talks the way they write. If the language is one that regularly gets written down, complexities filter their way into the spoken language, the possibilities of which become measurably more sophisticated. For a purely oral language, this "reservoir" of complexity is never available, and so the language stays relatively limited in the menu of syntactic and other options it offers.

With a deft touch, Cyril expanded the Slavs' language with Greek loanwords, *calques* (loan translations), and phraseology.

Moravia originally lay where incoming Slavs had displaced Celts and others along the Morava River, in roughly the area now comprising the Czech Republic. But by the 860s, the Moravian warrior-prince Rastislav had expanded his lands southward to the Danube, making Moravia the northern neighbor of Bulgaria. To the west Moravia's neighbor was the powerful Carolingian empire of Charlemagne's Frankish successors, to whom Moravia's princes owed fealty. The Franks were the dominant power in Moravia, and it was in an attempt to lessen their influence that Rastislav, who like Boris was interested in accepting Christianity, had dispatched an embassy to Constantinople asking for missionaries to be sent to his land. He was hoping they could displace the Frankish missionaries already active there.

Prince Rastislav welcomed the brothers warmly. They got busy recruiting and training a Slavic clergy and making further liturgical translations into Old Church Slavonic. But the situation in Moravia was less than propitious over the long term. Rastislav was opposed by a strong pro-Frankish faction among the Moravian nobility, and Frankish church officials back in Freising, Salzburg, and Passau, who had been working hard to convert the Moravians for a century, were naturally incensed at the Byzantines' arrival. They were also affronted at the brothers' use of Slavonic in the liturgy, since the Frankish missionaries had stuck to Latin, as was standard practice in the West.

Eventually, this would be yet another point of divergence between Catholic and Orthodox doctrine. Though it hadn't yet hardened, precedent already hinted at the future. From Ireland to Spain to Germany, Western Christians had generally used Latin. Meanwhile, Eastern Christians including the Armenians, Egyptians (Copts), and Syrians had developed strong liturgical traditions in their own languages. As with the *filioque*, it was the Frankish church that would eventually determine the Catholic line, lobbying to fix a practical difference into a doctrinal one. At this time, though, despite the Photian Schism, Rome and Constantinople still felt they had a church in common, and besides, Nicholas quite correctly harbored suspicions against the ambitions of the Frankish bishops for a powerful independent church in central Europe. Still, in 867, when the Frankish authorities complained to Rome about the activities of Cyril and Methodius in Moravia, Pope Nicholas I summoned the two Byzantine missionaries to Rome.

They got the summons in Venice, where they'd gone to ordain some of their followers as priests. There they also met and disputed with some other Latin priests who were hostile to the Slavonic liturgy. These critics argued that the holy rites might properly be celebrated in only three languages: Greek, Latin, and Hebrew. In response Cyril articulated an impassioned defense of the idea that a people ought to be able to celebrate the liturgy in their own language.

As a scriptural basis for this practice he quoted St. Paul, from 1 Corinthians 14: "In the church I had rather speak five words with my understanding, that by my voice I might teach others also, than ten thousand words in an unknown tongue." In years to come, this passage would offer the Orthodox their strongest scriptural authority for linguistic diversity in the various national churches, in staunch opposition to the Catholics, who clung to Latin right up to the 1960s.

Having summoned Cyril and Methodius to Rome, Nicholas died before they arrived, but the new pope, Adrian II, gave his official approval to their use of the Slavonic liturgy, rebuffing the Frankish representatives who also came to Rome.

The brothers were still in Rome when Cyril fell ill in early 869. He knew he was dying, and it was now that he took monastic vows under the name Cyril. He also urged Methodius to carry on their work in Moravia rather than returning to the monastery at Mount Olympus, as Methodius seems to have been thinking of doing. Cyril died on February 14, and was buried in Rome at the church of San Clemente.

Methodius held true to his brother's dying request. He returned to Moravia, though he must have supected the balance of power there lay with the Franks. Indeed, Methodius had not been back more than a year or so when Rastislav's nephew Svatopluk, backed by the sizeable pro-Frankish faction among the nobility, overthrew Rastislav and imprisoned him. Svatopluk's new government invited the Frankish missionaries back, and they wasted no time in having Methodius arrested and thrown in prison. There he stayed for nearly three years, until the pope, Adrian's successor John VIII, learned of Methodius' incarceration and intervened to have him released.

Undeterred, Methodius turned back once again to his missionary work. He kept it up, as well as continuing to translate many more religious works, for more than a decade after his release from prison. During that time the Franks constantly harassed him and his followers. Adrian II and John VIII had upheld Nicholas I's support for the brothers' Moravian mission, but after John's death in 882 the papacy caved to Frankish pressure, abandoning the Slavonic liturgy and lining up behind the Franks in Moravia and elsewhere.

Methodius himself died in 885. The Slavic disciples he had trained with such determination were arrested, deported to Bulgaria, or sold into slavery, and the Franks were left with an open field in Moravia. The life's work of Cyril and Methodius, it seemed, had come to nothing.

OPPORTUNITY KNOCKS FOR BORIS

In Byzantium and Bulgaria, events had unfolded with equal speed and complexity. In Byzantium, Michael III had been assassinated and replaced by Basil I, a supremely opportunistic former stable boy whom Michael had elevated to the role of advisor and confidant, and then dangerously alienated. Having taken this devious and unlikely road to power, Basil went on to found Byzantium's greatest ruling house, the Macedonian dynasty, which for two centuries would preside over the medieval empire at the height of its strength and prosperity.

In Bulgaria, the khan Boris, who had already converted to Christianity, wanted to Christianize his country, but at the same time he sought to maintain Bulgaria's independence from Byzantium. Accordingly, he asked Photius to appoint a patriarch for Bulgaria, which would establish a national Bulgarian Orthodox church on an equal footing with the Byzantine church, with full autonomy. When Photius refused to allow this, Boris turned to Rome and invited in a contingent of Frankish missionaries.

That was in the summer of 867. In the fall, Basil I reversed many of Michael's religious policies. In one of his first acts as emperor, Basil removed Photius from the patriarchate and reinstated Ignatius. This amounted to a victory for Nicholas I, who had opposed Photius. So, during the winter of 867–68, when Adrian II succeeded Nicholas I as pope, the papacy seemed poised on the edge of dominance. The Slavic world for all appearances lay ripe for the plucking before the Vatican, which with the deposition of Photius had seemingly imposed its will on the Byzantines as well.

But Adrian overplayed his hand. He angered Boris by rejecting Boris' nominee for archbishop of Bulgaria, and then he convened a council in Rome that not only condemned the deposed Photius but further declared that all bishops appointed by Photius during his tenure as patriarch were now themselves deposed. This high-handed attitude irked both Basil and Ignatius, who up till then had been favorably disposed toward Rome. By 870, Boris had turned back toward Constantinople, while in Byzantium Photius and Ignatius had taken steps to patch up their quarrel.

In returning to the Byzantine fold, Boris was only acknowledging the logic of his and his country's situation, which was strategically the reverse of Rastislav's and Moravia's. Both leaders had kicked against a powerful neighbor by appealing to a more distant power, but just as Moravia was ultimately sealed within its Frankish orbit, so was Bulgaria trapped by Byzantium's gravitational pull.

When Ignatius died in 877, the old tensions in Byzantium had been smoothed to the extent that Basil reappointed Photius back to the patriarchate, but this time in a much calmer political atmosphere. A few years later, a church council in Constantinople saw Photius reconciled with the papacy, ending the Photian Schism.

In Bulgaria, fate now presented Boris with a rare opportunity. Personally devout, he was also politically astute. From the start, he consciously used Christianity both to consolidate his own power and to further unify Bulgarian society. His main opponents in both endeavors were the remaining pagan and Turkic boyars, who had revolted immediately after Boris' conversion in the mid-860s. Boris put down that revolt without too much trouble, but for the time being the boyars remained a stubborn force opposing Boris' pro-Byzantine policies, including Christianization, and resisting as well the progressive Slavicization of the Bulgar ruling class.*

Against this pagan/Turkic influence among the nobility were balanced the couple of hundred Greek priests now spreading the word among the Slavic peasantry. Yet, they answered not to Boris but to the patriarch of Constantinople and the Byzantine emperor.

Both the boyars and the priests, in other words, constituted potent internal threats to Boris' own authority. Until a solution could be found, Boris' rule would amount to a balancing act between these opposing forces.

Cut to the northern shore of the Danube River in the year 885, perhaps seven or eight months after Methodius' death. It is winter. A contingent of Frankish soldiers has escorted a little band of his ragged and downcast disciples to the river, which is not blue but slate gray. Their leader is Clement, and with them also is Clement's lieutenant, Naum. They have likely been imprisoned for the past few months somewhere, perhaps in Svatopluk's palace at Nitra.

With them now they have their precious books and probably little else. They cross the Danube on a flimsy raft held together by ropes made of bark, and when they step off the raft into the cold water that laps the far shore of the river, they are on Bulgarian soil.

---

* It's significant in this regard that Boris was the first Bulgarian ruler to hold a Slavic name rather than a Turkic one.

CLEMENT AND BORIS SAVE THE SLAVONIC LEGACY

The death of Methodius and the expulsion of his followers from Moravia sealed the fate of the Slavonic legacy in central Europe, though in a few isolated pockets it hung on as late as the eleventh century. But Boris knew a good thing when he saw one, and he wasted no time in inviting the missionaries to his capital, Pliska, where he offered them accommodations at the homes of some of his prominent supporters.

He also held what appears to have been a series of confidential meetings with them, which resulted in a careful plan to establish and promote the Slavonic liturgy in Bulgaria. Owing to the success of this plan, Clement and Naum would eventually be venerated as Orthodox saints and the saviors of the Cyrillo-Methodian tradition.

The Slavonic liturgy offered the perfect solution to Boris' problems. As other Slavic rulers would discover, it held out all the benefits of membership in the emerging Byzantine Commonwealth, yet in theory at least it allowed them a high degree of religious and political independence. It also gave due place to Slavic pride, and helped Boris forge a new national identity based on common worship in a common language. Now for the first time we can truly begin to speak of a Bulgarian people, rather than of Slavs and Bulgars in uneasy coexistence.

Aside from Boris' political reasons for embracing the Slavonic liturgy, a number of other factors combined to give the tradition a better chance in its new environment than it ever had in Moravia. While the Moravians and other Slavs were able to understand the Old Church Slavonic that Cyril had created, it was based not on their own spoken dialect but on that shared by the Macedonians and Bulgarians, and so in Bulgaria it enjoyed a simple linguistic advantage. Bulgaria, in

that sense, was its home turf; Old Church Slavonic is sometimes called "Old Bulgarian."

And as Byzantium's next-door neighbor, Bulgaria was
close enough for easy access. While this worked for the Greek
priests who still came into Bulgaria, it also worked for the
Bulgarian priests who now increasingly went to Constantinople for their training in Slavonic. Like Boris, Basil and his
successors knew a good thing when they saw it, and they offered the Slavonic mission their full support. This policy was
well known at the time, since one of Basil's envoys, stopping
in Venice and seeing a group of Methodius' former disciples
offered up for sale as slaves, was so confident of the emperor's
blessing that he bought them and sent them back to Constantinople. From there, they most likely ended up rejoining
their brethren in Bulgaria.

Finally, Clement and Naum themselves were both Bulgarian by birth, though they had spent much of their adult
lives outside their homeland. Clement was probably in his
middle to late forties, which would put his birth sometime
around 840. Naum was perhaps ten years older. Both are
known to have accompanied Cyril and Methodius to Rome
in 868, where they were ordained as priests, and so presumably both had returned to Moravia with Methodius and
stuck by him through all the years of adversity.

Naum stayed in Pliska, teaching and carrying on the
seemingly endless work of translating, while Clement went
to the other end of the country, to the region of Lake Ohrid
in southwestern Bulgaria (now Macedonia). Where Pliska in
the Dobrudja was probably still largely Turkic in population,
the Macedonian hinterland was entirely Slavic. As a result
of the two priests' efforts, both soon turned into major centers of Slavonic culture. Ohrid in particular, where Clement
is said to have taught 3,500 students over the next thirty

years, became a hub from which the Slavonic tradition would radiate outward to nearby Serbia and eventually to the Rus in the far north.

In 889 Boris abdicated in favor of his oldest son, Vladimir, resigning his earthly power to pursue the contemplative life of a monk. The resentful boyars had been biding their time, and they now mounted a last-ditch defense of their pagan and Turkic birthright, intimidating the weak-willed Vladimir into reversing course. Over the next several years Bulgaria was dominated by a reaction against Christianity and Byzantium, in which priests were persecuted and the regime allied itself politically with the Franks. Finally, Boris came out of retirement and put his foot down. After removing Vladimir from power and having him blinded, Boris installed his third son, Symeon, on the throne.

Devoutly Orthodox, Symeon had spent much of his youth in Constantinople, where he enjoyed at least some of the fruits of a Byzantine education. Under his long rule, the Slavonic tradition in Bulgaria would return to the rapid growth it had enjoyed under Boris. However, if the Byzantines thought that Symeon's accession was going to usher in a period of peace and friendship between the two neighbors, they had sadly underestimated Symeon's world-class ambitions.

CHAPTER ELEVEN

WARS OF EMULATION

S ymeon the Great stands out as medieval Bulgaria's strongest and most determined ruler, an energetic visionary whose acquisitive ardor would nearly bring Byzantium to its knees. In a reign that lasted more than three decades, Symeon never once broke his gaze from the shimmering fascination of Constantinople, Tsargrad, as the Slavs knew it, the city of the caesars. He strove to emulate Byzantium, yet at the same time he longed to seduce it, to win it, and ultimately possess it.

Born around the time his father, Boris, converted to Christianity, the mid-860s, Symeon was raised as a Christian and was sent to Constantinople for religious training as a boy of thirteen or fourteen. He spent a decade studying in a monastery in the Byzantine capital, returning to Bulgaria a few years after the arrival of Clement and Naum and Boris' adoption of the Slavonic liturgy.

On returning to Bulgaria from his Byzantine sojourn, Symeon entered a monastery founded by his father in the city of Preslav, near Pliska in the Dobrudja but a bit closer to

Constantinople. There he took a leading role in the translation movement that was rapidly augmenting the amount of
Greek religious literature available in Slavonic. Preslav was
predominantly Slavic and Christian, while Pliska was a holdout of the Turkic and pagan boyars. When Boris installed
Symeon on the throne, the old khan also arranged for
Symeon to rule from Preslav as his capital.

Symeon added to the number of monasteries and
churches his father had already built there, and Preslav and
Bulgaria entered a period of growth and prosperity. Trade
between the two neighbors throve under a series of liberal
commercial treaties. In addition to raw materials such as
honey, fur, and wax, Bulgaria now boasted artisans who produced many fine goods. Bulgarian craftsmen were especially
famous for their coveted tile work, which soon became a favored luxury import of the Byzantines.

SYMEON GOES TO WAR

Boris had gone to great lengths to avoid military confronta-
tions with his powerful neighbor. Symeon appears to have
sought them out from the start. If he was looking for an ex-
cuse for war, he didn't have long to wait. Within a year of
Symeon's accession, influential Byzantine merchants used
their clout with the emperor to have Byzantine trade laws
changed to Bulgaria's disadvantage. Symeon protested stren-
uously and was ignored. Immediately, he invaded Byzantine
territory with a large army, inflicting a crushing defeat on the
Byzantine force sent to repel him and ravaging the Thracian
countryside around Constantinople.

The main Byzantine army was occupied in the east, and
so the Byzantines fell back on a time-honored diplomatic

ploy that had worked for them many times in the past: they bribed a warlike barbarian tribe, the Magyars, to attack Symeon's army from the rear. Symeon sued for peace, but— going the Byzantines one better—he also arranged for an even more warlike tribe of barbarians, the Pechenegs, to fall upon the Magyars from the rear. When they did so, the Bulgarians hit the Magyars from the front, with the result that the Magyars were trounced and fled in disarray to the Hungarian plain.* Symeon then inflicted another sharp defeat on the Byzantines.

In case anyone in Byzantium missed the point of his diplomatic maneuvering, Symeon sarcastically drove it home in the negotiations over prisoners of war. The emperor Leo VI, he observed, had impressed everyone the year before by predicting a solar eclipse.† He was rumored to have great astronomical knowledge. If the emperor's knowledge was so wonderful, Symeon told the Byzantine ambassador, then the emperor should also be able to say whether Symeon intended to return the prisoners. "So prophesy one thing or the other, and if you know my intentions, you shall get the prisoners as reward for your prophecy and your embassy, by God!"

In other words, Symeon would return the prisoners if the ambassador could tell him whether he intended to. This was an ancient logical conundrum of the sort with which any educated Greek was well familiar. Drawing on his Constantinopolitan education, the Bulgarian ruler was proclaiming his intention to out-Byzantine the Byzantines.

Symeon's military and diplomatic prowess wrung significant concessions from the Byzantines in the treaty that concluded the war in 897, and the ensuing peace lasted

---

* Originally nomads from Central Asia, the Magyars combined with the Slavs already inhabiting the Hungarian plain to form the modern Hungarian nation.
† Leo VI was the successor of Basil I.

for sixteen years, until the year after Leo VI's death in 912. During that time, however, Symeon hardly stood pat. Taking advantage of Byzantine reverses at the hands of the Arabs, Symeon expanded Bulgaria's territory south and west, occupying the new lands bit by bit, each encroachment carefully calculated to be just short of worth going to war over.

Leo's successor, his brother Alexander, reversed Leo's policy of appeasement, insulting Symeon by cutting off the tribute payment stipulated by the peace treaty, but dying only a year after coming to power, before Symeon could really demonstrate how eager he was for a scrap. In Constantinople, power devolved upon a council of regents, whom Alexander selected to stand in for his successor, Leo's sickly seven-year-old son, Constantine VII Porphyrogenitus.

From this inauspicious beginning, incidentally, Constantine VII would grow up not only to rule as emperor but also to compose the major historical source for this period, the *De Administrando Imperio*, "On Ruling the Empire." A sort of primer for emperors put together from Byzantine diplomatic reports, it covers the early history of many of Byzantium's neighbors, including the Bulgars and Serbs.

Constantine VII's regents now had to deal with the full force of Symeon's wrath. They were led by the imperious patriarch of Constantinople, Nicholas Mysticus, whose influence would soon be challenged by Leo's widow and Constantine's mother, the empress Zoe, currently exiled to a monastery.* The regents' difficulties were heightened when the commander of the army revolted. As Byzantium floundered,

---

* Zoe Carbonopsina ("of the coal-black eyes") was a famous beauty. Nicholas had incurred Zoe's displeasure by refusing to sanction Leo's uncanonical fourth marriage to her. Their son, Constantine VII, was called "Porphyrogenitus" or "born in the purple" as a way of asserting his legitimacy. The term referred to the purple imperial bedchamber, and was applied only to the legitimate offspring of reigning emperors, which Constantine was not.

Symeon once again marched his Bulgarians right up to the big walls, where they set up camp.

The war that ensued, the second and last of Symeon's wars of emulation, lasted a decade and a half. Aside from Constantine VII Porphyrogenitus, our view of it comes largely from the many letters written to Symeon by Nicholas Mysticus over its duration. The correspondence shows the war almost as a duel between these two strong-willed individuals. By turns flattering, cajoling, conciliatory, didactic, blandly menacing, and directly threatening, Nicholas over the years offered Symeon almost every comfort but the one he sought. The patriarch stood resolute that never could Symeon, a Christian perhaps but still a barbarian, occupy the Byzantine throne.

Like ambitious kings in the West, Symeon coveted the title "emperor of the Romans" above all else. At the symbolic heart of this second war lay Symeon's mysterious "coronation" by Nicholas Mysticus in September 913, soon after the Bulgarians' arrival before the city walls. But it seems to have been as emperor of the Bulgarians, not the Romans, that Nicholas crowned Symeon. More satisfying at the time would have been the betrothal of Symeon's daughter to the young Constantine VII. Being the father-in-law of an emperor was a well-established stepping-stone to the Byzantine throne, as Symeon would have known, and recognition as an emperor, even if only of the Bulgarians, was at least a step in the right direction.

Symeon was appeased for the moment and withdrew to await developments. He probably figured time was on his side. But the following year, the empress Zoe emerged from her monastery, ousted Nicholas Mysticus from the regency, and, taking over the regency herself, repudiated Symeon's new title and the betrothal agreement. This brought the

Bulgars crashing back down on Byzantium, and when Symeon captured the important city of Adrianople in Thrace, Zoe was forced to reaffirm both title and betrothal in exchange for getting Adrianople back. For several years, the war continued on a low level as each side engaged in diplomatic maneuvering, searching for allies to attack the other.

Then the Bulgarians scored a great victory at Achelous, on the Black Sea, virtually wiping out the Byzantine army. Zoe's regime was discredited. But from Symeon's perspective the victory only made things worse. Another regime change took place in Constantinople, as the admiral Romanus Lecapenus seized power and had his own daughter married to Constantine VII.

Symeon found himself decisively preempted on his hoped-for ascent to the Byzantine throne. He was predictably enraged, all the more so when Romanus had himself crowned co-emperor in 920. Romanus, not Symeon, was now the effective Byzantine emperor. Symeon rudely refused to answer Romanus' letters, acknowledging only those from Nicholas Mysticus. Burning with frustration, Symeon demanded that Romanus abdicate in his favor. Once again, Nicholas' own verbose missives, carefully styled with exquisitely infuriating condescension, offered everything to Symeon but that.

Symeon now controlled the Balkans. Over the next several years, he rampaged through rural Thrace, repeatedly burning and pillaging right up to the walls of Constantinople. Yet, he could not break through. In desperation he even turned to an infidel, the Fatimid caliph of Egypt, who apparently agreed to provide the needed naval fleet, but when Symeon assembled his army before the walls the Muslims failed to show.

Finally the stalemate brought both sides to the negotiating table, in a personal summit meeting between Symeon and Romanus. Because mutual suspicions ran so deep, they met on a specially constructed pier in the Golden Horn, just outside the city walls, so that Symeon could get there securely by land and Romanus could come from inside the walls by boat. Symeon's retinue made a point of conspicuously hailing him as emperor, but the Byzantine chroniclers who recorded the meeting (embellishing their accounts with firm, compelling speeches from Romanus and garbled, incorrect Greek from Symeon, both probably made up by the chroniclers) left no word on the outcome. All we're told is that an omen occurred: "They say that two eagles flew overhead while the emperors were meeting and cried out and copulated and that they immediately separated from each other and one went toward the city while the other flew toward Thrace." This may reflect a peace settlement of some kind, and it seems to put the two "emperors" on an equal footing with each other, which is interesting.

If there was a peace agreement, it didn't last long, as perhaps the omen also retrospectively suggests, with the eagles going their separate ways after copulating. After annexing Serbia outright in 924, Symeon would appear to have begun styling himself "emperor of the Bulgarians and Romans." At least, that's the clear implication in a letter to him from the emperor Romanus, written in 925 after the death of Nicholas Mysticus that May. Any original document in which Symeon may have called himself that has not survived. However, a seal from Symeon's administration does survive on which the Bulgarian ruler calls himself "emperor of the Romans." Though its exact date is uncertain, this seal would seem to reflect Symeon's own highest aspiration.

On the other hand, if he did crown Symeon emperor of the Bulgarians, Nicholas Mysticus isn't seen calling him that in the surviving version of his letters, which all (like those of

Romanus) address Symeon only as "prince." Symeon had pushed things so far, perhaps, that despite having crowned him, Nicholas may have thought better of addressing him as "emperor" of anything. Nicholas expunged all reference to the coronation in his own letters, editing them for posterity by removing allusions to an event that had become an embarrassment to him.

Having annexed Serbia, Symeon next set his sights on his powerful new neighbor to Serbia's west, Croatia, but met a sharp defeat in 926 at the hands of that Slavic kingdom's greatest medieval ruler, King Tomislav. Despite this chastening, the following spring Symeon readied a huge invasion force and marched toward Constantinople. In May 927, as he once again led an army toward the walls that had so effectively thwarted his life's ambition, Symeon's heart gave out. He was 63.

Symeon's obsession had cost his people dearly, for the years of warfare left Bulgaria devastated and broke. Though the country recovered, it would be decades before Bulgaria was a power in the Balkans again, and never the way it had been under Symeon. Serbia, annexed by Symeon, broke away right after Symeon's death. Symeon's son and successor, Peter, signed a peace treaty with Byzantium acknowledging the emperor Romanus as his "spiritual father," in return for which Peter was confirmed in the title accorded to Symeon, "emperor (*tsar*) of the Bulgarians."* In addition, Peter was rewarded with a prestigious marriage to Romanus' granddaughter, a Byzantine princess.

Forty years of peace followed between Byzantium and Bulgaria, during which Christianity in Bulgaria continued to

---

* Like the German *kaiser,* the Slavic word *tsar* comes from the Byzantine imperial title *caesar,* roughly "deputy emperor." That, of course, had originally been the family name of the first Roman emperor, Augustus Caesar, and his adoptive father, Julius Caesar.

grow and prosper. The biggest development of Symeon's reign was a new Slavonic alphabet, ironically called Cyrillic, which originated in Bulgaria decades after Cyril's death and may have been invented by Methodius' disciple Clement of Ohrid (though most scholars now doubt this). Based much more closely on Greek letters, it was also far simpler than Glagolitic, and now began rapidly to replace it in Old Church Slavonic literature.

While owing its inspiration to its Byzantine origins, this burgeoning Slavonic tradition preserved a degree of cultural autonomy that no doubt would have gratified Boris, Bulgaria's last khan. Clearly, though, it was not enough to satisfy his son Symeon, Bulgaria's—and the Slavic world's—first tsar.

CHAPTER TWELVE

SERBS AND OTHERS

The ancient world had been split in two linguistic halves, Latin and Greek. During the Middle Ages, a shadow version of this same dividing line was extended north from the Mediterranean to bisect the colder, wetter Slavic world. Running right through the Balkans and up into Eastern Europe, the line was drawn by missionaries such as Cyril and Methodius and their Western counterparts.

This shadow line marked the divide not between two languages, for the people nearly all spoke Slavic, but between two alphabets. Slavs on one side looked west, to Rome, accepting the Catholic faith and using the Latin alphabet. Today, they are Poles, Czechs, Slovenes. Slavs on the other side looked east, to Byzantium, accepting Orthodoxy and using the Cyrillic alphabet. They are Russians, Ukrainians, Bulgarians, Serbs, and others who in the past made up the Byzantine Commonwealth. Some, such as the Hungarians and

Czechs, straddled the line.* In most cases, the original Slavic has branched out into the separate languages spoken today, but the Orthodox Serbs and the Catholic Croats still speak the same language, Serbo-Croatian. They just write it differently. A shadow line runs between them.

The Slavs who became the Serbs and Croats had arrived around the time of Heraclius. Some scholars speculate that they took their names from two groups of Iranian mounted warriors who had ruled over a previously undifferentiated Slavic population in the northwest Balkans near the end of the seventh century. Others, following Constantine VII Porphyrogenitus, suggest that the name *Serb* comes from the Latin *servus*, "servant" or "slave": " 'Serbs' in the tongue of the Romans is the word for 'slave,' whence the colloquial 'serbula' for menial shoes, and 'tzerboulianoi' for those who wear cheap, shoddy footgear," Constantine, no doubt a stranger to menial shoes himself, informs us. "This name the Serbs acquired from their being slaves of the emperor of the Romans." A similar derivation has also been put forward for the English word *slave*, which is thought to have come from the name *Slav* (more likely than the other way round, which is sometimes also suggested).

Both etymologies show how common slaves were in the Mediterranean world. Menially shod or not, many were of Slavic origin, captured in war or caught for trade. Along with furs, honey, and wax, slaves were a basic export from Slavic lands.

Bulgaria had pushed itself into the Byzantine consciousness on its own, as a powerful neighbor and rival,

---

* Hungary's ethnic history is unusually complex, blending Slavic influences with non-Slavic ones including that of the Magyars. Under strong Byzantine influence in the eleventh and twelfth centuries, Hungary ultimately swung to the West.

before entering Byzantium's cultural orbit. Serbia was a Byzantine creature from the start. As an identifiable political entity, Serbia owed its very origins to Byzantium—and to Byzantium's need for a willing ally against the emerging might of the Bulgar state.

"The prince of Serbia has from the beginning, that is ever since the reign of Heraclius the emperor, been in servitude and submission to the emperor of the Romans, and was never subject to the prince of Bulgaria." So writes Constantine VII Porphyrogenitus, spreading, as he often does, a gauzy layer of imperial fantasy over what historians can only hope is a foundation of truth. Serbia instead begins to take shape in the decades after the terrifying reign of the Bulgar khan Krum in the early ninth century, as Byzantine diplomats and agents arrived and got to work with their purses and their promises.

Perhaps to counter Byzantine infiltration, the Bulgars invaded Serb territory in the 840s, but were driven out by the Serb ruler Vlastimir after several years of heavy fighting. Although Vlastimir expanded Serb lands, as was customary with the Slavs he divided his dominions among his three children. The resulting feud between the three branches of this ruling family helped ensure that for the time being Serbia remained a pawn in the contest between Byzantium and Bulgaria that reached its first crescendo in the time of Symeon.

SERBIA ENTERS THE BYZANTINE COMMONWEALTH

Serbia came under Bulgarian control during Symeon's rule, but after his death the Serbs won independence. They were led by a descendant of Vlastimir, Časlav, who had been born in Bulgaria and spent most of his life as a hostage there before escaping back to Serbia to lead the revolt. The exact date of Časlav's escape and the revolt aren't known, but it all probably happened within a few years of Symeon's death. Časlav ruled for three more decades, remaining a loyal Byzantine ally for all of that time.

For this reason, scholars assume that Byzantine influences spread in Serbia during Časlav's rule. Many Serb refugees had fled to Byzantine territory during the wars with Symeon and the Bulgarian occupation, and they now returned, perhaps bringing Christianity and other Byzantine ways with them. But little is known for sure, and we should keep in mind that, unlike Bulgaria, Serbia was not yet a cohesive nation but still a fluid ethnic confederation. Časlav's Serbian state, whose borders aren't known, was only one of several. Others included Zachumliya, Duklja (Dioclea), Trebinja, and later Raska, which by the twelfth century would become the most important center of Serb power.

It was from Raska that the Serbs began expanding in the twelfth and thirteenth centuries, struggling, like the Bulgarians earlier, to prove themselves and their identity against Byzantium even as they were drawn ever more tightly into its cultural orbit. By this time the Byzantine emperors considered the Serbs to be their subjects. Serb rulers, called grand zhupans, held power at the emperor's pleasure, and when they revolted—which they did with some regularity—they were seen as treacherous mutineers. This was dramatically illustrated in 1172, when the emperor Manuel Comnenus defeated the grand zhupan Stefan Nemanja. Stefan was brought before the emperor bareheaded and barefoot, with a rope around his neck, to proffer his sword and prostrate himself at the emperor's feet.

Such demonstrations make good theater, but this one

failed to take. A few years later, the emperor was dead, the empire fell into dissarray, and Stefan returned to the offensive, conquering or annexing considerable Byzantine territory in the Balkans. Eventually, the Byzantines defeated him all over again, but this time they placated him by marrying him into the imperial family and giving him the high rank of *sebastocrator*. Privilege served better than humiliation, with the result that Stefan and Serbia now became full-fledged members of the Orthodox Byzantine Commonwealth.

When Stefan abdicated in 1196, he took monastic vows, entering an Orthodox monastery he had founded at Studenica. Shortly afterward, he joined his son Sava, also a monk, on Mt. Athos, in an old monastery called Hilandar that the two had refounded as a Serbian establishment.

MT. ATHOS

Mt. Athos—the Holy Mountain, as it is still called—was the center of Orthodox monasticism long before Stefan's day. Athos is the easternmost of the three fingers that grope southward into the Aegean from the Chalkidike peninsula, between Thessalonica and the river Strymon in northern Greece. About thirty miles in length and five or six miles wide in most places, with a mountainous spine running down the middle, the rocky, hilly strip of land is joined to the Chalkidike by a slender isthmus just over a mile wide. Through this isthmus, Herodotus tells us, the Persian king Xerxes cut a canal in order to avoid taking his ships around the dangerous headlands during his abortive invasion of Greece in the fifth century BC. The canal's remains can still be seen. The mountain itself lies at the promontory's far tip, its white marble peak jutting sharply from the sea to some 6,000 feet above sea level.

This astonishingly beautiful and rugged landscape is dotted with twenty ancient monasteries, less than half of the forty-six that existed around the year 1000, Athos' medieval heyday. Most hug the coast, where they cling determinedly to the hillsides or squat in the fragrant valleys, surrounded by carefully tended olive groves, gardens, and orchards.

Today, Athos is a semiautonomous religious community governed by the church and controlled by Greece's Ministry of Foreign Affairs. Entry requires a special internal visa from the ministry (which to my great frustration was on strike when I visited Greece, so be warned). Tradition dictates that no women are allowed there, though lapses involving Vlach shepherds and their families were recorded around 1100. Generally, however, even donkeys, chickens, goats, and other livestock have been restricted to the males of the species. Eggs and milk have thus been imported in the past, though some of these restrictions have been relaxed in recent years.

The first monastery, called the Great Lavra, was founded near the tip of Athos in 963, though it's thought that eremetic (from the Greek *eremetikos*, "of the desert," which also gives us *hermit*) monks had begun arriving on the promontory perhaps a century earlier. While the monks of this first establishment were Greek, they were rapidly joined by Orthodox from other lands, and especially by Slavs, who came in great numbers during the twelfth century.

By 1200 or so, there were monasteries for Orthodox Armenians, Georgians, and Italians, as well as Russians, Bulgarians, and Serbs. The Russians took over the Panteleemon monastery, the Bulgarians moved into Zographou, and later in the century the Serbs refounded Hilandar, which would become especially famous. In these and other monasteries, the monks carried out the tasks of translating Byzantine theological and liturgical texts into Old Church Slavonic. From Athos the texts would be distributed to other monasteries throughout the Byzantine Commonwealth.

ST. SAVA AND THE GLORY OF MEDIEVAL SERBIA

Through Hilandar, and especially through the work of the brilliant Sava, Serbs came to constitute a leading presence at Mt. Athos. Stefan Nemanja had won much territory for Serbia and founded an important ruling dynasty, but his farthest-reaching contribution to Serbian culture was in fathering Sava. Both would later be canonized as Orthodox saints. It was Sava who played the biggest part in giving medieval Serbia its heavily Byzantine flavor.

A man of widely diverse abilities and interests, Sava had started life as a provincial governor under his father before fleeing to Athos, where he escaped his father's wrath at his desertion by joining the Russian monastery of Panteleemon and then the Greek one of Vatopedi. Later, the sources claim, it was Sava's influence that prompted the old warrior to don a monk's robes himself.

On his father's death Sava took over at Hilandar, working the Byzantine imperial establishment hard to obtain full autonomy and a secure income for the monastery. Hilandar was a great success, soon harboring close to a hundred monks, and assuming a vital place in Serbia's cultural and religious life. Sava himself became an influential figure on the Holy Mountain, acting as patron to a dozen other monasteries as well as to Hilandar. Yet, we're told by his hagiographers, it was the life of quiet contemplation that drew him most strongly, and he spent long periods in ascetic prayer in a special meditation room called a *hesychasterion*.

In 1204 the Latins took Constantinople, and a few years later they seized Athos. Sava made his way to Studenica, where he deposited his father's remains. He spent the next eight years as abbot there, often occupied with trying to control the bickering and malfeasance of his older brothers, but also writing works honoring their newly canonized father and founding new monasteries. The most important of these was Zica. Richly decorated by Byzantine artists, its church soon emerged as Serbia's leading place of worship.

In 1219, Sava was consecrated first archbishop of the autocephalous Serbian Orthodox Church by the Byzantine patriarch. After guiding his church through the perilous waters of papal encroachment, and twice making pilgrimages to Crusader-occupied Jerusalem, Sava died while visiting the Bulgarian capital of Turnovo in 1236. His body was laid to rest in a Serbian church founded earlier by the royal family at Mileseva, where a wall portrait survives of Sava that may have been painted from life in the 1220s.

Saint, mystic, pilgrim, warrior, and hero of many epic poems, Sava stood in popular imagination as Serbia's most inspiring national figure during the long Turkish occupation. The strength of his cult—even local Turkish Muslims venerated St. Sava—led Ottoman authorities to burn Sava's coffin in 1594.

Serbian art reached glorious heights in the decades after Sava's death. It's best exemplified in the majestic frescoes at the monastery church of Sopocani, which were done in the 1260s. Within decades, the Serbian artists' distinctive touch was lost, as Byzantine styles and influences from the Paleologan Renaissance won out.

Yet, in the mid-fourteenth century, even as its artistic originality declined, medieval Serbia reached its greatest military and political strength, during the reign of Stefan Dushan. His determined attempts to claim the Byzantine throne very much recall those of the Bulgarian tsar Symeon more than four centuries earlier. Just as Symeon had dreamed of establishing a Byzantine-Bulgarian empire with himself as emperor in Constantinople, so did Stefan Dushan now attempt to seat himself at the helm of a Byzantine-Serbian empire, taking advantage of the civil strife that wracked the empire in these years. Though unsuccessful in pressing his claim to be "emperor of the Serbs and Romans," he modeled his court and administration on those in Constantinople and Byzantinized Serbia's civil administration and law codes.

From the height of its strength, Serbia abruptly crumbled after Dushan's death as the Ottomans swiftly advanced into the Balkans, winning battles at the Maritsa River in 1371 and at Kosovo Polye, the "field of blackbirds," in 1389. This last battle, in which both the sultan Murad and the Serbian prince Lazar perished, marked the beginning of Serbian vassalage to the Turks, and for that reason took on an epic quality in later legend. Like the Byzantines, the Serbs enjoyed a brief respite after Tamerlane defeated the Ottomans at Ankara in 1402, but by 1459 all of Serbia was under direct Turkish occupation. Serbs still look back to the reign of Stefan Dushan as their golden age.

CHAPTER THIRTEEN

THE RISE OF KIEV

T radition holds that the Rus raiders who so terrified the inhabitants of Constantinople in 860 came from Kiev, the wealthy trading city on the Dnieper River in southern Russia that was the political center of the first Russian civilization, Kievan Rus. This idea is based largely on the earliest Russian account of this period, the *Primary Chronicle*. The *Primary Chronicle* tells how the various Slavic and other peoples in what is now northern Russia and the Ukraine invited a Scandinavian people called the Varangian Rus to rule over them. "Our land is great and rich," they said, "but there is no order in it. Come to rule and reign over us."

From the start, the story goes, the Slavs and their new overlords coveted Constantinople's shimmering magnificence. To the Slavs, the Byzantine capital was Tsargrad, the "city of emperors"; to the Varangians, it was Micklegard, the "great city." While moving to Constantinople with their families, two Varangian brothers named Askold and Dir stopped in Kiev, a "small city on a hill" by the Dnieper River. Askold and Dir stayed in Kiev and took it over, using it as a base for their attack on Constantinople in 860. The besieging fleet was wrecked by a storm that arose from nowhere when the emperor Michael and the patriarch Photius dipped "the vestments of the Virgin" in the sea.

Among the original Varangians had been a prince called Rurik, who became ruler of Novgorod in the north and progenitor of the future tsars of Russia up to 1568. Rurik's descendant Oleg overthrew and killed Askold and Dir, becoming ruler of Kiev. Under Oleg, Kiev extended its rule over other Rus population centers, taking its place as the Rus capital, "the mother of Russian cities."

Based on this account, the traditional interpretation has Kiev being founded sometime before the mid-ninth century. The city prospers, opening up the famous trade route "from the Varangians to the Greeks" along the Dnieper River to the Black Sea. This is the route that the *Primary Chronicle* depicts Askold and Dir as intending to take in emigrating to Tsargrad with their families. Kiev also attacks Byzantium from time to time, as in 860, but meanwhile Byzantine cultural influences are filtering back up the Dnieper. Kiev ultimately converts to Orthodox Christianity near the end of the tenth century.

Flattering as it was to Byzantium, for a long time this traditional interpretation was quite agreeable to modern Byzantinists. However, the *Primary Chronicle* has proved rather unreliable. It was compiled from various earlier sources, some of them oral, in the late eleventh and early twelfth centuries. Its compilers were Orthodox monks in Kiev looking backward from the era when Kiev's greatness had begun to fade. More recent scholars have concluded that the compilers had reason to exaggerate both Kiev's antiquity and its role in the founding of Rus power, in order to offer a more "appropriate" version of Kiev's origins.

THE EARLY RUS

New archeological evidence has left the scholars little choice, although the myth of Kiev's antiquity has died hard. Some books on Russian history from as recently as the late 1990s continue to assert that the attack of 860 came from Kiev. Yet, the new discoveries (along with the reinterpretation of old ones) have revealed conclusively that in 860 Kiev was nothing more than a primitive village of a few wooden huts, indistinguishable from other villages around it. There is certainly no evidence of voluminous trade with Byzantium going back to the mid-ninth century or before. It would have been a flat impossibility for a fleet of some two hundred vessels to originate there, sail down the Dnieper, and besiege Constantinople. The attack had to come from another Rus center.

There's no shortage of candidates. During the ninth century, the Varangian Rus—bold Viking traders who ventured across the frigid waters of the Baltic—established a string of trading posts along the forested rivers of northern Russia. Archeologists may have exploded the myth of the Dnieper route between the early Rus and Byzantium, but they have found ample evidence of commerce between the early Rus and the other two civilizations on their flanks, those of Western Europe and the Islamic world. Both the Franks and the Arabs, it turns out, got a head start on the Byzantines in trading with the adventurous Rus.

Not the Dnieper but the Don and especially the Volga

appear to have been the most important water routes from the early Rus to southern wealth. Both were well situated for trade with Islamic lands. Like the Dnieper, the Don ultimately gives onto the Black Sea, but farther east, through the Sea of Azov. The Volga gives onto the Caspian Sea, down which merchants could sail in the direction of the overland route to Baghdad. Navigable into their upper reaches, both rivers are accessible by a series of short portages from the Baltic Sea. Furthermore, they swing close to each other near the bottom, allowing boatmen to switch from one river (and thus one sea) to the other by another manageable portage.

By the 830s, we begin to hear of the Rus in the literary sources. The Frankish *Annals of St. Bertin* records a Byzantine embassy arriving at the court of the emperor Louis the Pious in 839. With the Byzantines was a group of travelers carrying a letter to Louis from the Byzantine emperor, who asked Louis to help the strangers return home. Their way home from Byzantium was blocked by some "barbarous and savage peoples of exceeding ferocity" whom the travelers had encountered on their outward journey. The letter said further that the strangers had identified themselves as "Rhos," and when Louis inquired further he found that "they were of the people of the Swedes."

It was long thought that these travelers had originated in Kiev, but since, as is now known, Kiev didn't exist at the time, recent scholars favor a trading post near the future Novgorod. The savages who blocked them were probably the Magyars, who would soon (as a result of Symeon's ploy, described earlier) give way to the Petchenegs north of the Black Sea and move into Hungary.

Despite the appearance of the Rus at the Byzantine court, there is little or no archeological evidence of trade between them and the Byzantines at this time. Instead, all the evidence—such as plentiful silver Arab coin hoards on the Volga and the Don—points to strong ties between the Rus and the Islamic world.

THE FOUNDATION OF KIEV

Around the year 900, however, the Varangian Rus found themselves blocked. To the east, their well-established route down the Volga to Baghdad was suddenly obstructed by a band of nomadic incomers, the Volga Bulgars, who demanded a cut of the profits from the lucrative Volga trade.* To the west, Rus traders on the Danube were subjected to similar pressures from those whose lands they passed through, mostly in the form of tariffs and tolls. This left them one option for expansion: south. That meant the Dnieper— as well as more extensive contacts with the Slavs who lived along its northern shores.

While the Dnieper River is the largest river flowing into the Black Sea, it doesn't offer the relatively smooth sailing found on Russia's other two major rivers, the Don and the Volga, both of which were navigable for virtually all of their lengths. In particular, a set of nasty rapids, formed by a series of massive granite ridges, extended for nearly fifty miles along the middle Dnieper, forcing boatmen either to make numerous lengthy portages or to face ruin or death.

The rapids occurred as the river flows through the steppes. Boatmen were forced to get out and laboriously drag their vessels and cargo just at the spot where they were highly vulnerable to attack by mounted nomads. Attacks by the

---

* The Volga Bulgars were a Turkic people related to the same group that founded Bulgaria.

Petchenegs on the middle and lower Dnieper, as Constantine Porphyrogenitus reports, would be the bane of the Kievan Rus.

At the same time that the Rus were looking south, the Byzantines had their own reasons to seek a new alliance in the north. The biggest reason was the attack of 860, which dramatically demonstrated that the old alliance with the Khazars was no longer enough to protect Byzantium from that direction. Khazar power was on the wane. The Byzantines flirted with nomadic peoples nominally in Khazar domains, such as the Magyars and then the Petchenegs, using them when they could, but such wandering warriors were too unreliable for the long term. They showed no interest in settling down as Christians or partaking in any cultural benefits they might derive from civilization. Nor were they much interested in trade beyond the trinkets-and-tools variety.

Trade, in contrast, was what the Rus were all about. Excavations in Kiev in the 1970s found the remains of log cabins on the waterfront that closely resemble similar structures found on the sites of Varangian Rus trading posts elsewhere. Now securely dated to around 900, these buildings would seem to mark the arrival in Kiev of the Rus from the north. Graveyards now begin to appear also, some Scandinavian but more Slavic, suggesting that increasing numbers of Slavs were drawn to Kiev and surrounding communities as jobs (such as shipbuilding) associated with trade became available.

To complement the archeological evidence, the *Primary Chronicle* preserves what appear to be two early trade agreements with the Byzantines. The first, from the year 907, gives the impression of being preliminary to the fuller provisions of the second, from 911. There's no guarantee these agreements were struck by the Rus in Kiev, though that's what the *Primary Chronicle* states. But for the first time the archeological evidence at least allows the *Primary Chronicle*'s claims about Kiev to be true. If so, these agreements can be seen as Kiev's founding documents.

The *Primary Chronicle* depicts the first one as being essentially extorted from the Byzantines by Oleg, the Varangian ruler who it says had earlier seized Kiev by overthrowing Askold and Dir. There's a detailed and dramatic narrative of an attack by Oleg on Tsargrad: the Varangian circumvents the city's fabled defenses by dragging ships overland into the Golden Horn, which the Byzantines had protected with a chain across its mouth. This was the same trick the Turks would use in 1453, and it also suggests the skills necessary for negotiating the Dnieper rapids. Only after being subjected to Oleg's virtuoso tactical skills and merciless rapine do the Byzantines agree to the Rus demands. Remarkably, nowhere do Byzantine sources mention this attack, which makes it almost certain that it never actually occurred. The whole thing seems carefully concocted to preserve the Rus' reputation as fearsome savages.

The terms of the agreements are unusually generous from the Byzantine point of view—right down to indulging the Scandinavians' penchant for unlimited bathing:

> The Russes who come hither shall receive as much grain as they require. Whosoever come as merchants shall receive supplies for six months, including bread, wine, meat, fish, and fruit. Baths shall be prepared for them in any volume they require. When the Russes return homeward, they shall receive from your emperor food, anchors, cordage, and sails and whatever else is needed for the journey.

But the agreements also laid down terms designed specifically to promote commerce and ensure the visitors' good behavior:

> If the Russes come hither without merchandise, they shall receive no provisions. Your prince shall personally lay injunction upon such Russes as journey hither that they shall do no violence in the towns and throughout our territory. Such Russes as arrive here shall dwell in the St. Mamas quarter. . . . They shall not enter the city save through one gate, unarmed and fifty at a time, escorted by an agent of the Emperor. They may conduct business according to their requirements without payment of taxes.

Without all these carefully negotiated provisions, the Dnieper route would not have been worth the trouble, expense, and danger. Kiev was hardly a propitious spot; being so far south it's extremely hard to defend. Novgorod and other early Rus trade centers lay in the northern forests, out of reach of the nomadic horsemen who have historically dominated the steppe. Kiev, in contrast, lies in the lightly forested zone on the steppe's northern edge, and was more accessible to any hordes of mounted nomadic warriors— Magyars, Petchenegs—who might sweep in for plunder and pillage. The original settlement sits on the right bank of the Dnieper, about six hundred miles upriver from the Black Sea, on a steep line of wooded bluffs looming three hundred feet over the river. It is a dramatic setting; today, at the top of the high bluffs, the spires and golden domes of its old churches can be seen from much of the modern city, which has spread out on the floodplain opposite. The climate here is more forgiving than in the heavy forests of the north, the trees more easily cleared, the soil more fertile. Counterbalancing such temptations lay the danger in the steppes.

But for a time the gamble, and the carefully negotiated concessions, paid off. This was the first Russian state, and its legitimacy was immeasurably bolstered by Byzantine recognition in the trade agreements. The *Primary Chronicle* names Oleg's advisors and representatives, and like him they all have decidedly Scandinavian names: Karl, Farulf, Vermund, Hrollaf, Steinvith, Ingjald, Gunnar, Harold, Karni, and the like. So we have a good idea of who founded it. Yet, within a century this new state and the emerging civilization over which it claimed supremacy would be thoroughly Slavic—truly Russian, if you will.

If Byzantinists liked the old interpretation for the role it gave Byzantium in influencing Kievan Rus after the city's foundation, how much more reason they have to like the new one. Our new picture of Kiev's early days gives Byzantium a far more prominent role even than before. Byzantium, it now seems clear, was a decisive factor in Kiev's very origins—which turn out to be later, more sudden, and more dramatic than had earlier been suspected.

COMMERCE AND COMBAT

It's an open question whether Askold, Dir, and Oleg were actually historical figures. By the decade of the 940s, the evidence is firmer. In 941, the first clearly identifiable Kievan ruler, Igor, led a huge fleet—though the Byzantine reports of ten thousand ships obviously exaggerated its size—down from the Black Sea and terrorized the coastal areas around Constantinople for several months. Only when the Byzantines brought some old ships out of retirement and armed them with Greek fire were the Russian ships driven away. Historians differ on what to make of this raid, but it was followed by a reaffirmation of commercial ties under a new and still more extensive treaty in 945, whose text is also given in the *Primary Chronicle*.

Igor died leading a small force against rebels in nearby Dereva soon after the new treaty was signed, and power in Kiev passed smoothly to his widow, Olga, who acted as regent for their small son, Svyatoslav. Olga's first act was to wipe out the Derevlian rebels to a man—at least as the *Primary Chronicle* tells it, dwelling lovingly on every gruesome detail of Olga's relentless quest to avenge her husband's death. In what can be taken as literary foreshadowing, the little boy Svyatoslav gamely tries to hurl a spear against his father's killers, barely clearing his horse's ears.

The *Primary Chronicle* then depicts Olga as going on to further consolidate Kiev's control over other cities as far distant as Novgorod, power that was mainly exercised by the collection of tribute in the form of valuable goods such as furs, wax, honey, slaves, and feathers. These raw goods could be traded for cash and manufactured luxury items such as silk, which is prominently mentioned in the 945 treaty. Like her predecessors Olga looked first and foremost to Byzantium for such ventures, not to other markets, though she later flirted briefly with the Germans.

In 957, right between Liudprand of Cremona's two journeys to Constantinople, Olga herself visited the Byzantine capital with a large retinue. The primary purpose of her visit was trade, but Olga also had something else on her mind. Nearly a century earlier, Photius had reportedly sent Christian missionaries to the Rus. They disappeared without a trace, but as contacts between Byzantium and the Rus grew closer with the rise of Kiev and the Dnieper trade, Christianity inevitably began winning converts among the Rus. Olga herself now asked to be baptized into Christianity. The ceremony was performed by the patriarch of Constantinople, presumably in Hagia Sophia. With the emperor Constantine VII Porphyrogenitus standing as her baptismal father, Olga was christened in state under the name Helena, after the mother of Constantine the Great.

This sort of intimate symbolic acceptance into the imperial family was taken very seriously. It was a rare honor, and it shows the importance that the Byzantines accorded their new ally to the north. But there may also have been a human element to the story, for the *Primary Chronicle* records Constantine VII—who seems genuinely to have been rather smitten with the remarkable Olga—as proposing marriage to the Rus ruler. She nimbly evades his advances, remarking that as her baptismal father he has called her his daughter, and so any union between them would be inappropriate under Christian law. His response is charmed but rueful: "Olga, you have outwitted me."

We might expect the conversion of a strong-willed ruler like Olga to have resulted in the final Christianization of her people, but that step was to be deferred just a bit longer. No matter how she tried, the devout Olga could never shake the firm paganism of her equally strong-willed son and heir, Svyatoslav.

Svyatoslav was the first Russian ruler to have a Slavic name, which suggests that the Varangian Rus had now, like the Bulgars before them, been largely absorbed by their more numerous Slavic subjects. A restless and hard-charging warrior, gray-eyed and snub-nosed, Svyatoslav modeled himself on the nomadic horsemen of the steppes, right down to hair-style (shaved head with single side sprig of hair, barbarian style):

> Stepping light as a leopard, he undertook many campaigns. Upon his expeditions he carried with him neither wagons nor kettles, and boiled no meat, but cut off small strips of horseflesh, game, or beef, and ate it after roasting it on the coals. Nor did he have a tent, but he spread out a horse-blanket under him, and set his saddle under his head; and all his retinue did likewise.

Leaving the formidable Olga to run things in Kiev, Svyatoslav at first devoted himself to further expanding Kievan power to the east. In the early 960s he undertook a series of expeditions against the Khazars, sacking their capital, Itil, and finally putting an end to the limping Khazar state. He then subjugated other tribes whose names the chronicle preserves—Kasogians, Yasians, Vyatichians—as well as attacking the Volga Bulgars. His objective seems to have been to gain access to the still lucrative Don and Volga trade routes, but if so, he was only partly successful.

Then, in 967, the Byzantine emperor Nicephorus II Phocas asked Svyatoslav to lead an army against the Bulgarians. This was a standard sort of request for the Byzantines to make of an ally, and it was accompanied by the usual bribe, or in this case perhaps slightly larger than usual, 1,500 pounds of gold. Svyatoslav duly crossed the Danube, easily defeated the Bulgarians, and occupied Little Preslav (Pereslavyets) in the Dobrudja, where he spent the winter.

While he was there, the Petchenegs seized the opportunity to attack Kiev, which they blockaded and besieged with a large force. Svyatoslav rushed back north and relieved the city, driving the Petchenegs back out into the steppes. But his time in prosperous Bulgaria had given him ideas, and after rescuing Olga he had a surprise for her, announcing his intention to transfer the seat of Rus power to Bulgaria. Already ill, Olga died a few days after numbly receiving the news that her son and heir wished to move their capital south. Svyatoslav marched back to Bulgaria and again captured Little Preslav. It took the Byzantine emperor John Tzimisces (who had murdered and replaced Nicephorus II Phocas) three bloody defeats of Svyatoslav, and a long blockade on the Danube, to get him to agree to leave Bulgaria.

On their way back to Kiev via the Dnieper, laden with booty, Svyatoslav and his small retinue were set upon at the rapids by the Petchenegs. Svyatoslav was killed, and the Petchenegs (perhaps to show who the real barbarians were) gave his carefully shaved skull the now familiar Dixie-cup treatment. Svyatoslav had specifically asked the Byzantines to negotiate a safe passage. Either they had not bothered, or their request had been less compelling than the rich Bulgarian loot that Syatoslav and his men carried with them.

There is no indication that Svyatoslav's misbehavior in the Balkans did anything much to disrupt Kiev's close relationship with Byzantium. That relationship was based on trade, although that was about to change, and business is business. Both the Byzantines and, after Svyatoslav's death, the Russians were caught up in domestic tensions that would have blurred the lines of any antagonism.

In Byzantium, John Tzimisces replaced Nicephorus Phocas (whom he had killed) as regent for Constantine VII Porphyrogenitus' young grandson Basil II until Tzimisces' death in 976. At that point, the eighteen-year-old Basil II, Byzantium's rightful emperor, faced more than a decade of civil war in his struggle to rule the empire in his own name.

In Russia, where Svyatoslav had left several of his sons in charge of different cities, the 970s were similarly taken up in a succession struggle among those sons, with the youngest, Vladimir, finally emerging as victor in 980.

Basil II and Vladimir both faced daunting challenges in their respective struggles for power, and as it turned out, each had crucial support to offer the other just where and when it was needed most. These two outstanding rulers helped each other bring their countries, medieval Byzantium and Kievan Rus, to their respective peaks of prosperity and strength. In doing so, they firmly and finally cemented the unique partnership between Byzantine civilization and the emerging civilization of Russia.

CHAPTER FOURTEEN

THE GOLDEN AGE OF KIEVAN RUS

T he ruler known variously as Vladimir the Great and St. Vladimir had been born to one of Svyatoslav's peasant concubines around 956. His two older brothers, Yaropolk and Oleg, therefore had breeding and legitimacy as well as seniority on their sides. Svyatoslav had put Yaropolk in charge of Kiev and Oleg in charge of nearby Dereva (whose inhabitants had earlier rebelled against Igor), sending Vladimir to be prince of distant Novgorod. Trouble soon broke out between the two older brothers. Yaropolk defeated Oleg, who was killed in battle, and Vladimir fled to Sweden, leaving Yaropolk in sole control of Kievan Rus.

But if Vladimir had nothing else, he had nerve. As the *Primary Chronicle* relates, he gathered together a band of adventurers in Sweden, returned to Novgorod, and easily expelled Yaropolk's lieutenants there. Wasting no time, he marched on Kiev with a large army of mixed northerners, where he induced Yaropolk to flee by suborning his key general. Inviting Yaropolk to negotiations, Vladimir then had him stabbed by two Varangians as he came in the door.

Upon winning power Vladimir faced a potentially crippling lack of political legitimacy. He turned immediately to religion to solve that problem—but not to Christianity. Not at first, anyway. In the *Primary Chronicle,* Vladimir's very first act as ruler is to identify himself publicly with the pagan gods of traditional Slavic worship, headed by the thunder god, Perun: "Vladimir then began to rule alone in Kiev, and he set up idols on the hills outside the castle with the hall: one of Perun, made of wood with a head of silver and a mustache of gold, and others of Khors, Dazh'bog, Stribog, Simarg'l, and Mokosh." Many of these gods reflect the local deities of communities over which Kiev now exercised control. A brother-killing bastard who was identified with Kiev's distant rival Novgorod, Vladimir desperately needed a way to establish himself with his still-heterogeneous subject population, and conspicuously adopting their gods was an obvious way to do that.

"On Earth There Is No Such Beauty"

Yet, such a course also had pitfalls. Local gods evoke local ties, not loyalty to a central government. And like his father and grandparents, Vladimir made the expansion of Kievan authority his overriding concern, constantly campaigning against outlying towns, attacking, conquering, subjugating, exacting tribute.

Many of the inhabitants of these towns were Christians, as indeed were many in Kiev by now, and they objected to making mandatory sacrifices to pagan gods. There were also Muslims and Jews living under Kievan rule, indeed almost certainly within Kiev itself. The Khazars had been Jewish, and the Volga Bulgars were Muslim, so that any Rus ruler possessed at least a passing familiarity with both of those faiths as well as with Christianity. From an early stage Vladimir also seems to have begun exploring the possibility of adopting one of these more prestigious, scripture-based monotheistic religions.

The famous set piece of Vladimir's conversion in the *Primary Chronicle* has been accepted by most historians as plausible at least in its broad outlines. Vladimir was entertaining some envoys from the Volga Bulgars, and he asked them about their faith. "They replied that they believed in God, and that Mahomet instructed them to practice circumcision, to eat no pork, to drink no wine, and, after death, promised them complete fulfillment of their carnal desires." The last part sounded good to Vladimir, but not so the prohibition of pork and especially wine. " 'Drinking,' said he, 'is the joy of the Russes. We cannot exist without that pleasure.' " This last passage, it seems, is commonly cited as especially strong evidence of the chronicle's plausibility.

There followed similar visits from the Germans, representing the Latin church, and the Khazars, representing Judaism, both of whom also failed to win Vladimir's allegiance. The Germans prompted his rejection by revealing that their faith called for fasting, while the Khazars derailed themselves by bringing up the Diaspora. This led Vladimir to expostulate, "If God loved you and your faith, you would not be thus dispersed in foreign lands. Do you expect us to accept that fate also?"

Each of these episodes gets a paragraph in the *Primary Chronicle*. But then from Byzantium comes "a scholar" who gets more than ten pages, giving a long summary of world history à la the Old and New Testaments, which is moved along in the text by periodic questions from the obviously rapt Vladimir. The "scholar" introduces his lengthy disquisition by saying that the Byzantine version of Christianity is similar to that of the Germans, but that the Germans "have modified the faith" by introducing novelties such as unleavened bread in the Eucharist.

After consulting his boyars, Vladimir then sent out emissaries to visit in turn the Volga Bulgars, the Germans, and the Byzantines and report on how they worshiped. The Bulgars and Germans received the envoys cordially enough, but couldn't compete with Hagia Sophia, where the emperor and patriarch invited the Russians to join a service. On entering the great church, the envoys later reported, "We knew not whether we were in heaven or on earth. For on earth there is no such splendor or such beauty, and we are at a loss how to describe it. We only know that God dwells there among men." Vladimir and his boyars, the *Primary Chronicle* says, now resolved to be baptized into the Byzantine version of the Christian faith.

That's the story from the Russian sources, looking back. The Byzantine sources have their own perspective on the conversion of the Rus, one that may be better grounded in reality.

During much of the tenth century, during Basil's minority and that of his grandfather Constantine VII Porphyrogenitus before him, the Byzantine government had been controlled by powerful generals acting as regents and co-emperors. These figures have intruded themselves into our narrative more than once. Such men were the scions of the great military families in the provinces, especially in Asia Minor, families who were in large part responsible for the victories over the Arabs that expanded imperial territory eastward over the course of the century. As the great families jockeyed for influence at court, rivalries developed among them, and it was such a rivalry that had led to the murder of Nicephorus Phocas by John Tzimisces in 969.

Over the next two decades of civil strife, the feud between the Phocas family and its enemies dominated Byzantine politics. Basil hung on, patiently working to reclaim power from the feuding generals, who commanded what were essentially private armies, imperial in name only, and larger than anything Basil could muster. Finally, after dispatching his rivals, Nicephorus Phocas' nephew Bardas rebelled openly against Basil in 987, and was proclaimed emperor by his troops. He controlled virtually the whole empire, while Basil had only Constantinople itself, where he was surrounded and cut off.

But in Byzantine politics, whoever ruled in Constantinople retained the aura of legitimate power, no matter how bad things were elsewhere. And they were bad. Basil was challenged not only by Bardas Phocas but by a rebellion in Bulgaria, where the tsar Samuel had taken advantage of Byzantine confusion to throw off imperial rule. This had been imposed directly on Bulgaria by John Tzimisces, as part of the campaigns in which Svyatoslav had participated. In 986, the Bulgarians had caught Basil's army unawares and wiped it out in ambush as the Byzantines retreated through a steep mountain pass. From this point on, Basil would be grimly obsessed with Bulgaria's utter reduction, and his bloody fulfillment of that goal would ultimately win him the epithet Bulgaroctonos, "Bulgar-slayer."

In 988, Basil's victory over Bulgaria lay far in the future. His most urgent priority was simple survival. Most importantly, to meet the armies of Bardas Phocas, Basil needed soldiers, and for that there was really only one place to turn.

Basil sent a delegation to Vladimir asking for a large detach-
ment of troops, and in the negotiations that followed, the
Byzantine emperor showed exactly how desperate the situation was by offering Vladimir his own sister Anna—a born-
in-the-purple Byzantine princess, no less—in marriage.

This was a great opportunity for Vladimir, and an
unheard-of concession to a barbarian ruler from the north.
It would have absolutely scandalized Basil's grandfather,
Constantine VII Porphyrogenitus, who in his voluminous
writings on imperial comportment was very clear that sully-
ing the royal bloodline with such an alliance was out of the
question.

Aside from the troops, Basil's only conditions in making this unprecedented offer were that Vladimir be baptized
into Christianity and renounce his other wives. Vladimir accepted the offer, sent a reported six thousand troops to Basil,
and was duly baptized. With the Russian troops Basil defeated the rebels and won sole control of the empire. The
Russians stayed, eventually forming the famous crack unit
known as the Varangian Guard, the emperor's elite, distinctive, and highly loyal personal guard at the Great Palace in
Constantinople.

Back in Kiev, Vladimir instituted Christian worship
with the same zeal he had earlier shown for the pagan gods,
which he now publicly spurned:

> When the Prince arrived at his capital, he directed that the
> idols should be overthrown, and that some should be cut to
> pieces and others burned with fire. He thus ordered that
> Perun should be bound to a horse's tail and dragged down . . .
> to the stream. He appointed twelve men to beat the idol with
> sticks. . . . After they had thus dragged the idol along, they
> cast it into the Dnieper.

He ordered the Kievans to undergo baptism as well, an order they received with exemplary good cheer and trust, saying (at least according to the monks who wrote the *Primary Chronicle*), "If this were not good, the Prince and his boyars would not have accepted it." Surely not.

Vladimir also took steps to spread the new faith throughout Kiev's growing empire. "He began to found churches and to assign priests throughout the cities, and to invite the people to accept baptism in all the towns and cities." But the most impressive churches were erected in the capital itself, with Byzantine help and inspired by Byzantine models. Where he had stood and uprooted the pagan idols Vladimir built a large church dedicated to his patron saint, Basil. On an even grander scale, he brought in Byzantine artists and craftsmen to construct a great church dedicated to the Holy Virgin, as part of a new, richly appointed royal palace complex on Old Kiev Hill, where he lived with his *porphyrogenita* bride.

From Byzantium came not only clerics to spread the gospel and man the new churches but also architects, artists, and craftsmen to decorate them, and to pass on their knowledge to Slavic apprentices. Within just a few years, the skyline of Kiev was completely altered; a visitor from the West, one Thietmar, bishop of Merseberg and a contemporary of Vladimir's, reported Kiev to be a magnificent city with some forty churches and eight marketplaces.

This transformation was nonetheless dwarfed by cultural changes that proceeded in tandem with the material ones. Vladimir's prestigious marriage alliance and his conversion to Christianity helped him secure his own position in Kiev. He was soon minting Byzantine-style gold and silver coins showing his royal self enthroned on one side, and the Byzantine Christ Pantocrator ("ruler of all") on the other.

Most of all, in converting his people Vladimir gave them a collective identity—as Christians and, before long, as Russians.

THE LEGACY OF CYRIL AND METHODIUS IN RUSSIA

Immediately after "inviting" his people to convert, Vladimir took steps to see that they had at least some idea of what they were converting to. In addition to sending out priests to the towns and cities, he initiated an educational program that targeted the children of his most influential subjects: "He took the children of the best families," the *Primary Chronicle* tells us, "and sent them for instruction in book-learning. The mothers of these children," the chronicler continues blandly, "wept bitterly over them, for they were not yet strong in faith, but mourned as for the dead."

What Vladimir was doing here was more than just cleverly if coldheartedly indoctrinating his future ruling class. Since, like the Bulgarians before them, the Russians had had no alphabet before becoming Christians, Vladimir was also founding what would turn out to be one of the world's greatest literary traditions.

The "book-learning" with which these young students were inculcated was nothing other than the by now substantial body of Old Church Slavonic writings that constituted the legacy of saints Cyril and Methodius. That same Slavonic heritage, still flourishing in Bulgaria, found an even more momentous incarnation in Russia, where it became the dominant factor in the shaping of early Russian civilization.

The *Primary Chronicle* clearly recognizes this. The unknown chronicler prominently covers the missions to

Moravia and Bulgaria, pointing out the Russians' cultural debt and proudly celebrating the common Slavic heritage as shaped by the Cyrillo-Methodian legacy. "It was for these Moravians that Slavic books were first written, and this writing prevails also in Rus and among the Danubian Bulgarians."

Under Vladimir's son Yaroslav the Wise, this legacy reached its apogee, giving rise to the golden age of Kievan Rus. Under Yaroslav, Byzantine artists and artisans continued their work in Russia. Among the scores of churches Yaroslav built with Byzantine help, the most famous is St. Sophia in Kiev (1037–46), clearly inspired by the Constantinopolitan original, and where the visitor can see some of the finest surviving examples of eleventh-century Byzantine mosaics and frescoes.

Yaroslav's epithet hints at what the *Primary Chronicle* says explicitly over and over: that the Russian ruler was above all a "lover of books."

> He applied himself to books, and read them continually day and night. He assembled many scribes, and translated from Greek into Slavic. He wrote and collected many books through which true believers are instructed and enjoy religious education. . . . For great is the profit from book-learning. Through the medium of books, we are shown and taught the way of repentance, for we gain wisdom and continence from the written word. Books are like rivers that water the whole earth; they are the springs of wisdom. For books have an immeasurable depth; by them we are consoled in sorrow.

We don't know where Yaroslav's translators came from. Some were Russians, while others were probably Byzantine Greeks or Slavs, and it seems almost certain that there were Bulgarian monks, priests, and scholars among them as well.

Nor do we know exactly what works were translated, since Old Church Slavonic manuscripts are notoriously hard to date with certainty. Until the twelfth century or so Old Church Slavonic was unusually uniform, so that a tenth-century Bulgarian manuscript looks and reads much like an eleventh-century Russian one. This homogeneous quality itself testifies to the quality and staying power of Cyril's philological achievement.

But scholars have suggested a number of works that may have been translated at this time. Not all are from the Byzantine religious corpus. They include of course numerous lives of saints, monastic rules, and liturgical works, but also legal texts, the *Christian Topography* of the explorer Cosmas Indicopleustes, and a handful of secular works such as Josephus' *History of the Jewish War* and, perhaps, the Byzantine epic of the ninth-century Arab border wars, *Digenes Akritas.*

As the Slavic dialects evolved into national tongues marked by mutual incomprehensibility, Old Church Slavonic carried on as the international language of the Byzantine Commonwealth. Only when taken up by the Russians, however, was this status ensured. Its unlikely ricochet success, more than a century after its near extinction in Moravia, helped seal forever the prestige of Cyril's unique and brilliant invention.

On the other hand, by allowing the Slavs to receive Christianity in their own language, Old Church Slavonic delayed their exposure to the rich pre-Christian past, to which the Catholics' insistence on Latin acted as a gateway for churchmen in the various Western European countries, and to which educated Byzantines had access by virtue of their expertise in Greek. Likewise, if Old Church Slavonic offered the Slavs their own distinctive idiom, it also isolated them from ongoing developments in the rest of European civilization, which expressed its high culture in Latin and Greek. In this way, the glittering legacy of Cyril and Methodius has been both a blessing and a burden for the Slavic world.

KIEV'S GOLDEN AGE

Yaroslav expanded on the foundations laid by his father, Vladimir, to bring Kiev to its fullest flowering under Byzantine tutelage, as architects, artists, and artisans arrived from Byzantium to build, work, and teach in this new Orthodox Christian venue. Militarily, too, the Kievan state, which now took in a vast territory, flaunted its confidence during Yaroslav's reign by crushing the Petchenegs and again attacking Constantinople, in 1043.

This dispute arose over trade issues, after a brawl between Byzantine and Russian merchants in which a prominent Russian was killed. The fighting was bitter and bloody, and the Russian force of some four hundred ships was virtually destroyed, its men either killed or captured. Some of the prisoners had their right hands cut off, which were then displayed on the city's walls for the edification of the public. Others, some eight hundred of them, were blinded, which was the traditional Byzantine punishment for those who had rebelled against the imperial government (Basil II had famously inflicted the same treatment on Bulgarian prisoners). It was the last time the Russians would carry out such an attack.

As earlier, armed conflict proved no impediment to commerce and cultural diffusion. After protracted negotiations the fighting was settled by another trade agreement, and the Russians continued apace their thirsty consumption of Byzantine Christianity and the whole ready-to-wear cultural ensemble that came with it.

Shortly after the war, another marriage alliance between the two ruling houses demonstrated the continuing strength of these ties. The marriage itself was between Yaroslav's son Vsevolod and an unnamed daughter of the Byzantine emperor Constantine IX Monomachus. The offspring of that marriage, known as Vladimir II Monomakh, would eventually take the lead in the losing battle to shore up Kiev's central authority, which proceeded to dissipate among the various Russian principalities after Yaroslav's death in 1056.

This process is often presented in textbooks as "the decline of Kievan Rus," which is somewhat misleading. The basic political problem for Kiev was the persistent tension between influences that favored centralized political power in Russia and influences that hindered it. Kiev's rulers struggled to build a centralized state. Yet, working against this effort was the Russian custom of dividing an inheritance equally among the sons, which as it expressed itself in the division of political power within ruling dynasties is called the appanage system. The appanage system is a good example of an area in which Byzantine practices were not picked up by the Russians (another was in the codification of Russian law, the Russkaya Pravda, that took place under Yaroslav).

Vladimir the Great, for example, had twelve sons, and each had to get his inheritance, with Kiev itself as the grand prize—literally, since its ruler was styled the "grand prince." Later, other principalities would wrangle over the aggrandizing title. Because the various sons of a Kievan grand prince would typically each hope to be given a city over which to rule, the appanage system tended to pit these princes against each other. And of course it made succession in Kiev, theoretically the capital, a perennially tricky issue. Such problems were reinforced by the often intense commercial rivalries between the cities.

Vladimir II Monomakh's reign as grand prince of Kiev, which lasted from 1113 to 1125, represents the last hurrah of central authority against the internecine strife endemic to the appanage system. It's tempting to characterize Vladimir's push to uphold Kiev's authority as a reflection of his Byzantine heritage, Byzantium being generally regarded as a bastion of absolutism, but to make this connection in more than a symbolic way would be a stretch.

More concrete evidence of Vladimir's Byzantine background comes from a cycle of frescoes, probably done during his reign, in Kiev's Church of St. Sophia. The frescoes decorate the walls and vaults of two staircases leading up to the area where the prince's family sat for worship. Set in Constantinople, they depict scenes from the Hippodrome, showing the famous chariot races, as well as jugglers, acrobats, and jousters. The emperor is seen presiding over the games, in crown and imperial robes, and in one scene he rides a white horse in a triumphal procession. The scenes may have been described to Vladimir by his mother, the Byzantine princess whose name has been lost to history.

These frescoes reveal the intimate connection between Byzantine and Russian politics at this time. In Byzantium, such games publicly symbolized the emperor's majesty and authority, and modern scholars have seen the frescoes as Vladimir's attempt to extend the emperor's symbolic sway over Russia as well. Not that there was any notion of actual political sovereignty. But as the supreme head of the Orthodox empire, in Byzantine theory at least the emperor held a position of special authority over all Orthodox Christians, no matter what political regime they actually lived under.

This conception of the emperor's idealized rule as transcending the merely political would survive Kiev's decline to influence Byzantine patronage of Moscow. In the age to come, when the emperor's actual dominion was slight, his symbolic dominion would still count for much.

The Byzantine world was changing fast now. Byzantium's power collapsed dramatically in the latter half of the eleventh century. By the accession of Alexius I Comnenus in 1081, it was once again hard pressed by new enemies on three fronts. Pushed closer by their defeat at the hands of Yaroslav, the Petchenegs harried the empire from the north, while the Normans in southern Italy threatened from the west, and the Turks pressed into Asia Minor from the east after their victory at Manzikert in 1071.

Though the empire managed to recover under its three brilliant Comnenan emperors—Alexius I, John II, and Manuel I—their successes were those of nimble goalkeepers. And goalkeepers, however miraculous their parrying and deflecting, can only do so much. On Manuel's death, Byzantium was left with an open goal and no shortage of onrushing attackers.

Meanwhile, in Russia, in 1108 Vladimir Monomakh's son Yuri Dolgoruky—"Yuri of the long arm," so called for his notorious territorial acquisitiveness—founded a new fortified outpost on the Klyazma River in the far northeastern forests, which he named for his father. The town of Vladimir grew in importance, and a half century later Yuri's son and heir, grand prince Andrei Bogolyubsky, moved the capital there from Kiev. He also went on a building spree in and around Vladimir, erecting several exquisitely beautiful churches, built from the area's distinctive white stone, which no traveler's itinerary should overlook. In addition to being the seat of the grand prince, the principality of Vladimir soon also controlled the prosperous nearby cities of Rostov and Suzdal.

Around the same time, in 1147, we see mentioned for the first time in the sources the small outpost of Moscow, which lay just west of Vladimir on the Moscow River. In 1156, the year before he moved the capital to Vladimir, Andrei Bogolyubsky built the first fortifications around Moscow's center, a ring of earthenwork ramparts known as the Kremlin. Moscow would grow in prosperity, eventually succeeding Vladimir as the seat of the principality.

Relations between Byzantium and the fractious Russian principalities suffered as a new group of Turkic nomads, the Cumans, moved into the steppes during the twelfth century.[*] The southern principalities of Kiev and Galicia both temporarily broke with Byzantium, allying themselves with Hungary, at that time Byzantium's deadly foe. During these and other tribulations, Byzantine historians noted the steadfast loyalty of the principality of Vladimir. Later, a similarly close relationship would prevail between Byzantium and Vladimir's successor, Moscow.

CRUSADERS AND MONGOLS:
THE DISASTROUS THIRTEENTH CENTURY

In the following century, the Orthodox Christian world of the Byzantine Commonwealth suffered two grievous blows. The first came in 1204, when Constantinople fell to the

---

[*] The Cumans (also called the Kipchaks, and in Russian the Polovtsy) were a loose confederation of nomadic tribes that replaced the Petchenegs in the southern steppes.

Western soldiers of the Fourth Crusade. Then, less than two decades later, in 1223, a combined Cuman and Russian army was defeated by the Mongol armies of Genghis Khan at the battle of Kalka. In the winter of 1237–38, his grandson Batu Khan returned to finish the job with a massive invasion of northeastern Russia, starting with the sacks of Riazan in December, Moscow in January, and Vladimir in March.

One by one the Mongols proceeded to pick off the disunited principalities, pillaging and looting as they went, their sophisticated siege techniques easily overpowering the Russian defenses. Kiev fell after a two-week siege in December 1240. Only in 1242 did the Mongols stop their westward advance. Having reached Poland and Hungary, they withdrew inexplicably—for they remained undefeated—to hold the conquered lands of the Central Asian steppe. Their empire now stretched from China to the lower Danube. Batu built his capital of Sarai on the lower Volga. It was to Sarai that the Russian princes would come, humbled and subjugated for two long centuries, bearing their tribute, and serving at the pleasure of the Mongol khan, whom they called tsar.

These two disasters dealt a seemingly fatal blow to the Byzantine world. Only in one institution did the Byzantine idea survive intact: the Byzantine Orthodox Church, as headed by the patriarch of Constantinople. This fact had momentous political consequences as the disastrous thirteenth century unfolded, and would continue to do so as Byzantium—empire and commonwealth—recovered somewhat during the fourteenth. If the emperor's power was increasingly symbolic, the patriarch's was entirely real, in that he controlled the administration of the Orthodox churches that remained under his jurisdiction. He also, of course, retained great spiritual authority over the others.

Of the several Byzantine successor states that vied to win back Constantinople after 1204, the one that ultimately succeeded, the so-called empire of Nicaea, was the one that early on received the blessing of the patriarch of Constantinople. Patriarchal support gave the Nicaean emperors an aura of legitimacy that their rivals lacked, and it was a Nicaean emperor, Michael VIII Paleologos, whose forces retook Constantinople from the Latins in 1261.

Similarly, among the competing Russian principalities that jostled with each other under the Mongol yoke, the Orthodox church provided the only institution whose prestige (not to mention its official administrative structure) transcended all borders. Headed by the metropolitan of Kiev and All Russia, who was appointed by the patriarch of Constantinople, the church in Russia was controlled from Byzantium. For 150 years, until near the end of the fourteenth century, the patriarchate's unofficial but remarkably consistent policy was to take turns regarding the metropolitan's nationality, alternating a Russian-born metropolitan with a Byzantine-born one.

By the time of Russia's subjection to the Golden Horde, however, in political terms Kiev was no longer the leading principality. So far, no other had emerged to replace it.

The Mongols preferred that no one did. Their grip was firmest in the northeast principalities, where political leadership went with the grand principality of Vladimir. The khan bestowed this honorific on whatever prince won his temporary favor, switching the grand principality of Vladimir back and forth so that no one local dynasty might become strong enough to pose a threat. For the first quarter of the fourteenth century, the honor was held by the prince of Tver, Moscow's rival. But Byzantium also had much to say about the focal point of Russian political prestige. Once the patriarchal decision was taken to move the metropolitan's seat from Kiev, the choice of where to relocate it became a political question of the highest importance. And as with the Byzantine successor states, the principality that ended up with the prize, Moscow, also reaped the immeasurable reward of political legitimacy and ultimately came out on top.

By the early fourteenth century, a three-way entente had arisen among the Byzantines, the Golden Horde, and the Genoese, whose maritime empire now dominated the Black Sea trade. From the Byzantine point of view, one benefit of the Mongol invasion was that it shattered the power of the Seljuk Turks, who had been the biggest threat to Byzantium. For that reason, and then also because the Mongols never impinged directly on Byzantine territory or disrupted the business of the church in Russia, the Byzantines accepted the Golden Horde's presence without hostility. In time, close relations developed between the two governments, which actively cooperated in settling political (Golden Horde) and ecclesiastical (Byzantium) matters in Russia.

The Byzantine-Mongol *rapprochement* over Russia was one element in the status quo that had developed by the beginning of the fourteenth century. Another was the Byzantine government's frequent dependence upon Genoa, a major maritime power that—as Venice's rival—had assisted Michael VIII in recovering the capital from the Venetian-run Latin government. Genoa often called the shots in Constantinople under the early Paleologan emperors, though Venice (which dominated eastern Mediterranean trade) was always on the lookout for a pretender to support or some other form of leverage over the perennially shaky Byzantine ruling house. Finally, Genoa was also in bed with the Mongols, and out of that alliance got rights to rich Black Sea trading ports such as Kaffa in the Crimean peninsula.

This comfortable status quo had two big fault lines.

Byzantine and Mongol interests ultimately diverged when it came to the question of Russian unity. The church in Russia was by its very nature a unifying force both institutionally and spiritually, and it stood to benefit if Russians looked to a single power center. In contrast, the Mongols had much to gain from Russian disunity and everything to lose if a single center arose to take the lead in Russian affairs. Genoa, anxious to protect its trade, fell in with the Mongols on this issue.

In addition, the Orthodox church in Russia took in more territory than answered to the Golden Horde. To the west, Lithuania was a major power (much larger than today's nation of that name), with large numbers of Orthodox Russians under an ethnic Lithuanian ruling house. In the far north, wealthy Lord Novgorod—that's how this feisty merchant republic styled itself—looked back on a proud tradition of independence but increasingly fell under the sway of either Moscow, Tver, or Lithuania. Both Lithuania and Novgorod looked nervously over their shoulders at the Germans of the Teutonic Order, who were fond of launching Catholic Crusades into Orthodox territory.

Thus things stood in the middle decades of the fourteenth century, when the Hesychast movement took over the resurgent Byzantine religious establishment.

CHAPTER FIFTEEN

THE RISE OF MOSCOW

O n September 8, 1380, a rebellious Russian army commanded by grand prince Dimitri II of Moscow met and defeated a large Mongol force at a meadow called Kulikovo on the upper Don, about two hundred miles south of Moscow. The battle was long and bloody, with terrible losses on both sides. And in political terms, its significance was slight. The Mongols would return with a vengeance two years later, looting and burning Moscow and bringing the city once again under the "Tatar yoke."

But the battle of Kulikovo immediately took on great symbolic significance. For the first time in a century and a half, a Russian army had stood up to and repulsed a concerted attack by the Mongol tsar. Dimitri himself would be accorded the status of a national hero, known forever after as Dimitri Donskoi ("of the Don") in commemoration of the victory.

The prestige of Kulikovo cemented Moscow's claim to leadership of Russia's competing principalities. This is ironic because the city had risen to prominence earlier in the fourteenth century largely through opportunistic toadying to the Mongols. Dimitri's rebellion represented an about-face in this long-standing policy.

Despite its vengeance on Moscow two years after the battle, the Golden Horde never achieved quite the same degree of control over the Russians as before, though at first that was due more to the Mongols' internal problems than to Russian assertiveness. Within another fifty years or so Russia would finally shake off the Tatar yoke forever, again under Muscovite leadership. Moscow would then take its place as Russia's capital, the heir to Kievan greatness—and soon after that, to Byzantine greatness as well. So Kulikovo, even if lacking in immediate consequences, is still viewed as a major turning point in Russian history.

The Russian chroniclers who recorded the battle play up the religious angle, portraying the devout Dimitri as a defender of the Orthodox faith against the Muslim Mongols, whose khan Mamai they malign as an "accursed, godless, impious, and dastardly eater of uncooked flesh." St. Sergius of Radonezh, who revived and expanded Russian monasticism in this period, is prominently associated with the victory: he is portrayed as exhorting Dimitri before the battle, thereby assuming the role of Russia's saint protector, for which he is still venerated.

Some accounts also claim that before the battle Dimitri was advised by Cyprian, metropolitan of Kiev and All Russia, the Byzantine-appointed head of the Orthodox church in Russia, enshrining him, too, as a national liberator in popular memory. This is interesting, since historians believe that Cyprian was nowhere near Moscow or Kulikovo at the time of the battle. In fact, until very shortly before it, he was in Constantinople, defending his claim to the metropolitanate. In the years leading up to Kulikovo, Cyprian had been embroiled in a bitter struggle with Dimitri, who had opposed his accession as metropolitan and had tried to have his own candidate installed instead. Yet, shortly after the battle, Dimitri abruptly reversed himself and welcomed Cyprian to Moscow, fêting him with a celebratory banquet in the prince's palace and according him all honor and respect as metropolitan.

Behind this puzzling turn of events lies a tale of cynical intrigue, political backstabbing, and, on Cyprian's part, a gritty determination that survived years of adversity before its final vindication. That story begins around the middle of the century, with the rise of Hesychasm.

HESYCHAST POLITICS AND RUSSIA

While for Byzantium's humanists the Hesychast victory felt like a tragedy, for the Hesychasts' many supporters in the Byzantine mainstream it was a glorious affirmation of divine truth. The most immediate result of the Hesychasts' victory was to give them and the monastic establishment they led control of the patriarchate and the invigorated official church structure.

The remarkable John VI Cantacuzenos—Byzantine statesman, regent turned emperor, bookworm, theological speculator, and finally historian and monk—was the main exponent of what can be described as the Hesychast political program. Among other things, that entailed opposition to Genoa, which supported the pro-Western empress Anne of Savoy against Cantacuzenos in the civil war that brought him to the throne.* Instead, Cantacuzenos allied himself with the

---

* Anne was the widow of Cantacuzenos' friend Andronicus III, who died in 1341. The ensuing civil war lasted from 1341 to 1347.

nascent Asian power of the Ottoman Turks, whose soldiers helped Cantacuzenos against Anne and the Genoese. The Ottomans were not yet the threat they soon—partly because of Cantacuzenos' policy—came to be.

Since the patriarchate was now the most potent means of projecting Byzantine power abroad, Cantacuzenos relied on his patriarchs to implement the foreign policy side of the Hesychast program. He had begun developing the basic principles of this foreign policy as early as 1328, when as a young man he helped engineer the succession of his friend Andronicus III, after which he served as Andronicus' prime minister.

When it came to Russia, the watchword was unity. Cantacuzenos' highest priority was to preserve the unity of the Russian metropolitanate, which essentially meant opposing any princes or grand princes who wished to establish a separate metropolitan for their own territory. Another aim was to preserve Byzantine control of the metropolitanate, which would be much easier if there was only one metropolitan of Kiev and All Russia. Other aspects of the policy included suspicion of Lithuania, whose imperialist rulers showed signs of both Western sympathies and Russian territorial ambition, and cooperation with the Golden Horde, at least for the time being.

Cantacuzenos' Hesychast foreign policy was based on more than lofty abstract principles. Russia was big, rich, and populous, far more so now than the struggling Byzantine empire. Trade was no longer dominated by the Byzantines, but generous donations flowed through ecclesiastical channels in a steady stream to Constantinople, and there was always the hope of military help as well. Byzantines also found a reassuring ideological loyalty and solidarity in the rising Slavic world, and especially in Russia, during an otherwise frightening time.

In practice Hesychast policy in Russia translated into support for Moscow, which reciprocated by proving the most consistently loyal of all the Russian principalities. The relationship started almost by accident. In 1326 the metropolitan Peter, a Russian from Galicia, settled in Moscow, where he was buried after dying later that year. Despite the precedent of close Byzantine relations with Moscow's predecessor, Vladimir, Peter seems to have favored Moscow for the simple reason that the prince of Tver, Moscow's rival, had opposed Peter's nomination to the metropolitanate. But Peter's Greek successor Theognostos, appointed after Cantacuzenos' government took over in 1328, upheld Peter's policy of support for Moscow, which in that year helped the Mongols sack rebellious Tver, no doubt with Byzantine approval. Theognostos' long and successful metropolitanate (which lasted from 1328 to 1353) helped to cement Cantacuzenos' policy in place.

THE CHALLENGE TO UNITY

During that time, under the patronage of both Constantinople and Sarai, Moscow grew in what we might call its "borrowed" prestige: ecclesiastical prestige as the seat of the metropolitan of Kiev and All Russia, political prestige as the seat of the grand prince of Vladimir. It grew in size and power, too. Perched on a bend in the placid Moscow River, the city resembles the cross-section of a tree, with concentric circles that can be counted inward from newest to oldest. Today, the outermost circles are ring roads that buzz with automobile traffic. But the inner rings were once fortifications—wooden palisades, stone walls, and earthen ramparts, arranged target-like to protect the traders and merchandise within. The original central stockade was the log fortress or kremlin erected by Yuri Dolgoruky. In the early fourteenth century, grand prince Ivan I, called Kalita ("Moneybags"), replaced its relatively flimsy pine walls with thick oaken timbers—a privilege granted him by his master, the Mongol tsar.

Genoa had concerns about Moscow's growing power, and problems for the Hesychast unity policy arose when Cantacuzenos was forced to abdicate in 1354. With Genoese assistance, John V Paleologos resumed the throne as sole emperor. Cantacuzenos' patriarch, Philotheos, was deposed, and the new government installed his rival, Callistos.*

The new Genoese-controlled government in Constantinople now swung toward Olgerd, the powerful grand prince of Lithuania, as a counter to Moscow. Callistos offered Olgerd his own "metropolitan of the Lithuanians," for which position the Lithuanian ruler nominated a Russian from Tver named Roman. The patriarchal archives record Byzantine impressions of Olgerd's motive: "to find a means, with Roman's help, of ruling Great Russia," as the northeastern principalities were now called. Since he already ruled "Little Russia," including Kiev, it was clear that Olgerd was making a bid to take over all of Russia.

In keeping with Olgerd's ambitions, Roman soon began styling himself metropolitan of Kiev and All Russia, moving his residence to Kiev and ignoring Callistos' injunctions that he respect the claims of Alexis, the rightful metropolitan, whom Philotheos had installed before Cantacuzenos'

* A year earlier, Cantacuzenos had deposed Callistos and replaced him with Philotheos. Callistos, a Hesychast, had himself been appointed by Cantacuzenos, but had refused to crown Cantacuzenos' son Matthew as co-emperor.

resignation, and who resided in Moscow. But Roman died in 1362, and Callistos—perhaps under Cantacuzenos' renewed influence behind the scenes—reunified the Russian metropolitanate under Alexis.

Olgerd wasn't about to give up so easily. Over the next decade and a half, until his death in 1377, the energetic Lithuanian grand prince challenged Moscow for control of Russia. That struggle was a major watershed in Eastern European history. It reached its peak in his unsuccessful siege of Moscow in 1368, which was repelled by Moscow's grand prince Dimitri II, not yet the victor of the Don. Olgerd's campaign continued even after that defeat. It turned Alexis and the metropolitanate into political footballs, presenting Hesychast policy in Russia with grave challenges. Philotheos, not Callistos, had to face those challenges first, since Callistos died the year after Roman. By that time, Cantacuzenos had reasserted himself as an influence behind the throne, and Philotheos resumed the patriarchate.

Philotheos, whose surname Kokkinos means "the redhead," proved the most influential of the Hesychast patriarchs, and the ablest promoter of Cantacuzenos' foreign policy. Born in Thessalonica to a poor family (perhaps of Jewish converts), Philotheos was a few years younger than his fellow Thessalonican Gregory Palamas. As a boy Philotheos had worked in the kitchen of Thomas Magister, a humanist scholar and philologist, who had taken him on as a student. He had then entered a monastery at Mt. Athos, where he became initiated into Hesychasm, rising to become superior of the Great Lavra and then metropolitan of Heraclea.

During his second term as patriarch, Philotheos chose the brilliant Bulgarian monk Cyprian as his Hesychast "ambassador" in Russia. Some three decades Philotheos' junior, Cyprian was coincidentally also the exact contemporary, as near as anyone can tell, of Coluccio Salutati. The two offer mirror images of each other, embodying the different ways that Italians and Bulgarians acted as conduits for the two sides of the Byzantine legacy. While Salutati was discovering the allure of ancient Greek literature and organizing Chrysoloras' teaching trip to Florence, Cyprian was serving as Philotheos' agent in Russia, helping to establish what one scholar has called "Hesychast International." By realizing the Hesychast foreign policy that Cantacuzenos and Philotheos had envisioned, this informal but cohesive network of monks and others would reshape the political and cultural landscape of the Byzantine Commonwealth.

Hesychasm's international headquarters was Mt. Athos, where sometime in the early fourteenth century a wandering monk named Gregory of Sinai had introduced the mystical technique of the "prayer of the heart." It was based on the "Jesus prayer," which he had picked up while studying in Jerusalem. The method consisted of constant repetition of the phrase "Lord Jesus Christ, Son of God, have mercy on me," accompanied by controlled breathing in a continuous, imageless, mantra-like loop. If properly executed, the prayer allowed its performer to perceive a special light, which in his *Discourses on the Transfiguration* Gregory identifies with the light that bathed Christ at Mt. Tabor. This was the seed of Hesychasm, which was soon taken up by other monks on Athos and from there eventually spread throughout the Orthodox world.

One of the first places it spread was Bulgaria, for Gregory eventually left Athos and founded four monasteries at Paroria, on the Bulgarian-Byzantine border. Among his disciples there was the future patriarch Callistos I, as well as a number of Bulgarians.

Before the rise of Hesychasm, the Athonite monasteries

had often been associated with emperors, who had founded many of them and had generously supplied imperial patronage. With the religious resurgence that invigorated Athos after Hesychasm, the Holy Mountain became closely linked instead with the patriarchate of Constantinople. Many of the most powerful patriarchs of the fourteenth century, including Callistos and Philotheos, were among the thousands of men from all corners of the Orthodox world who trained in its Hesychast monasteries.

Above all, Athos was an international phenomenon, a traveler's polyglot way station, a place of endless comings and goings, and of energetic networking. It was here more than anywhere else that Byzantine and Slavic monks such as Philotheos and Cyprian established the far-flung friendships and long-range affiliations that allowed them to promote the Hesychast agenda with such effectiveness.

Unfortunately, we know little of Cyprian's early life other than that he was Bulgarian. He emerges from the shadows in 1373, when he was in his early forties. It was at that point that Philotheos tapped him to serve as his confidential agent in Russia.

For some time, alarming complaints had been reaching Constantinople about the metropolitan Alexis, who had acted as regent for the young grand prince Dimitri II and whose extensive political activities on Moscow's behalf had irked both Olgerd and Prince Michael of Tver. Philotheos had at first firmly supported Alexis, but by about 1370 he began to have second thoughts. In a prolonged scandal, Michael of Tver had accused Alexis of complicity when Michael was illegally imprisoned while visiting Moscow.

More ominously, Olgerd of Lithuania had complained that Alexis concentrated exclusively on Moscow at the expense of his Orthodox flock in Lithuania's extensive Russian lands. "Not even our fathers knew such metropolitans as this metropolitan!" Olgerd had expostulated in a letter to Philotheos. "He blesses the Muscovites to commit bloodshed. He never visits us. He never goes to Kiev. . . . We invite the metropolitan to visit us, but he never comes to us. Give us another metropolitan for Kiev, Smolensk, Tver, Little Russia, Novosil, and Nizhni-Novgorod!" Clearly, both Olgerd and his ally Michael saw Alexis as a wedge to drive between Byzantium and its ally Moscow, their bitter rival.

Philotheos seems to have agreed that Olgerd had a valid point. In 1371 the patriarch had expressed his concern in a letter to Alexis:

> Your sacredness certainly knows that, when we performed our consecration, we consecrated you as metropolitan of Kiev and all Russia: not of a portion, but of all of Russia. But now I hear that you visit neither Kiev, nor Lithuania, but remain in one place, leaving the rest without pastoral care, without supervision, without fatherly instruction. This is offensive and foreign to the tradition of the sacred canons. The right attitude for you is to visit the whole land of Russia, to have love and fatherly disposition toward all of the princes, to love them all equally, to show them the same and equal disposition, good-will and love.

Philotheos' scolding of Alexis shows how seriously he took the pastoral commitment that went with the metropolitan's job, and his own, for that matter. More importantly, it also illustrates how, in the end, he considered Byzantium's alliance with Moscow to be subordinate to the overarching ideal of unity. It wasn't just Moscow that counted, but all of Russia, and Moscow should not be favored inordinately over other locales if such favoritism led to disunity. In other words, the alliance with Moscow was to be pursued only when (and because) it promoted unity, not when it worked against it.

Philotheos now assigned Cyprian the delicate tasks of ensuring Alexis' compliance with his patriarchal directives and of calming the tensions between Moscow and its rivals, Tver and Lithuania. Above all, Philotheos wished to avoid being buffaloed by Alexis' negligence into granting Lithuania its own metropolitan, which Olgerd had been demanding with some justification. Cyprian seems to have succeeded, and in short order, for peace was soon established between Michael of Tver and Dimitri of Moscow.

More remarkably, the two Russian princes now aligned themselves with Olgerd against the divisive efforts of the Golden Horde, which at this point was weakened by internal dissension. Yet, Olgerd still hungered to run the whole show, and moreover it was obvious that Alexis, now elderly, wasn't going to be tramping around Lithuania anytime soon. On top of that, Olgerd had made it clear that he was quite ready to turn to the Latin church for comfort if necessary.

Under increasing pressure from Lithuania, Philotheos realized his time had run out. He had to do something to placate Olgerd. The problem was to do so without destroying the unity of the metropolitanate, for which he and others had fought so long and hard.

His solution to this dilemma was unconventional, even ingenious, and it seems likely to have been inspired partly by Philotheos' observation of Cyprian's obvious ability. It was probably also inspired by the fact that Philotheos had already responded to similar complaints about Alexis from King Casimir of Poland, who had conquered Galicia, by consecrating a *temporary* metropolitan of Galicia. This office was to revert back to the metropolitanate of Kiev and All Russia on its holder's death.

Galicia was one thing, but Olgerd's demands were far more extensive. Nevertheless, Philotheos ordered Cyprian back to Constantinople. On December 2, 1375, as a temporary expedient, the patriarch consecrated Cyprian as metropolitan of Kiev, Russia, and Lithuania, with the express provision that upon Alexis' death Cyprian should reunite the whole metropolitanate in his person once again by succeeding Alexis as sole metropolitan of Kiev and All Russia.

It was an imaginative attempt to manage the formidable political pressures that were hammering on the metropolitanate's unity, but it had a big weakness: it relied on the cooperation of whoever was patriarch at the time of Alexis' death. And Philotheos' consecration of Cyprian, as it turned out, was one of his last acts as patriarch.

Cyprian Rides Out the Storm

A few months later, the Genoese engineered a coup against John V by his son Andronicus IV, who promptly deposed Philotheos and installed his own patriarch, Macarios. Other changes quickly ensued. Olgerd and Philotheos died in 1377, and Alexis died early the following year.

In Constantinople the ruling family of Paleologos had hit a new low. The Genoese, the Venetians, and the now dominant Ottoman Turks competed over the dynasty like bickering puppeteers over the strings of a dilapidated marionette. John V and his loyal son Manuel—Chrysoloras' friend, the future Manuel II—languished in prison, where they would remain for a year until the Venetians were able to arrange their escape. "Each evening men expect the dawn to bring some new development, and every day they fear the night will bring some terrible calamity," wrote Demetrius Cydones of the events surrounding Andronicus IV's coup and its aftermath. "It is like a storm at sea where we are all in danger of going down."

The storm would continue on and off for more than a decade, until Manuel II brought some measure of calm with his assumption of the throne in 1391. Throughout that period, Byzantium remained incapable of implementing a sustained and consistent policy in Russia, as it had done with such success under Philotheos' firm hand. Like the throne itself, Byzantine policy jumped around from one moment to the next, depending on whether Venice or Genoa could best suck up to the Turks at any given time.

The situation in Moscow was equally unstable, reflecting the new divergence of interest between the church's overall unity in a politically divided Russia and Moscow's narrower purposes. The Hesychast party of Cyprian and his allies in the Russian monastic establishment struggled to uphold the unity policies of Cantacuzenos and Philotheos. Against them were arrayed the powerful boyars, who had grown accustomed under Alexis to the church's unconditional support of the Muscovite agenda.

Into these buffeting political winds rode Cyprian in the spring of 1378, soon after Alexis' death, as he journeyed north on horseback into Russia from Constantinople to claim his place as metropolitan under the terms of Philotheos' decree. Stopping along the way, he wrote to his close friend and collaborator, Sergius of Radonezh, leader of the monastic party in Russia. "Let it be known to you: I have arrived in Lyubutsk on Thursday 3 June, and I am on my way to see my son, the Grand-prince, in Moscow."

What happened when he approached Moscow we know from another letter, again to Sergius, that Cyprian wrote in anger three weeks later. Dimitri, under the influence of his boyars, had had no intention of letting Cyprian assume the metropolitanate: "But he sent envoys instructing them not to let me pass. He blocked the roads, placing military detachments and officers, giving them instructions to treat me harshly, up to the point of even putting us to death mercilessly."

Circumventing the guards, Cyprian and his retinue snuck into Moscow by a different route, but when he confronted Dimitri, the grand prince had him imprisoned. "He locked me in the dark, naked and hungry, and I am still sick from that dark cold place." The prince's henchmen even abused Cyprian's servants: "[T]hey drove them out of the city having stolen all their belongings, including shirts, knives and leggings. Not even shoes and hats they left them!" Cyprian also bitterly berates Sergius for not sticking up for him: "But you . . . why did you remain silent, seeing such evil?" His treatment at Dimitri's hands, Cyprian continues, is all the more outrageous because never once since he assumed the metropolitanate has Cyprian spoken or acted in any way against Dimitri or against Moscow. Yet, now he finds himself confronted by a rival Muscovite "metropolitan," Mityai, uncanonically selected by Dimitri—who claims to have the backing of the patriarch.

Then Cyprian gets to the heart of the matter, showing his keen understanding of the political mess in which he has become ensnared:

He accuses me of having gone first to Lithuania [a reference to Cyprian's earlier residence in Kiev]: but what evil did I commit while I was there? . . . I am trying to reunite lost areas to the metropolitanate and want to make things firm, so that they may remain forever, for the honour and majesty of the metropolitanate. But the Grand-prince plans to cut the metropolitanate in two! What advantage would be gained through such a plan? Who are his advisors? What are my faults before the Grand-prince?

Cyprian concludes, "I am travelling to Constantinople, seeking protection from God, the holy patriarch, and the great synod." Even as he signs off, Cyprian injects a note of cynicism about the support he can expect at home: "Whereas these people rely on money and the Genoese, I rely on God and my right."

His pessimism was fully justified. As Cyprian was now aware, the Genoese-controlled patriarch, Macarios, had already hung him out to dry. Paid off by Moscow immediately after the death of Alexis in a deal brokered by Genoese bankers, Macarios had removed his support from Cyprian even as Cyprian traveled north. He'd agreed that Dimitri should not recognize Cyprian as metropolitan, and agreed furthermore to create a separate metropolitan for "Great Russia," that is, Moscow and the surrounding territory, to be chosen by Dimitri. All the infuriated Cyprian could do was maintain his claim to be the rightful metropolitan of Kiev and All Russia—and excommunicate all those back in Russia who stood in his way, which he proceeded to do. To top it all off, as he crossed the Danube on his way home he was held up and robbed.

After a restorative stay in his native Bulgaria, where he visited his old friend the Bulgarian patriarch Euthymius, Cyprian arrived back in Constantinople in the spring of 1379. Now the political winds swung back in his favor. No sooner had he confronted the Genoese-backed government

of Andronicus IV than Andronicus' father, John V, and
brother, Manuel, made their break from prison with Venetian and Turkish help and reentered the capital. Andronicus
promptly absconded by rowboat across the Golden Horn to
the Genoese quarter in Galata, taking his mother, Helena,
and her now ancient father, John Cantacuzenos, as hostages.
Macarios was immediately deposed; as Cyprian wrote with
discernable satisfaction, "Together with the other bishops, I
was present at that synod and signed the act of his deposition."

Over the next few years the Venetians and Genoese
would fight it out in the waters around the capital, each backing their own candidate for the throne and vying with each
other for Turkish support. "At that time," Cyprian continues,
"I remained in the imperial city, named Constantinople, for
thirteen months. I could not go out of it, because the imperial city was beleaguered by much disorder and trouble: the
sea was held by the Latins, whereas the earth and dry ground
was controlled by the God-hating Turks."

Into this fluid situation now sailed the Muscovite
delegation accompanying the man Dimitri had chosen to
supplant Cyprian, whose name was Mityai. Unaware of
the recent turn of events in Constantinople, they had voy-
aged down the Don expecting to find a friendly welcome—
and rubber-stamped confirmation of Mityai—from Macarios.
On the way they enjoyed a leisurely sojourn at Sarai, since
the Golden Horde backed Mityai's nomination, which had
been orchestrated in Moscow by the pro-appeasement
boyars.

Then, almost unbelievably, when the delegation was
already in view of Constantinople, Mityai—described in the
sources as a physically imposing man—suddenly dropped
dead. The Muscovites were completely thrown for a loop,

"confused and agitated," a chronicler reports, "like drunken men." Their Genoese allies had been overthrown, the patriarchate was still vacant, Cyprian had beaten them to the punch in Constantinople, and now their candidate for metropolitan was dead. They buried Mityai in the Genoese quarter. Recovering somewhat from their bewilderment, they then put forward one of their own, a priest named Pimen, to replace Mityai, reportedly forging Pimen's name on the official documents to make it look as though his replacement of Mityai had Dimitri's approval.

By this time, the spring of 1380, John V had filled the vacant patriarchate, appointing the prominent Hesychast Neilos Kerameus, who convened a synod to resolve the issue of the metropolitanate. The Russians played their best card, invoking grand prince Dimitri's bottomless credit and passing around loads of cash among the members of the synod: "[T]he Russians, acting in the name of the grand-prince, borrowed silver from the Genoese and the Turks. . . . They made promises and distributed gifts left and right, barely satisfying everyone."

Despite strong support for Cyprian from both Byzantine and Russian Hesychast leaders, Neilos proved unable to resist completely the pressures from Moscow. The result was a compromise, splitting the metropolitanate once again. Pimen was consecrated as metropolitan of Kiev and Great Russia, while Cyprian's purvue was limited to Lithuania and Little Russia.

However, before this new arrangement could be put in place, the situation in the far north once again realigned itself in another dramatic reversal. The Mongol tsar Mamai mobilized against Moscow, where Dimitri had pushed his luck too far in holding back his annual tribute, not realizing that

Mamai himself was in a shaky position and required the cash. To help him play enforcer, Mamai had enlisted the support of his ally Genoa, as well as Ryazan and, most ominously, mighty Lithuania, now under the capable rule of Olgerd's son Jagiello. At the last minute, Dimitri sent out some representatives with the overdue tribute, but they were too late. Mamai was on the march already, and they came back with the money.

The pro-Mongol, pro-Genoa appeasement policy advocated by the boyars had failed. Dimitri now perforce turned to the monastic party of Sergius and the other Russian Hesychasts, who since Philotheos' day had called for opposing the Mongols and the Genoese. Receiving Sergius' public blessing, Dimitri gathered his forces and marched out to meet the approaching armies of Mamai.

The Russian victory at Kulikovo was significant more for its symbolic value than for its practical consequences. Closely associated with that symbolic value was Dimitri's abrupt change of heart toward Cyprian after the battle. Immediately after Kulikovo, Dimitri Donskoi (as we can now call him) welcomed Cyprian in Moscow, according him full status as metropolitan. It was now Pimen's turn to be hung out to dry, and eventually, after returning to Dimitri's domains, he was imprisoned.

We don't know what caused Dimitri's sudden change in attitude toward Cyprian. We possess only a few tantalizing facts that may or may not be connected. One is that Cyprian had abruptly and mysteriously left Constantinople before Pimen's consecration, and he'd headed for Lithuania, not Moscow. Another is that although Jagiello brought his Lithuanian army to Kulikovo, as he'd agreed with Mamai, at the last minute he broke the agreement and held back from the fighting. The Lithuanians' nonparticipation on Mamai's side was a critical factor—perhaps *the* critical factor—in Dimitri's victory.

It's been suggested that Cyprian had received "confidential information" about Mamai's coalition, and especially about Lithuania's part in it, and that Cyprian had rushed northward in an attempt to dissuade Jagiello from honoring his agreement with Mamai. In other words, Cyprian once again put Orthodox unity above everything else, even above his own burning resentment at the treatment to which Dimitri had earlier subjected him. The result was Russia's—and Moscow's—great symbolic victory over the hated Mongols. This would certainly explain Dimitri's change of heart, as it would also explain why later sources associated Cyprian with the victory at Kulikovo.

It's possible (if less dramatic) to explain Dimitri's reversal by simply noting that he had now come under the influence of Cyprian's Hesychast friends such as Sergius. In any event, Cyprian now returned in full pomp to Moscow in the spring of 1381, where a chronicler relates that he was greeted with great rejoicing among the people. He resumed his active promotion of ecclesiastical unity, conspicuously ministering to the Orthodox in Lithuanian-controlled "Little Russia" (which included Kiev).

But he also made it clear that this unity now cohered around Moscow, exalting it as the divinely favored center of Orthodoxy in Russia. His *Life of Peter,* written at this time, pointedly celebrates his illustrious predecessor, the metropolitan who had first taken up residence in Moscow. Dimitri and his dynasty benefited immensely from such influential propaganda. The *Life of Peter* glorifies them as the legitimate heirs of Kievan rule, specially anointed to hold sway over the lands of the Orthodox Russians.

Cyprian's travails were by no means finished. The new Mongol tsar Tokhtamysh, who had overthrown Mamai after Kulikovo, sacked Moscow with a large army. Cyprian fled to Tver in mysterious circumstances—his enemies accused him of cowardice—and Dimitri reverted to his earlier hostility. Among Cyprian's greatest detractors now was the patriarch Neilos, whose nose had been put severely out of joint by the way events had voided his synodal judgment of 1380. In addition, the Genoese were back in control in Byzantium. After the sack of Moscow, with Neilos' backing Dimitri again booted Cyprian out of the city and reinstalled Pimen as metropolitan.

But Pimen proved too small for the job and soon lost Dimitri's support, although Dimitri would never again accept Cyprian back in Moscow. For several turbulent years things remained unresolved, with much discreditable intrigue bubbling around the metropolitanate and much back-and-forth between Moscow and Constantinople.

During this same time, the Turks advanced inexorably into the Balkans. Constantinople itself underwent further confused regime changes, and seemed liable to capture by the Turks at any time.

Meanwhile, another momentous event occurred on the international scene with the union of Lithuania and Poland in 1386, when the Lithuanian grand prince Jagiello married the Catholic Polish princess Hedwig.* Lithuania and its rulers now turned decisively to the West and the Latin church.

Only at the end of the decade did things settle down. Neilos died in 1388, Dimitri and Pimen both died the following year, and in 1390 Cyprian—"after a stormy passage on the Black Sea in which he nearly lost his life"—was able to

---

* The uniting of Lithuania and Poland is called the Union of Krewo.

reenter Moscow with the full support of both political establishments. With the death of John V Paleologos and the succession of the brilliant Manuel II the year after that, a period of relative stability began. Now the sole and unchallenged metropolitan of Kiev and All Russia, Cyprian had survived the tempest, winning his long struggle to assert the legacy of his mentor, Philotheos.

Chapter Sixteen

The Third Rome

F or a decade and a half Cyprian had kept the faith against the vacillations of Dimitri and the venality of Philotheos' two successors, Macarios and Neilos. Now, for the next decade and a half—until his death in 1406—he consolidated his victory with fruitful labor. This period of intense productivity—writing, translating, teaching, organizing, administering—made Cyprian the most influential exponent of Byzantine civilization in Russia.

Behind it all, woven into all of these activities, was Cyprian's loyalty to the Hesychast policies of Cantacuzenos and Philotheos. Always Cyprian's overall aim was to strengthen the unity of the Slavic churches and bind them ever more closely to the patriarchate. The web of friendship among teachers, students, and colleagues was anchored by common adherence to Hesychast ideals and to their spiritual father in Constantinople. While political events would soon overturn the world in which these ties were formed, their cultural influence would continue to shape the Slavic world decisively and permanently.

Despite its crumbling power, Byzantium continued until the end to play a key part in Moscow's expansion. Indeed, that process would survive Constantinople's fall to culminate in Moscow's eventual emergence as the capital of imperial Orthodox Russia, the vast realm that for so long lay in thrall to the awesome power of the tsars.

Cyprian's immense stature by the time of his death amounted to a deep well of prestige from which his successors Photius and Isidore were able to draw. It also contributed to the remarkable loyalty to Byzantium that Moscow continued to show until almost the very end. In return, the church that Byzantium controlled showered Moscow's grand princes with material and other blessings.

On the material level, the establishment of fortified monasteries throughout Russia but especially around Moscow added strength and depth to the city's defenses. More importantly, through missionary activity the church took the lead in colonizing new lands in eastern Russia, and since Moscow was the seat of the church these lands also naturally came under Muscovite political control. This increased Moscow's political strength, also adding greatly to its economic might.

But the most significant contributions came, as they always had, on the symbolic level. It is through such channels that political legitimacy flows. In 1408, for example, two years after Cyprian's death, his workshop produced the *Trinity* chronicle, a compilation of local chronicles that—like Cyprian's *Life of Peter*—linked Moscow with Kiev and underscored its role as the new center of Russian Orthodox culture. And already in the fourteenth century, hints had appeared that Moscow might stand as heir to Byzantium itself, should Constantinople fall to the Turks.

This idea—summed up in the phrase *translatio imperii,* or the transference of imperial authority—would never be an exact fit, since Russia would always be a nation first and an empire second. Even at their autocratic worst, the tsars would never claim the universal rule that Byzantine theory always ascribed to the emperors of Byzantium. Yet, while never fully embraced, the idea that Moscow stood as Byzantium's heir was certainly never fully rejected, either. It found its most resonant formulation in the famous theory of Moscow as "the Third Rome." This arose from the confluence of three events, each of radical significance to Russian history, around the middle of the fifteenth century: the Council of Florence, the fall of Constantinople, and the final overthrow of Mongol power in Russia.

The Council of Florence, which united the Catholic and Orthodox churches on terms entirely favorable to the Catholics, was the knife that finally cut Moscow's long string of loyalty to Byzantium. One of the main supporters of union (siding with Cardinal Bessarion) was Isidore, the metropolitan of Kiev and All Russia at the time, who helped his friend Bessarion draft the unionist decree. Unfortunately for Isidore, his deeply conservative Russian flock rejected the decree well before the Greeks themselves, spurning Isidore on his return from Florence and eventually taking the unprecedented step of electing their own patriarch. Never again would the Russian Orthodox Church take orders from the Greeks, although cultural ties certainly continued.

The fall of Constantinople came so soon after the Council of Florence that the connection between them was clear, at least from the Russian perspective: God had punished the Byzantines for deviating from the true faith and compromising their principles. This was also the line taken by many Greeks, especially those of the Hesychast, anti-Catholic persuasion. The fall of Constantinople validated the Russians' break with Byzantium that the council had caused.

The end of Russia's subjection to the Mongol yoke had no definitive date but came instead with the gradual disintegration of Mongol power after Kulikovo in 1380, and especially after the Golden Horde was shattered by the armies of Tamerlane around the turn of the fifteenth century. By 1425, Moscow had no rival capable of challenging its place as leader of the Russian principalities.

The idea of Moscow as the Third Rome was worked out during and after the reign of Dimitri Donskoi's great-grandson Ivan III in the late fifteenth century. Also called Ivan the Great, it was he who undertook the "gathering of the lands" that laid the foundations of centralized authority in Russia under Muscovite rule.

After coming to power in his early twenties, Ivan received a letter from Cardinal Bessarion, who suggested that the Russian ruler wed Bessarion's young ward, Zoe Paleologa, niece of the last Byzantine emperor. Ivan did so, and his government also began using Byzantine-style regalia to back up the obvious symbolism of the marriage. Best known is the famous double-headed eagle, long a symbol of Byzantine imperial power, which Ivan appropriated to symbolize his own autocratic rule. This would remain the tsars' imperial emblem right down to the Russian Revolution.

It was during Ivan's reign that Dimitri Gerasimov, a wandering Russian churchman, allegedly brought back from his travels to the West a text known as *The Legend of the White Cowl*. This engagingly anachronistic tale purports to tell of a miraculous white cowl that the pope had received from Constantine the Great after his conversion. Just before the Catholics deviated from Orthodox dogma, the last good pope sent the cowl to Philotheos and the emperor John Cantacuzenos in Byzantium. In foreknowledge of Constantinople's fall, they in turn sent it to the lands of the Rus for safekeeping. The tale's narrator explains that ancient Rome had deviated from the true faith "because of its pride and ambition," while the new Rome of Constantinople has fallen to the Turks. "In the third Rome, which will be the lands of the Rus, the Grace of the Holy Spirit will shine forth."

This idea was further elaborated soon after Ivan III's reign, becoming a commonplace in Russian religious literature, especially that of an eschatological bent. It was put in still more apocalyptic language by the monk Filofei (Philotheos), abbot of a monastery in Pskov around the year 1525:

> The Church of old Rome fell for its heresy; the gates of the second Rome, Constantinople, were hewn down by the axes of the infidel Turks; but the Church of Moscow, the Church of the New Rome, shines brighter than the sun in the whole universe. . . . Two Romes are fallen, but the third stands fast; a fourth there cannot be.

THE MYSTICS' LEGACY

While Hesychasm's political consequences were momentous, its cultural impact was just as profound and far-reaching, and by no means limited to Russia. A picture has emerged in recent scholarship that posits Hesychasm as a second stage in Byzantine cultural diffusion to the Slavic world, one that succeeded the Cyrillo-Methodian first stage and was fully its equal. Its surprisingly broad effects can be seen not just in religion but also in related areas such as art and literature. They began elsewhere in the Byzantine Commonwealth, in places such as Bulgaria and Serbia, though Russia was to be their final destination.

In the late fourteenth century a distinctive literary movement arose in the Balkans that helped further spread Byzantine influences to northern Slavic lands such as Russia. Closely associated with Hesychasm, this international movement has been called "the second South Slavic influence," to distinguish it from the earlier Slavonic legacy of Cyril and Methodius, which also was spread by South Slavs, largely Bulgarians but also others.

Bulgaria once again took the lead in this new wave of cultural dissemination, which was originated and overseen by the Bulgarian patriarch Euthymius of Turnovo, the old friend whom Cyprian visited after being robbed on the Danube. Euthymius began the movement in the period when Cyprian was struggling to assert himself as metropolitan, the 1370s. When Cyprian finally claimed victory in 1390, the decade and a half of his greatest productivity that followed was squarely within the context of his old friend's "second South Slavic" movement. The movement continued into the same time that Salutati, Chrysoloras, Bruni, and the other early humanists were doing their work in Italy, that is, the early fifteenth century. As an exercise in linguistic recovery, it offers some interesting parallels and contrasts.

The movement blended the two Orthodox traditions of Cyril and Methodius on one hand and Hesychasm on the other. As a young man Euthymius had studied at Kilifarevo, just south of Turnovo, where a disciple of Gregory of Sinai named Theodosius of Turnovo had founded a Hesychast monastery. Euthymius became a staunch Hesychast, Theodosius' leading disciple, going to spend nearly a decade in Constantinople and then at Mt. Athos, meditating and copying Slavonic manuscripts. It was there, most likely, that he met Cyprian, if not before. Returning to Bulgaria, Euthymius was elected patriarch in 1371, a position he held until 1393, when Turnovo's capture by the Turks ended the independent Bulgarian patriarchate.

Euthymius' great ability, like that of Cyril before him, was as a scholar, and it was as a scholar that he conceived and undertook a concerted effort to improve the standards of Slavonic translations from Greek, which he held to have slipped below acceptable norms. Over time the original Slavic dialects, once mutually intelligible to all, had evolved into various national languages, essentially rendering Old Church Slavonic a dead language.

Euthymius' attempt at reform was first and foremost a conservative effort, an attempt to recover the linguistic purity of the older Slavonic translations. It was also an attempt to evoke a golden age when the Byzantine Commonwealth was vibrant and expansive, not cowering before the Turkish advance. In making his reforms Euthymius also injected a strong Hesychast element into the mix of texts that were being translated, focusing on writers who were favorites of the Hesychasts: John of the Ladder, Symeon the New Theologian, Gregory of Sinai, and Gregory Palamas, among others.

The scholars of this literary movement were the peripatetic foot soldiers of the Hesychast International: Bulgarians, Serbs, Russians, Byzantines, Romanians, and others. These young men worked in Hesychast monasteries in Constantinople, at Mt. Athos, in Thessalonica, at Paroria, at Kilifarevo. They came and copied their manuscripts, laboring side by side with others before scattering back to their homelands, bringing their precious books, their precious knowledge, and their precious new contacts with them. In imitation of their work, they also inspired the creation of original literary works by other writers in the Slavic lands, thus giving rise to local outbursts of Hesychast-flavored native literature in Slavonic, from Serbia to Romania and on up into Russia.

HESYCHASM AND RUSSIAN CIVILIZATION

In all of these lands, the second South Slavic influence spread from the realm of religious literature into other areas of culture, but nowhere was this ferment more productive than in Russia. The primary agents, of course, were the monks.

The reviver of Russian monasticism after the Mongol invasion was St. Sergius of Radonezh, Cyprian's close friend and colleague. What we know about him comes from two *vitae* written by his disciples Epifan Premudry (Epiphanius the Wise), a Russian, and Pachomius, a Serb. Both of these famous monks exemplified the second South Slavic influence, Epifan by his ornate literary style, known as "word weaving," and Pachomius by his emphasis on Hesychast principles such as the divine light.

Sergius, a big, strong man who loved physical labor and solitude, went out into the forests north of Moscow to be alone in the "desert" (in Russian monastic literature, forest equals desert). Soon, however, urged by his many followers who would not leave him alone, he founded the monastery of the Holy Trinity there. He was offered the metropolitanate on Alexis' death, but he turned it down, perhaps out of deference to Cyprian. Sergius and his many disciples are associated above all with the foundation of a huge number of monasteries, perhaps as many as 150 in just a few decades. Sergius, who was involved in some questionable political adventures, stayed in close contact with both the Muscovite leadership and with Hesychast leaders such as Philotheos and metropolitan Cyprian.

After Sergius, the most influential Russian monk was probably his younger friend St. Stephen of Perm, a scholar and missionary. Again, his *vita* was written by Epifan Premudry, who tells us that Stephen had many books in his cell, including Greek ones, which he learned how to read. In a career reminiscent of Cyril and Methodius, and redolent of the second South Slavic ethos, Stephen undertook a famous mission to a remote Finnish people called the Zyrians, for whom he created an original alphabet and translated many religious works.

The literary trends that influenced these monks spilled over most notably into the field of painting, where Byzantine methods and models had long been taken up wholesale by the Russians along with religious culture. In the late fourteenth and early fifteenth centuries, Russian icon and fresco painting reached a peak of artistic quality that is associated with two towering figures, the Byzantine master Theophanes the Greek (Feofan Grek) and his brilliant Russian student Andrei Rublev. Both worked squarely in the monastic milieu inspired by Byzantine Hesychasm and the second South Slavic influence.

A close friend of Epifan Premudry's, Theophanes arrived in northern Russia from Byzantium around 1378, just as Euthymius' international movement was gathering momentum. While little of his work survives (that which does is exquisite), he is known to have decorated several churches in Novgorod and Nizhni Novgorod before coming to Moscow. There he painted an iconostasis in the Church of the Annunciation, working as well in the Church of the Archangel Michael. Epifan praised his work in terms that leave no doubt about its spiritual intent and its otherworldly aesthetic, so essential to Byzantine art: while painting he "never looked on worldly models," but instead "in his spirit, encompassed distant and intellectual realities, while his spiritual eyes contemplated spiritual beauty."

Andrei Rublev started out as a monk at Sergius' monastery of the Holy Trinity, but it's thought that by the early years of the fifteenth century he was acting as Theophanes' assistant during the latter's work in Moscow. Later he painted a number of famous icons, among them the Savior icon and the Trinity icon (for his old monastery), as well as a series of frescoes for the Cathedral of the Assumption in Vladimir. Rublev's distinctive ethereal style inspired a number of imitators, giving rise to an influential school of Russian icon painting. His work also strengthened the idea, already prominent in the writings of Cyprian and others, that the center of the Russian church had moved from Kiev to Moscow.

While owing so much to its Byzantine model, Russian spirituality lacked the defensive polemicism that distinguished Byzantine Hesychasm after Palamas. This argumentative impulse arose in response to the rationalist critiques of humanists such as Barlaam, but in Russia, Hesychasm didn't encounter that sort of hostility. For the moment, at least, Russian mysticism was free to bloom without the withering frost of such unsympathetic scrutiny.

THE LAST BYZANTINE

O n an early spring day in the year 1516, an envoy from Vasily III, grand prince of Moscow, arrived at Mt. Athos. He brought money for the monasteries, with instructions that the monks were to pray for the souls of Vasily's deceased parents, Ivan the Great and the Byzantine princess Zoe Paleologa. They were to pray also for an heir to be born to Vasily's childless wife, Solomonia.

The envoy brought a further request that the monks send to Moscow a certain Sava, an elderly and learned monk from the Vatopedi monastery, so that Sava might perform some important translation work in Moscow. Once Sava had completed the translations, the grand prince promised the abbot of Vatopedi, "we will release him again to you."

Sava, it turned out, was too infirm for the rigorous trip north. Instead, the abbot settled upon a younger monk named Maximos. The abbot explained in a letter to the grand prince that Maximos was a suitable replacement, as he was "experienced in the divine scripture and capable of interpreting all sorts of books, both church and Hellenic, because from his youth he has grown up in them."

It is interesting that the abbot would mention Maximos' proficiency with "Hellenic" books, which meant ancient Greek literature, or what Byzantines had also called the Outside Wisdom. Such attainments seem unlikely to have been of much use in Moscow. They were certainly rare among the monks of the Holy Mountain, which may be the reason the abbot mentioned them. The monks' scholarship generally ran more to Church Fathers and Old Church Slavonic.

But Maximos was a most unusual monk. In his midforties when the abbot nominated him for the trip to Russia, he had been born Michael Trivolis (c. 1470) to an aristocratic Greek family in Arta, the capital of Epirus, on the coast of what is now Albania. His parents, Manuel and Irene, had emigrated from Constantinople to Arta, where Manuel may have served as a military governor before the city fell to the Turks in 1449. The family was well connected. The patriarch Callistos, Philotheos' rival of a century earlier, had been a Trivolis.

More recently, Michael's uncle Demetrius was a well-known scholar and collector of ancient Greek literature. A protégé of Cardinal Bessarion, Demetrius Trivolis was also acquainted with the Byzantine humanist and diplomat John Lascaris, who had settled in Florence probably sometime in the 1470s.* By the early 1490s, Lascaris held Manuel Chrysoloras' old chair in Greek studies at the Florentine *studio*. He also worked as Lorenzo the Magnificent's librarian, traveling widely in Ottoman lands in search of Greek manuscripts for his Medici patron. During those travels, in 1491, Lascaris visited Arta, where he stayed with Demetrius Trivolis.

---

* We met John Lascaris briefly at the end of Part I.

Young Michael, who had already studied Greek philosophy and rhetoric with a well-known teacher on Crete, was no doubt thrilled to meet the famous Lascaris. And when Lascaris returned to Florence the following year, he brought Michael Trivolis with him.

Through Lascaris, Michael gained immediate access to the highest level of Florence's thriving intellectual life. Lorenzo the Magnificent was an accomplished humanist and poet in his own right, and he had revived his grandfather Cosimo's Platonic Academy, under the guidance of the still-vigorous Marsilio Ficino. Now the grand old man of Renaissance philosophy, Ficino sought above all to demonstrate that Platonic doctrine anticipated Christianity, and that independent reason could confirm the truth of Christian revelation.

Michael met Ficino soon after arriving in Florence, joining the charmed circle of the Platonic Academy. It included Angelo Poliziano (Politian), the poet and philologist who had studied with John Argyropoulos in the 1470s and had nearly been killed defending Lorenzo during the attempt on the latter's life in 1478; Giovanni Pico della Mirandola, who combined an interest in Plato with an attraction to the thought of Averroës on one hand and the mysticism of the Jewish cabbala on the other; and the brilliant young Michelangelo, still a teenager, whom Lorenzo had taken into the Medici household.

Among the people who most impressed Michael in Florence was an influential Dominican friar from Ferrara named Girolamo Savonarola, whom, with Giovanni Pico della Mirandola and Michelangelo, Michael frequently went to hear preach. Savonarola had long attacked the blatant corruption in the church, demanding reform. Called by Lorenzo to Florence in 1490, Savonarola had also begun denouncing the materialism of Florentine society and, provocatively, the tyranny of Medici rule.

Florence changed rapidly in the few years after Michael's arrival. Lorenzo died in 1492 and was succeeded by his less talented son Piero. In 1494 Giovanni Pico della Mirandola and Poliziano both died, while Michelangelo went to Bologna and John Lascaris left Italy for France. That same year the French army of Charles VIII invaded Italy, overthrowing the now highly unpopular Piero de Medici in Florence. Propped by popular enthusiasm, Savonarola embarked on his turbulent four-year reign over Florence, burning humanistic books and imposing a puritanical severity on Florentine life and art. Finally, having gone too far in opposing the pope, he was excommunicated and burned at the stake before a crowd of disenchanted Florentines.

By then Michael himself had moved on, first to Bologna and then to Venice. There, in early 1498, it is thought that he spent several months working for Aldus Manutius, helping the other Byzantine scholars who were preparing Greek texts for publication by the Aldine Press. That spring he accepted an invitation to come live and work with Gianfrancesco della Mirandola, the nephew of his friend Giovanni, who had succeeded to the family estate at Mirandola on Giovanni's death.

But Michael was restless at Mirandola, and the news of Savonarola's execution that May shocked him deeply. Gianfrancesco's Christianity was more conservative than his uncle's had been, and, working closely with Gianfrancesco, Michael now turned for the first time to a serious study of the Church Fathers. Though broken by periodic trips to the area of his birth, his studies at Mirandola ultimately resulted in his conversion. In 1502 Michael Trivolis renounced humanism, turning away from what he later called an excessive reliance on reason and secular learning, instead joining the

Dominican monastery of San Marco in Florence, where Savonarola himself had served as prior.

Michael's conversion had been not to Catholicism but to Christianity, and his entry into San Marco attests more to his respect for Savonarola than to any attachment to Dominican ideals. The Church Fathers he had studied at Mirandola were Greek, not Latin, and his faith was a matter of recovery, not discovery—of rediscovering the faith in which he had been raised, not uncovering a new belief system.

So it comes as no surprise to find him leaving Italy for his homeland sometime around 1505 and settling at Mt. Athos, which despite the Turkish conquest was still the vibrant center of Orthodox monasticism. And given Michael's literary bent, it was natural that he gravitate to Vatopedi, the wealthiest monastery, which boasted an extensive library. John Lascaris had bought two hundred manuscripts from Vatopedi in the 1490s for Lorenzo's library, which was at San Marco, where Michael may have read them.

At Vatopedi Michael Trivolis took the name Maximos. Although we know little about the decade he spent there, we do know that later, in Moscow, he would look back on Athos with great longing. San Marco had been urban, politicized, and Italian. During his time there, the monastery was rife with bickering over the meaning of Savonarola's tumultuous career. Vatopedi was comparatively peaceful—pastoral yet at the same time more cosmopolitan, in that the Greeks there lived, prayed, ate, and worked shoulder to shoulder with Bulgarians, Serbs, Macedonians, Romanians, Russians, and others from the Orthodox world, some three hundred monks in all. Maximos had a knack for languages. Though he did not learn Russian yet, he would have picked up a smattering of the various Slavic tongues from his brother monks.

He also had a knack for timing. Traveling with a small

party, Maximos broke the journey north with sojourns in Constantinople and the Crimea, arriving in Moscow in March 1518. And just as had happened earlier in Florence, he unknowingly landed himself in a political and religious cauldron that was on the point of boiling over. This time, however, he would find himself not on the periphery but at the dangerous center. From this point, Maximos is properly called by the Russian version of his name, Maxim Grek— "Maxim the Greek," Michael Trivolis' third and final incarnation. It was as Maxim Grek that he became embroiled in the controversy that would seal his fate.

For some time, a dispute had been going on between two factions in the Russian monastic world. Since the time of Cyprian, a powerful new group of monks had arisen in many of Russia's most densely settled areas. They were called Josephites after their leader, Joseph, abbot of the large and influential Volokolamsk monastery, which was their stronghold not far from Moscow. They were also known as Possessors, since their monasteries comprised extensive feudal estates on which the land was owned by the monks and worked by the peasants, with the monks receiving the income. The monks lent money to peasants at exorbitant rates, driving them further into poverty while growing wealthier themselves.

As the riches of the Possessors accumulated, they were increasingly opposed by monks who lived very differently, building small, isolated hermitages for themselves in patches of cleared land deep in the northern forests. These were the Non-Possessors, and it was they who represented the conservative Hesychast tradition as established by such figures as Cyprian and St. Sergius of Radonezh.

Cyprian himself had preached strongly in Russia against the monastic possession of large estates. After his death, the opposition had been led by Nil Sorsky, later St. Nil, who had visited Mt. Athos and was the first Russian to write about mystical contemplation. When Maxim arrived, the Non-Possessors' leader was Vassian Patrikeyev, a monk of noble birth and a dynamic advocate who wasted no time enlisting Maxim in the cause. The two eventually became close friends as well as collaborators.

Joseph died a few years before Maxim's arrival, and with the support of the metropolitan Varlaam, Vassian and Maxim enjoyed a period of seeming ascendancy. They did battle with the Josephites on a number of issues, only one of which was the possession of extensive estates and exploitation of the peasants, which Maxim—like Cyprian long before him—was able to affirm went quite against the Byzantine tradition. Not only that, but he also placed it in sharp contrast with the practices of the Dominicans and Franciscans, whose poverty and asceticism he had seen firsthand. While the example of Savonarola remained always before his eyes, Maxim was careful to conceal his erstwhile membership in a Dominican monastery.*

But Vassian's strength was illusory. The Non-Possessors had the past on their side, but the Possessors had the future. Joseph had earlier struck a deal with Vasily III, who (like his contemporary Henry VIII of England) coveted the great monastic estates of his realm. Vasily would let the Possessors keep their vast estates, and in return they would support his bid for absolute control over the church. Despite the continued opposition of figures such as the metropolitan Varlaam, who struggled to maintain the church's independence from secular authority, the logic of this alliance proved irresistible.

---

* Maxim hid this potentially incendiary information so effectively that not until 1942 was his original identity as Michael Trivolis uncovered, by the French scholar Elie Denissoff in his book *Maxime le Grec et l'Occident*.

Another aspect of the situation (and another parallel with Henry VIII) was the grand prince's failure to produce an heir. Backed by Vassian and Maxim, the metropolitan Varlaam refused to sanction the grand prince's uncanonical divorce from the still-barren Solomonia, on behalf of whose fertility the Athonite monks' prayers had themselves been barren.

In 1522 Varlaam was deposed and Daniel, the new leader of the Possessors, was chosen to replace him as metropolitan. Daniel was Joseph's disciple and his successor at Volokolamsk before being elevated to the metropolitanate. Now he went after Maxim, who had overreached himself by criticizing Vasily III. Daniel used Maxim's indiscretions to win Vasily over. During the winter of 1524–25 Maxim was arrested, and that February he was tried before a court presided over by the metropolitan Daniel and grand prince Vasily.

The list of charges was long. It included accusations such as sorcery and heresy, along with more substantive—and truer—ones including criticizing Vasily, maintaining that the Russian church's separation from the patriarchate of Constantinople was uncanonical, and railing against the corrupt abuses of the Possessors. The verdict was a foregone conclusion. Maxim was excommunicated, clapped in irons, and imprisoned deep within the walls of Volokolamsk. There, in solitary confinement, he remained for six years, deprived not only of freedom, communion, and companionship but also of books, pens, ink, and paper. Later that year Vasily got his divorce, and in 1530 an heir, the future Ivan IV ("the Terrible"), was born.

The year after that, Maxim was hauled out and tried again, this time together with Vassian, who would seem to be the main target of this second round of persecution. Now Vassian himself was sent to Volokolamsk, while Maxim was moved to a different monastery, where his treatment gradually improved. He was allowed books and writing equipment, and after a time was permitted to take communion. The double trial and condemnation of Vassian and Maxim effectively marked the end of the Non-Possessor movement as a political force.

As for Maxim, his situation continued to improve. With Vasily's death soon afterward, the three-year-old Ivan IV became grand prince. Eventually the hostile metropolitan Daniel was deposed, but Ivan—who began asserting himself as ruler while still in his teens—fell under the influence of the new metropolitan, the elderly Makary, whose attitude toward Maxim was hardly more sympathetic. Maxim pleaded over and over to be allowed to return home to Mt. Athos, but his pleas were refused. Although he was finally released from imprisonment when he was around eighty, he never left Russia.

Instead, he found refuge of a sort in the famed monastery of the Holy Trinity near Moscow, which had been founded by St. Sergius of Radonezh. There Hesychast and Non-Possessor ideas still quietly percolated, and there Maxim continued to read and write, though his eyesight was failing and his hands were arthritic. He also taught the monks enough Greek to make copies of the Psalms.

In 1553 Maxim was reportedly visited by Ivan the Terrible, who was making a pilgrimage with his wife and infant son to a monastery in the far north to give thanks for his delivery from a near-fatal illness. The conversation between the young ruler and the old monk was later recounted by a disenchanted retainer of Ivan's, Prince Kurbsky. Kurbsky was one of many Russians who retained Non-Possessor sympathies and greatly admired Maxim for his modest fortitude in the face of so many torments.*

---

* A recent scholar has argued that Kurbsky's account of Ivan's reign is a forgery. Even if so, it suggests much about later attitudes to Maxim.

According to Kurbsky, Ivan had fallen under the influence of evil Possessor monks, who promised him absolution in exchange for granting them land and making useless pilgrimages. Maxim instead advised Ivan to look after the widows and orphans of soldiers killed in a recent military campaign against the Tatars. If Ivan persisted in the pilgrimage, Maxim prophesied, his young son, Vasily, would perish. "Flattered and urged to do this by those monks who love the world and love possessions," Kurbsky writes, the arrogant Ivan insisted on ignoring the advice, and the boy indeed fell ill and died. A few years after this (possibly fictional) meeting took place, Maxim himself died quietly at the Trinity monastery, on January 21, 1556, by the old Orthodox calendar.

Maxim and the Hesychast tradition he stood for had become symbols of resistance to the autocratic power that was now claimed by Moscow's expansionist rulers. A few years before his meeting with Maxim, Ivan the Terrible was the first Russian ruler to be crowned as tsar, although his father and grandfather had used the title on occasion. This was part of a deliberate campaign to appropriate the Byzantine legacy and use it to enhance Moscow's imperial power; as part of that campaign, the old idea of the Third Rome was now picked up and burnished for public consumption. In effect, the new Russia turned its back on Byzantium's spiritual legacy and instead embraced a propaganda version of its political legacy. Despite such claims, the imperial tsars were a Russian creation, not a Byzantine one.

Echoes of the Hesychast tradition would continue to resound in Russian culture. The mystical Tolstoy would have had much to talk about with Maxim Grek. And in the West, the ancient Greek heritage that at first had so entranced Michael Trivolis would also find new life and new meaning.

But Byzantium itself had ended a century earlier. It was

now a fading memory, not a point of embarkation for travelers bearing the fruits of civilization. No one would follow in the footsteps of Michael Trivolis, the man who became Maxim, and whose fate so strangely recapitulates Byzantium's own: a passage into long captivity at the end of the road from Athens to Jerusalem.

Author's Note

I originally met Byzantium in the eighth grade, when my Russian teacher and good friend, James Morris, suggested Cyril and Methodius as a topic for my first long research paper. Years later, as an undergraduate at UCLA, I was lucky enough to take several Byzantine history courses with Speros Vryonis, Jr., whose teaching brought a long-forgotten subject back to life for me. I'm grateful to every teacher I've ever had, but I'd especially like to thank Jim Morris and Speros Vryonis for enriching my life by introducing me to Byzantium with such warmth, enthusiasm, and skill.

This book originated in a comment that Professor Vryonis made one day in class: One of the most fascinating things about Byzantium, he said, was the way it influenced the younger civilizations that grew up around it. Despite a busy schedule, Speros Vryonis continued to offer his warm support as I undertook the research and writing of *Sailing from Byzantium*, generously reading some early versions of the outline and manuscript. I am very grateful to him for his efforts. If the book has strengths, they likely originate with him; its mistakes, I hasten to add, I have made entirely on my own.

With the same stipulation very much in mind, I thank Michael J. B. Allen, Dimitri Gutas, Henrietta Leyser, and Ingrid D. Rowland for help and advice at various stages of researching and writing this book; I owe a special additional debt to Henrietta Leyser for her ongoing encouragement and support. For inspiration, I thank Peter Brown, Averil Cameron, Fred Halliday, Dimitri Obolensky, Diana Wells, and Mark Whittow. Bob Loomis gave me a fair hearing long before I was ready, and I thank him for that. My father, Charles Wells, and my mother, Liz Jones, offered helpful comments on early drafts, as did Gordon Davis, George Davis, Charlie Davis, Dan Henderson, and Simone Stephens. They were wonderful exemplars of my intended audience, the curious general reader. I'm indebted also to the staffs of the following institutions: the University Research Library at UCLA; Firestone Library at Princeton University; the New York Public Library; Starr Library at Middlebury College; Feinberg Library at SUNY Plattsburgh; the Archiginnasio (Biblioteca Comunale) in Bologna, Italy; and the Westport Library Association and the Wadhams Free Library of Westport, NY.

My agents, Edward Knappman and Elizabeth Frost-Knappman of New England Publishing Associates, have given me the best professional representation anyone could hope for, along with sage counsel and warm support. The talents of John J. Flicker, my editor at Bantam Dell, contributed significantly to this book's final shape and tone; anyone who says that old-school editing is a thing of the past hasn't worked with John. David Lindroth turned a tangle of notes into a series of crisp, attractive, and informative maps; Marietta Anastassatos' beautiful dust jacket and Glen Edelstein's elegant interior design handsomely complement the content. Thank you all. Finally, the late Clyde Taylor believed in the book also, and I remain grateful for his efforts on my behalf.

ACKNOWLEDGMENTS

This is a work of popular synthesis with no pretensions to original scholarship. Byzantium's interactions with its three neighboring civilizations constitute separate areas within the larger field of Byzantine studies, and to each of these areas some first-rate scholars have devoted all or part of their careers. In addition, Byzantium per se has also been blessed by the attention of some superb scholars; likewise the separate areas of Italian Renaissance history, Islamic and Arabic history, and Slavic studies, not to mention related fields such as the transmission of classical literature. Without the work of scholars in all of these fields this book would not have been possible.

While many of the points made in passing are my own, many have also come from the work of these scholars. Most often they have been picked up by other scholars and entered the common reservoir, so to speak, but doubtless sometimes they have not. Regardless, I have given notes not for individual ideas and insights, as one would ideally try to in a scholarly work, but only for quotations. To anyone familiar with the field in question, my debts should be readily apparent, but I would like to sketch them below on a chapter-by-chapter basis, not only for the sake of giving credit where credit is due, but also for the sake of helping the general reader who would like to learn more.

My greatest general debt is to the late John Meyendorff, whose learned and stimulating writings have done so much to illuminate the role of Hesychasm in the dissemination of Byzantine civilization to the Slavic world. Most importantly, I have adopted his conception of Byzantine civilization as a long dialogue between humanists and monks, between faith and reason, between Athens and Jerusalem, and of the Hesychast controversy as the final stage of that dialogue. Meyendorff also stresses the dismay and discomfort of the humanists with the controversy's outcome, and so my own thesis of the Hesychast controversy as an engine of Byzantine cultural influence in the West as well as in the Orthodox world owes much to his insightful scholarship. I have extended Meyendorff's picture of the Hesychast controversy and its implications to include Byzantium's influence on the West, and then used the tension between faith and reason on which the controversy turned to frame my discussion of Byzantine cultural diffusion to the Islamic world. Much of this, I think, is implicit in Meyendorff's analysis, but it needed to be worked out. Focusing on Byzantium's Orthodox legacy, Meyendorff had no interest in either of these latter two fields.

An Orthodox priest as well as a historian, Meyendorff was remarkably objective in many of his judgments, but he resisted mightily the imputation of obscurantism to the Hesychast monks that has commonly been made by sometimes hostile modern historians of a secular humanist bent. On one hand, though I share these historians' secular outlook, my view of the monks is less dismissive than they tend to be; on the other hand, I cannot follow Meyendorff in rescuing the monks from the charge of obscurantism. In the end I have been less interested in passing judgment than in telling the story—a story to which both sides made valuable contributions as well as perhaps more discreditable ones.

Prologue: My greatest debts are to the work of John Meyendorff, and especially to his article on the Chora in Paul A. Underwood, *The Kariye Djami;* and to the article by Ihor Ševčenko in the same volume.

Part I

Chapter One: See the work of Averil Cameron, Judith Herrin, Peter Brown, Margaret Gibson, and James J. O'Donnell as cited in the Bibliography. **Chapter Two:** John Meyendorff, as cited in the Bibliography. **Chapter Three:** Kenneth Setton, "The Byzantine Background to the Italian Renaissance"; Donald Nicol, *The Last Centuries of Byzantium;* and the articles of Frances Kianka as cited in the Bibliography. **Chapter Four:** Michael Baxandall, *Giotto and the Orators;* George Holmes, *The Florentine Enlightenment;* Roberto Weiss, "Jacopo Angeli da Scarperia"; and N. G. Wilson, *From Byzantium to Italy.* **Chapter Five:** Eugenio Garin, *Portraits from the Quattrocento;* the works of Deno John Geanakoplos as cited in the Bibliography; Joseph Gill, *Council of Florence;* George Holmes, *Florentine Enlightenment;* and N. G. Wilson, *From Byzantium to Italy.*

PART II

Chapter Six: See Averil Cameron as cited in the Bibliography; Patricia Crone, *Meccan Trade;* Garth Fowden, *From Empire to Commonwealth;* H. A. R. Gibb, "Arab Byzantine Relations Under the Umayyad Caliphate"; Walter Kaegi, *Byzantium and the Early Islamic Conquests;* and Speros Vryonis, Jr., "Byzantium and Islam, Seven–Seventeenth Century." **Chapter Seven:** The works of Sebastian Brock as cited in the Bibliography; Garth Fowden, *Empire to Commonwealth;* Dimitri Gutas, *Greek Thought, Arabic Culture;* Marshall Hodgson, *The Venture of Islam;* and Hugh Kennedy, *The Early Abbasid Caliphate.* **Chapter Eight:** The works of Dimitri Gutas as cited in the Bibliography; the works of Fred Halliday as cited in the Bibliography; Majid Fakhry, *A History of Islamic Philosophy;* and Marshall Hodgson, *The Venture of Islam,* vols. I and II.

PART III

Chapters Nine through Twelve: See the works of John Fine, Dimitri Obolensky, Ihor Ševčenko, and Mark Whittow as cited in the Bibliography. **Chapters Thirteen and Fourteen:** Obolensky and Whittow as cited in the Bibliography, and Simon Franklin and Jonathan Shepard, *The Emergence of Rus.* **Chapters Fifteen and Sixteen:** Dimitri Obolensky, *The Byzantine Commonwealth* and *Six Byzantine Portraits;* John Meyendorff, *Byzantium and the Rise of Russia;* Daniel Pipes, *Russia Under the Old Regime;* and Janet Martin, *Medieval Russia, 980–1584.*

Epilogue: See Dimitri Obolensky, *Six Byzantine Portraits,* and Jack V. Haney, *From Italy to Muscovy.*

ⓃⓞⓣⒺⓈ

Page		
4	*for all times to come.*	Underwood, *Kariye Djami*, 51–52.
12	*and manliness.*	Procopius, *History*, 11.
12	*from the beginning.*	Procopius, *History*, 13.
16	*perspicacious Theoderic.*	Procopius, *History*, 13.
24	*of most copious light.*	Cassiodorus, *Institutiones*, I xxx (in Jones, *Introduction*, 134–35).
27	*and quivering tongue.*	Liudprand, *Works*, 208.
27	*tiny mole's eyes.*	Liudprand, *Works*, 236.
28	*oil and fish sauce.*	Liudprand, *Works*, 254.
28	*of neither gender.*	Liudprand, *Works*, 267.
31	*all the world.*	Geoffroy de Villehardouin, *Chronicles*, 58–59.
31	*at the sight.*	Geoffroy de Villehardouin, *Chronicles*, 59.

33	*streaming in.*	Nicetas Choniates, *O City,* 316.
34	*grown dark.*	Nicetas Choniates, *O City,* 317.
37	*from the outside.*	St. Basil, *Letters,* 384.
52	*of Greek lore.*	Boccaccio in Osgood, 114.
53	*in the curia.*	Setton, "Byzantine Background," 44.
53	*pertains to Greek?*	Boccaccio in Osgood, 113.
53	*in my purpose.*	Petrarch, *Le Familiari,* Letter 12.
54	*manners and behavior.*	Boccaccio in Osgood, 114.
58	*tasted the lotus.*	Cydones, *Apology,* 363.
59	*December 24, 1354.*	Setton, "Byzantine Background," 53.
60	*stupid and gauche.*	Cydones, *Apology,* 365–66.
61	*word of the expedition.*	Cydones, *Letters II,* 31.
63	*other Venetian citizens.*	Loenertz, "Demetrius Cydones," 125–26.
77	*taste in Latin.*	Wilson, *From Byzantium to Italy,* 12.
100, 101	*of an Academy.*	Holmes, *Florentine Enlightenment,* 257.
120	*have a son.*	Grabar, "Umayyad Dome," 53.
125	*with the righteous.*	Koran, 325.
126	*it was sword-shaped.*	Kaegi, *Byzantium,* 65.
129	*the* Arabian Nights.	Ibn Khaldun, *Muqaddimah,* 216.

129	*of this world.*	Ibn Khaldun, *Muqaddimah*, 215.
129	*like an emperor.*	Vryonis, "Byzantium and Islam," 211.
130	*versed in it.*	Ibn Khaldun, *Muqaddimah*, 191.
139	*in the world.*	Wiet, *Baghdad*, 11.
144	*them with him.*	Geanakoplos, *Byzantium*, 419.
144	*confirm the orthodox.*	Geanakoplos, *Byzantium*, 26.
146	*Nothing else.*	Rosenthal, *Classical Heritage*, 48–49.
146	*this was done.*	Rosenthal, *Classical Heritage*, 49.
148	*of the Greeks.*	O'Leary, *Greek Science*, 165.
148	*incomplete, in Damascus.*	Gutas, *Greek Thought*, 179.
153	*ruler prohibits this.*	Gutas, *Greek Thought*, 119.
154	*in that direction.*	Meyerhof, "New Light," 717.
154	*today's American dollars.*	Gutas, *Greek Thought*, 138.
155	*Muhammad ibn Musa.*	Meyerhof, "New Light," 711.
157	*remained to me.*	Meyerhof, "New Light," 689.
157	*the confiscated library.*	Meyerhof, "New Light," 689–90.
158	*more useful matters.*	Rosenthal, *Classical Heritage*, 19.

170	*accessible to men.*	Urvoy, *Ibn Rushd,* 32.
178	*to the divine?*	Geanakoplos, *Byzantium,* 351.
179	*the farthest north?*	Obolensky, *Byzantine Commonwealth,* 240.
179	*of the land . . .*	Geanakoplos, *Byzantium,* 350.
181	*outside the woods . . .*	Obolensky, *Byzantine Commonwealth,* 75.
189	*accept the assignment.*	Obolensky, "Sts. Cyril and Methodius," 2.
193	*an unknown tongue.*	Obolensky, *Byzantine Commonwealth,* 191–92.
203	*embassy, by God!*	Fine, *Early Medieval Balkans,* 138–39.
211	*of the Romans.*	Constantine Porphyrogenitus, *De Administrando,* 153.
212	*prince of Bulgaria.*	Constantine Porphyrogenitus, *De Administrando,* 161.
219	*reign over us.*	*Primary Chronicle,* 59.
219	*on a hill.*	*Primary Chronicle,* 59.
220	*of the Virgin.*	*Primary Chronicle,* 59.
220	*of Russian cities.*	*Primary Chronicle,* 61.
222	*of the Swedes.*	Franklin and Shepard, *Emergence,* 29.
226	*payment of taxes.*	*Primary Chronicle,* 64–65.
229	*have outwitted me.*	*Primary Chronicle,* 82.

230	*retinue did likewise.*	*Primary Chronicle,* 84.
234	*Simarg'l, and Mokosh.*	*Primary Chronicle,* 93.
235	*their carnal desires.*	This and the following quotations are from the *Primary Chronicle,* 97ff.
236	*there among men . . .*	*Primary Chronicle,* 111.
238	*into the Dnieper.*	This and the following quotations are from the *Primary Chronicle,* 116ff.
240	*for the dead.*	*Primary Chronicle,* 117.
241	*the Danubian Bulgarians.*	*Primary Chronicle,* 62.
241	*consoled in sorrow.*	*Primary Chronicle,* 137.
253	*of uncooked flesh.*	*A Source Book for Russian History,* 55.
259	*"Hesychast International."*	Cited without attribution by Dimitri Obolensky in Laiou and Maguire, *Byzantium,* 47.
261	*and Nizhni-Novgorod!*	John Meyendorff offers an English translation of Olgerd's letter (from which I quote here) in *Byzantium and the Rise of Russia,* 288–89.
261	*good-will and love.*	John Meyendorff offers an English translation of Philotheos' letter (from which I quote here) in *Byzantium and the Rise of Russia,* 290–91.

264	*danger of going down.*	Nicol, *Last Centuries of Byzantium*, 280.
264	*Grand-prince, in Moscow.*	John Meyendorff offers an English translation of Cyprian's letter (from which I quote here) in *Byzantium and the Rise of Russia*, 292.
265	*to death mercilessly.*	John Meyendorff offers an English translation of this second letter of Cyprian's (from which I quote here) in *Byzantium and the Rise of Russia*, 293ff. The following quotations are taken from it as well.
267	*of his deposition.*	From Meyendorff's translation of Cyprian's *Life of Peter*, in *Byzantium and the Rise of Russia*, 300ff.
267	*the God-hating Turks.*	From Meyendorff's translation of Cyprian's *Life of Peter*, in *Byzantium and the Rise of Russia*, 300ff.
268	*like drunken men.*	Meyendorff, *Byzantium and the Rise of Russia*, 218.
268	*barely satisfying everyone.*	Meyendorff, *Byzantium and the Rise of Russia*, 219.

270   *agreement with Mamai.*   Meyendorff, *Byzantium and the Rise of Russia,* 221.

272   *political establishments.*   Obolensky, *Six Byzantine Portraits,* 193.

277   *will shine forth.*   Geoffrey Hosking, *Russia and the Russians,* 103.

277   *there cannot be.*   Geanakoplos, *Byzantium,* 447.

282   *spiritual beauty.*   Meyendorff, *Byzantium and the Rise of Russia,* 143.

283   *again to you.*   Haney, *From Italy to Muscovy,* 32.

284   *up in them.*   Haney, *From Italy to Muscovy,* 33.

292   *ill and died.*   Kurbsky, *History,* 79.

BIBLIOGRAPHY

To help the general reader, I have marked with an asterisk (*) those primary and secondary sources that I consider especially valuable, accessible, or both.

TEXTS

Boethius. *The Theological Tractates and The Consolation of Philosophy.* Translated by H. F. Stewart, E. K. Rand, and S. J. Tester. Cambridge, MA: Harvard University Press, 1973. Bilingual Latin and English text in the Loeb series.

St. Basil (Loeb Classical Library). *The Letters* (vol. IV). Translated by Roy J. Deferrari. Cambridge MA: Harvard University Press, 1934. Bilingual Latin and English text in the Loeb series.

Boccaccio. *The Genealogy of the Gods.* In Charles Osgood, *Boccaccio on Poetry.* Princeton: Princeton University Press, 1930.

Cassiodorus. *Institutiones.* Edited by R. A. B. Mynors. Oxford: Oxford University Press, 1937. English translation by L. W. Jones in *An Introduction to Divine and Human Readings.* New York: 1946.

Cassiodorus. *Variae*. Translated and edited by S. J. B. Barnish. Liverpool: Liverpool University Press, 1992.

Choniates, Nicetas. *O City of Byzantium: Annals of Niketas Choniates*. Translated by Harry J. Magoulias. Detroit: Wayne State University Press, 1984.

*Comnena, Anna. *The Alexiad of Anna Comnena*. Translated by E. R. A. Sewter. Harmondsworth: Penguin, 1969. A good read. Combine with Michael Psellos and Procopius' *Secret History* (see p. 311) for a Penguin sampler of Byzantine history.

Constantine Porphyrogenitus. *De Administrando Imperio*. Greek text edited by Gy. Moravcsik. English translation by R. J. H. Jenkins. New, revised edition. Washington, DC: Dumbarton Oaks, 1967. Bilingual Greek and English text.

Cydones, Demetrius. *Apology for His Own Faith* = Mercati, G., *Notizie di Procoro e Demetrio Cidone*. Vatican: Biblioteca apostolica vaticana, 1931.

Cydones, Demetrius. *Letters I* = *Démétrius Cydonès Correspondance*. Edited by R.-J. Loenertz. (2 vols.) Vatican, 1956–60.

Cydones Demetrius. *Letters II* = *Démétrius Cydonès Correspondance*. Edited by G. Cammelli. Paris: Les Belles Lettres, 1930.

*Geanakoplos, Deno John. *Byzantium: Church, Society, and Civilization Seen Through Contemporary Eyes*. Chicago and London: University of Chicago Press, 1984. Selections from a wide variety of Byzantine sources, arranged thematically.

Geoffroy de Villehardouin. "The Conquest of Constantinople," in *Chronicles of the Crusades*. Translated with an introduction by M. R. B. Shaw. Harmondsworth: Penguin, 1963.

Ibn Khaldun. *The Muqaddimah: An Introduction to History*. Translated by Franz Rosenthal. Edited and abridged by N. J. Dawood. Princeton: Princeton University Press, 1967. A handy one-volume abridgment of this classic work of historiography.

Kantor, M., trans. *Medieval Lives of Saints and Princes*. Ann Arbor: University of Michigan Press, 1983. Includes *vitae* of Cyril and Methodius.

Koran. Translated by N. J. Dawood. Harmondsworth: Penguin, 1968.

Kurbsky, A. M. *Prince A. M. Kurbsky's History of Ivan IV*. Edited with a translation and notes by J. L. I. Fennell. Cambridge: Cambridge University Press, 1965.

Patrologia graeca. Edited by J.-P. Migne. Paris, 1866. This monumental collection of Greek patristic texts is the place to find (in Greek) the writings of John Cantacuzenos, Barlaam, Chrysoloras, Manuel II, and a great many of the other Byzantine authors referred to in the text and in the secondary sources.

Petrarch. *Francesco Petrarcha: Le Familiari*. Edizione critica per cura di Vittorio Rossi, vol. 3. Florence: Sansoni, 1937.

Photius. *The Homilies of Photius*. Translated by Cyril Mango. Cambridge, MA: Harvard University Press, 1958.

*Procopius. *History of the Wars III*. Translated by H. B. Dewing. Cambridge, MA: Harvard University Press, 1919. Bilingual Greek and English text in the Loeb series. Covers Justinian's Gothic Wars in Italy.

*Procopius. *The Secret History*. Translated by G. A. Williamson. Harmondsworth: Penguin, 1966. Racy gossip on Justinian and Theodora. See note on Anna Comnena above.

*Psellus, Michael. *Fourteen Byzantine Rulers*. Translated by E. R. A. Sewter. Harmondsworth: Penguin, 1966. See note on Anna Comnena above.

Robert of Clari. *The Conquest of Constantinople*. Translated by Edgar Holmes McNeal. New York: Octagon, 1966.

*Rosenthal, Franz. *The Classical Heritage in Islam*. Translated by Emile and Jenny Marmorstein. London and New York: Routledge, 1992 (1975). Includes English translations of selections from Hunayn ibn Ishaq, Ibn an-Nadim (*Fihrist*), and other Arabic sources. An easily available and extremely helpful book for the curious reader, since many of these writings are not otherwise available in English.

Russian Primary Chronicle (Laurentian Text). Translated and edited by Samuel Hazzard Cross & Olgerd P. Sherbowitz-Wetzor. Cambridge, MA: Medieval Academy of America, 1973.

A Source Book for Russian History from Early Times to 1917. Vol. I: Early

Times to the Late Seventeenth Century. George Vernadsky, senior editor. New Haven: Yale University Press, 1972.

Two Renaissance Book Hunters: The Letters of Poggius Bracciolini to Nicolaus De Niccolis. Translated with notes by Phyllis Walter Goodhart Gordan. New York: Columbia University Press, 1991 (1974).

Modern Scholarship

Angold, Michael. *The Byzantine Empire 1025–1204.* Second edition. London: Longman, 1997. Good political history of the late Macedonian and Comnenan periods.

Armstrong, Karen. *A History of God: The 4,000-Year Quest of Judaism, Christianity and Islam.* New York: Ballantine, 1993.

———. *Islam: A Short History.* New York: Modern Library, 2000.

Bark, William. "Theoderic vs. Boethius: Vindication and Apology."

American Historical Review 49 (1943–44): 410–26.

Baron, Hans. *The Crisis of the Early Italian Renaissance.* Princeton: Princeton University Press, 1955. In this influential work Baron introduces the widely accepted idea of Florentine civic humanism.

*Baxandall, Michael. *Giotto and the Orators: Humanist Observers of Painting in Italy and the Discovery of Pictorial Composition, 1350–1450.* Oxford: Oxford University Press, 1971. Credits Chrysoloras with inspiring the development of pictorial composition and linear perspectives in painting.

Baynes, Norman. *The Byzantine Empire.* Oxford: Oxford University Press, 1925.

Berlin, Isaiah. *Russian Thinkers.* Henry Hardy, ed. Harmondsworth: Penguin, 1979.

*Billington, James H. *The Icon and the Axe: An Intepretive History of Russian Culture.* New York: Vintage, 1970 (1966). A well-written and insightful narrative account of Russian cultural history, with an enlightening discussion on Hesychast mysticism vs. rationalism in Russian history.

Bolgar, R. R. *The Classical Heritage and Its Beneficiaries.* Cambridge: Cambridge University Press, 1954.

Bowersock, Glenn. *Hellenism in Late Antiquity.* Ann Arbor: University of Michigan Press, 1996 (1990).

Brock, Sebastian. "Greek into Syriac and Syriac into Greek." Reprinted with original pagination (Study II) in Sebastian Brock, *Syriac Perspectives on Late Antiquity.* London: Variorum, 1984.

———. *Syriac Perspectives on Late Antiquity.* London: Variorum, 1984.

*Brown, Peter. *Augustine of Hippo.* Berkeley: University of California Press, 1969. Indispensable.

———. *The Cult of the Saints.* Chicago: University of Chicago Press, 1981.

*———. *The Making of Late Antiquity.* Cambridge, MA: Harvard University Press, 1993 (1978).

———. *Power and Persuasion in Late Antiquity.* Madison, WI: University of Wisconsin Press, 1992.

*———. *The Rise of Western Christendom.* Oxford: Blackwell, 1996. Insightful exploration of early Christianity by the master of Late Antiquity. Despite the title, offers much on Christianity's early context in the eastern Mediterranean world.

*———. *Society and the Holy in Late Antiquity.* Berkeley: University of California Press, 1982. Contains an excellent article on the Iconoclast controversy, "A Dark Age Crisis: Aspects of the Iconoclast Controversy," and much else of value besides.

*———. *The World of Late Antiquity AD 150–750.* New York: Norton, 1989 (1971). The book that opened up Late Antiquity as a hot academic field.

*Browning, Robert, ed. *The Greek World: Classical, Byzantine, and Modern.* London: Thames and Hudson, 1985. Articles by leading scholars in a handsome coffee-table book.

*———. *The Byzantine Empire.* Revised edition. Washington, DC: Catholic University of America Press, 1992. Excellent introduction to Byzantine history and civilization by a respected scholar.

————. *Byzantium and Bulgaria.* Berkeley: University of California Press, 1975.

————. *Church, State, and Learning in Twelfth Century Byzantium.* London: Dr. Williams's Trust, 1980.

Brooker, Gene. *Renaissance Florence.* New York: John Wiley and Sons, 1969.

*Bullock, Alan. *The Humanist Tradition in the West.* New York: Norton, 1985.

Burckhardt, Jacob. *The Civilization of the Renaissance in Italy.* New York: Phaidon, 1950.

Burke, Peter. *The European Renaissance: Centres and Peripheries.* Oxford: Blackwell, 1998.

Bury, J. B. *A History of the Later Roman Empire.* 2 vols. New York: Dover, 1958 (1923). Classic, if dated.

*Cameron, Averil. *Christianity and the Rhetoric of Empire: The Development of Christian Discourse.* Berkeley: University of California Press, 1991.

————. "Early Christian Territory After Foucault." *Journal of Roman Studies* 76 (1986): 266–71.

————. "Images of Authority: Elites and Icons in Late Sixth-Century Byzantium." *Past and Present* 84 (1979): 3–35.

*————. *The Later Roman Empire, AD 284–430.* Cambridge, MA: Harvard University Press, 1993. Excellent narrative history of this transitional period for the vigorous general reader.

*————. *The Mediterranean World in Late Antiquity, AD 395–600.* London and New York: Routledge, 1993. Read with her *Later Roman Empire* for superb coverage of the Mediterranean world in the centuries before Islam.

————. "New Themes and Styles in Greek Literature: Seventh–Eighth Centuries." In *The Byzantine and Early Islamic Near East, Vol. I: Problems in the Literary Source Material,* edited by Averil Cameron and Lawrence I. Conrad. Princeton: Darwin, 1992.

*————. *Procopius and the Sixth Century.* London and New York: Routledge, 1996 (1985). Essential reading on Procopius and his times by a leading scholar of early Byzantium.

————. "The Theotokos in Sixth-Century Constantinople: A City Finds Its Symbol." *Journal of Theological Studies,* new series 29 (1978): 79–108.

————. "The Virgin's Robe: An Episode in the History of Early Seventh-Century Constantinople." *Byzantion* 49 (1979): 42–56.

Cammelli, Giuseppe. *I Dotti Byzantini e le Origini Dell'Umanismo I: Manuele Crisolora.* Florence: Vallecchi Editore, 1941.

Cardwell, Donald. *The Norton History of Technology.* New York: Norton, 1994.

*Cavallo, Guglielmo, ed. *The Byzantines.* Chicago: University of Chicago Press, 1997. Excellent thematic introduction to Byzantine society with articles by leading scholars.

Crone, Patricia. *Meccan Trade and the Rise of Islam.* Princeton: Princeton University Press, 1987.

Dawson, Christopher. *Religion and the Rise of Western Culture.* Doubleday, 1991 (1950).

Demus, Otto. *Byzantine Art and the West.* New York: New York University Press, 1970.

*Diehl, Charles. *Byzantium: Greatness and Decline.* Translated by Naomi Walford. Edited and with an introduction by Peter Charanis. New Brunswick, NJ: Rutgers University Press, 1957. Holds up well, a classic. Especially good on the Byzantine cultural legacy.

Drijvers, Jan Willem, and Alasdair MacDonald. *Centres of Learning: Learning and Location in Pre-Modern Europe and the Near East.* Leiden: E. J. Brill, 1995.

Dvornik, Francis. *Byzantine Missions Among the Slavs.* New Brunswick, NJ: Rutgers University Press, 1970.

————. *The Making of Central and Eastern Europe.* Second edition. Gulf Breeze, FL: Academic International Press, 1974.

————. *Photian and Byzantine Ecclesiastical Studies.* London: Variorum, 1974. Collected studies; valuable for Photius.

Edgerton, S. *The Renaissance Discovery of Linear Perspective.* New York, 1975.

Fakhry, Majid. *A History of Islamic Philosophy.* Second edition. New York: Longman, 1983.

————. *A Short Introduction to Islamic Philosophy, Theology and Mysticism.* Oxford: Oneworld, 1997.

Fine, John V. A., Jr. *The Early Medieval Balkans.* Ann Arbor: University of Michigan Press, 1983.

*Fowden, Garth. *Empire to Commonwealth: Consequences of Monotheism in Late Antiquity.* Princeton: Princeton University Press, 1993.

Flogaus, Reinhard. "Palamas and Barlaam Revisited: A Reassessment of East and West in the Hesychast Controversy of 14th Century Byzantium." In *St. Vladimir's Theological Quarterly* 42, 1 (1998): 1–32.

Franklin, Simon. "Greek in Kievan Rus." *Dumbarton Oaks Papers* 46 (1992): 69–87.

*Franklin, Simon, and Jonathan Shepard. *The Emergence of Rus 750–1200.* London: Longman, 1996. Very good survey of recent archeological evidence on early Russia.

Frend, W. H. C. "Nomads and Christianity in the Middle Ages." *Journal of Ecclesiastical History* 26 (1975): 209–21.

Gabrieli, Giuseppe. "Hunayn Ibn Ishaq." *Isis* 6 (1924): 282–92.

*Garin, Eugenio. *Portraits from the Quattrocento.* Translated by V. A. Velen and E. Velen. New York: Harper and Row, 1972.

*Geanakoplos, Deno John. *Constantinople and the West: Essays on the Late Byzantine (Paleologan) and Italian Renaissances and the Byzantine and Roman Churches.* Madison: University of Wisconsin Press, 1989.

————. *Greek Scholars in Venice: Studies in the Dissemination of Greek*

Learning from Byzantium to Western Europe. Cambridge, MA: Harvard University Press, 1962.

———. *Interaction of the "Sibling" Byzantine and Western Cultures in the Middle Ages and the Italian Renaissance (330–1600).* New Haven: Yale University Press, 1976.

Gibb, H. A. R. "Arab-Byzantine Relations under the Umayyad Caliphate." *Dumbarton Oaks Papers* 12 (1958): 223–33.

Gibson, Margaret, ed. *Boethius: His Life, Thought and Influence.* Oxford: Blackwell, 1981.

Gill, Joseph. *The Council of Florence.* Cambridge: Cambridge University Press, 1961.

Goffart, Walter. *The Narrators of Barbarian History.* Princeton: Princeton University Press, 1988.

Goodman, Lenn E. *Islamic Humanism.* Oxford: Oxford University Press, 2003.

Grabar, Oleg. "The Umayyad Dome of the Rock in Jerusalem." *Ars Orientalis* 3 (1959).

Gurevich, Aaron. "Why Am I Not a Byzantinist?" *Dumbarton Oaks Papers* 46 (1992): 89–96.

*Gutas, Dimitri. *Greek Thought, Arabic Culture: The Graeco-Arabic Translation Movement in Baghdad and Early Abbasid Society (2nd–4th/8th–10th Centuries).* New York and London: Routledge, 1998. Excellent if occasionally polemical revisionist account of the translation movement.

———. "Islam and Science: A False Statement of the Problem." *Islam and Science* 1, 2 (2003): 215–20.

———. "The Study of Arabic Philosophy in the Twentieth Century: An Essay on the Historiography of Arabic Philosophy." *British Journal of Middle Eastern Studies* 29, 1 (2002): 5–25.

Hale, J. R., ed. *The Thames and Hudson Encyclopedia of the Italian Renaissance.* London: Thames and Hudson, 1981.

*Halliday, Fred. *Islam and the Myth of Confrontation: Religion and*

Politics in the Middle East. London: I. B. Tauris, 1995. Absolutely essential reading for anyone hoping to understand Islam, its place in the world, and Western attitudes to it.

————. *Two Hours That Shook the World: September 11, 2001: Causes and Consequences.* London: Saki, 2002.

Hankins, James. "Introduction." In *Leonardo Bruni: History of the Florentine People.* Edited and translated by James Hankins for the I Tatti Renaissance Library. Cambridge, MA: Harvard University Press, 2001.

Haskins, Charles Homer. *The Renaissance of the Twelfth Century.* Cambridge, MA: Harvard University Press, 1927.

Herrin, Judith. "Aspects of the Process of Hellenization in the Early Middle Ages." *Annual of the British School of Athens* 68 (1973): 113–26.

*————. *The Formation of Christendom.* Princeton: Princeton University Press, 1997. Insightful and well written; for the general reader with a scholarly bent.

*Hodgson, Marshall. *The Venture of Islam: Conscience and History in a World Civilization.* 3 vols. Chicago: University of Chicago Press, 1974.

*Holmes, George. *The Florentine Enlightenment 1400–50.* New York: Pegasus, 1969. Credits Chrysoloras with inspiring the secular outlook in the early Florentine humanists.

Hosking, Geoffrey. *Russia and the Russians.* Cambridge, MA: Harvard University Press, 2001.

Hourani, Albert. *A History of the Arab Peoples.* Cambridge, MA: Harvard University Press, 1991.

Hussey, J. M. *Ascetics and Humanists in Eleventh Century Byzantium.* London: Dr. Williams's Trust, 1960.

*————. *The Byzantine World.* New York: Harper, 1961. Still an excellent brief introduction to Byzantine history and civilization, including the cultural legacy.

Jaeger, Werner. *Early Christianity and Greek Paidea.* Cambridge, MA: Harvard University Press, 1961.

Johnson, Mark J. "Toward a History of Theoderic's Building Program." *Dumbarton Oaks Papers* 42 (1988): 73–96.

Kazhdan, Alexander, and Anthony Cutler. "Continuity and Discontinuity in Byzantine History." *Byzantion* 52 (1982): 429–78.

Kaegi, Walter E. *Byzantium and the Early Islamic Conquests.* Cambridge: Cambridge University Press, 1992.

Kennedy, Hugh. *The Early Abbasid Caliphate.* London: Croom Helm, 1981.

Kianka, Frances. "The Apology of Demetrius Cydones: A Fourteenth-Century Autobiographical Source." *Byzantine Studies/Études Byzantines* 6, 1–2 (1979): 56–71.

———. "Byzantine-Papal Diplomacy: The Role of Demetrius Cydones." *International History Review* 7 (1985): 175–200.

———. "Demetrius Cydones and Thomas Aquinas." *Byzantion* 52 (1982): 264–86.

———. "Demetrius Kydones and Italy." *Dumbarton Oaks Papers* 49 (1995): 99–110.

Kraemer, Joel. *Humanism in the Renaissance of Islam: The Cultural Revival During the Buyid Age.* Second revised edition. Leiden: E. J. Brill, 1992.

Kristeller, Paul Oskar. *Renaissance Concepts of Man and Other Essays.* New York: Harper, 1972.

———. *Renaissance Thought: The Classic, Scholastic, and Humanist Strains.* New York: Harper, 1961.

———. *Renaissance Thought and the Arts.* Princeton: Princeton University Press, 1990.

———. "The School of Salerno." *Bulletin of the History of Medicine* 17 (1945): 138–94.

Laiou, Angeliki. "Italy and the Italians in the Political Geography of the Byzantines (Fourteenth Century)." *Dumbarton Oaks Papers* 49 (1995): 73–98.

Laiou, Angeliki E., and Henry Maguire, eds. *Byzantium: A World Civilization.* Washington, DC: Dumbarton Oaks, 1992.

Lemerle, Paul. *Le Premier Humanism Byzantin.* Paris: Presses Universitaires de France, 1971.

Lewis, Bernard. *Islam and the West.* Oxford: Oxford University Press, 1993.

————. *What Went Wrong? The Clash Between Islam and Modernity in the Middle East.* New York: Harper, 2002.

Leyser, Karl. "The Tenth Century in Byzantine-Western Relationships." In *Relations Between East and West in the Middle Ages,* Derek Baker, ed. Edinburgh: University of Edinburgh Press, 1973.

Loenertz, Raymond. "Demetrius Cydones, Citoyen de Venise." *Echos d'Orient* 37 (1938): 125–26.

McCormick, Michael. *Eternal Victory: Triumphal Rulership in Late Antiquity, Byzantium, and the Early Medieval West.* Cambridge: Cambridge University Press, 1990 (1986).

McManners, John, ed. *The Oxford Illustrated History of Christianity.* Oxford: Oxford University Press, 1990.

MacMullen, Ramsay. *Christianity and Paganism in the Fourth to Eighth Centuries.* New Haven: Yale University Press, 1997.

————. *Christianizing the Roman Empire (A.D. 100–400).* New Haven: Yale University Press, 1984.

Maguire, Henry. *Art and Eloquence in Byzantium.* Princeton: Princeton University Press, 1981.

Makdisi, George. *Religion, Law and Learning in Classical Islam.* London: Variorum, 1991.

————. *The Rise of Humanism in Classical Islam and the Christian West.* Edinburgh: Edinburgh University Press, 1990.

Mandalari, Giannantonio. *Fra Barlaamo Calabrese: Maestro del Petrarca.* Rome: Carlo Verdesi, 1888.

*Mango, Cyril. *Byzantium: The Empire of New Rome.* New York: Scribners. The best topical treatment of Byzantine civilization, if occasionally a bit hard on the Byzantines.

*————. *Byzantium and its Image: History and Culture of the Byzantine Empire and its Heritage.* London: Variorum, 1984. Collected articles by one of the most influential of Byzantinists.

*Mango, Cyril, ed. *The Oxford History of Byzantium.* Oxford: Oxford University Press, 2002. If you get one book on Byzantine history, this should probably be it—snappy, up-to-date articles by leading scholars.

Margolin, Jean-Claude. *Humanism in Europe at the Time of the Renaissance.* Translated by John L. Farthing. Durham, NC: Labyrinth, 1989.

Martin, Janet. *Medieval Russia, 980–1584.* Cambridge: Cambridge University Press, 1995.

Martines, Lauro. *The Social World of the Florentine Humanists.* Princeton: Princeton University Press, 1963.

Mathews, Thomas F. *Byzantium: From Antiquity to the Renaissance.* New York: Abrams, 1998.

Mernissi, Fatema. *Islam and Democracy: Fear of the Modern World.* Translated by Mary Jo Lakeland. Second edition. Cambridge, MA: Perseus, 2002.

Meyendorff, John. *Byzantine Hesychasm: historical, theological, and social problems: collected studies.* London: Variorum, 1974.

———. *Byzantine Theology: Historical Trends and Doctrinal Themes.* New York: Fordham University Press, 1974.

*———. *Byzantium and the Rise of Russia: A Study of Byzantino-Russian Relations in the Fourteenth Century.* Crestwood, NY: St. Vladimir's Seminary Press, 1989.

———. "Mount Athos in the Fourteenth Century: Spiritual and Intellectual Legacy." *Dumbarton Oaks Papers* 42 (1988): 157–65.

———. "Spiritual Trends in Byzantium in the Late Thirteenth and Early Fourteenth Centuries," in Paul A. Underwood, ed., *The Kariye Djami, Volume 4: Studies in the Art of the Kariye Djami and Its Intellectual Background.* Princeton: Princeton University Press, 1975, 95–106.

*———. *A Study of Gregory Palamas.* Translated by George Lawrence. Crestwood, NY: St. Vladimir's Seminary Press, 1998 (1964).

———. "Wisdom-Sophia: Contrasting Approaches to a Complex Theme." *Dumbarton Oaks Papers* 41 (1987): 391–401.

Meyerhof, Max. "New Light on Hunain Ibn Ishaq and His Period." *Isis* 8 (1926): 685–724.

*Momigliano, Arnaldo. *Alien Wisdom: The Limits of Hellenization.* Cambridge: Cambridge University Press, 1975.

————. "Cassiodorus and the Italian Culture of His Time." *Proceedings of the British Academy* 41 (1955): 207–45.

*Nicol, Donald. *The Byzantine Lady: Ten Portraits.* Cambridge: Cambridge University Press, 1994.

————. *Byzantium: its ecclesiastical history and relations with the western world: collected studies.* London: Variorum, 1972.

*————. *Byzantium and Venice: A Study in Diplomatic and Cultural Relations.* Cambridge: Cambridge University Press, 1988. Excellent treatment of a fascinating relationship.

*————. *The End of the Byzantine Empire.* London: Edward Arnold, 1979. Excellent brief treatment of late Byzantium (1261–1453) by the leading scholar of the field.

*————. *The Last Centuries of Byzantium, 1261–1453.* Second edition. Cambridge: Cambridge University Press, 1993. Longer version of above, worth every inch.

*————. *The Reluctant Emperor.* Cambridge: Cambridge University Press, 1996. Excellent biography of the enigmatic John Cantacuzenos.

*Obolensky, Dimitri. *The Byzantine Commonwealth: Eastern Europe, 500–1453.* Crestwood, NY: St. Vladimir's Seminary Press, 1974 (1971). The seminal account of Byzantine cultural influences on the Slavic world.

*————. *The Byzantine Inheritance of Eastern Europe.* London: Variorum, 1982. More collected studies.

*————. *Byzantium and the Slavs: collected studies.* London: Variorum, 1971.

*————. *Six Byzantine Portraits.* Oxford: Oxford University Press, 1988. Biographical sketches of many of the individuals discussed in this book, including Clement, Vladimir Monomakh, Sava, Cyprian, and Maxim the Greek.

———. "Sts. Cyril and Methodius, Apostles to the Slavs." *St. Vladimir's Seminar Quarterly* 7 (1963): 1–11. Reprinted with original pagination (Study VIII) in Dimitri Obolensky, *Byzantium and the Slavs: collected studies*. London: Variorum, 1971.

O'Donnell, James J. *Cassiodorus*. Berkeley: University of California Press, 1979.

O'Leary, De Lacy. *How Greek Science Passed to the Arabs*. London: Routledge, 1949.

Ostrogorsky, George. *A History of the Byzantine State*. Third edition. Translated by J. Hussey. Oxford: Oxford University Press, 1968.

Phillips, Jonathan. *The Fourth Crusade and the Sack of Constantinople*. New York: Viking, 2004.

Pipes, Daniel. *Russia Under the Old Regime*. Second edition. Harmondsworth: Penguin, 1995.

Pirenne, Henri. *Medieval Cities: Their Origins and the Revival of Trade*. Translated by Frank D. Halsey. Princeton: Princeton University Press, 1969 (1925).

Reynolds, L. D., and N. G. Wilson. *Scribes and Scholars: A Guide to the Transmission of Greek and Latin Literature*. Third edition. Oxford: Oxford University Press, 1991.

*Runciman, Steven. *Byzantine Civilization*. New York: New American Library, 1956.

———. *Byzantine Style and Civilization*. Harmondsworth: Penguin, 1987 (1975).

———. *The Eastern Schism: A Study of the Papacy and the Eastern Churches During the Eleventh and Twelfth Centuries*. Oxford: Oxford University Press, 1955.

*———. *The Fall of Constantinople, 1453*. Cambridge: Cambridge University Press, 1965. Informative and highly readable.

———. *The Great Church in Captivity: A Study of the Patriarchate of Constantinople from the Eve of the Turkish Conquest to the Greek War of Independence*. Cambridge: Cambridge University Press, 1985 (1968).

————. *A History of the Crusades.* 3 vols. Cambridge: Cambridge University Press, 1987 (1951–54). The best popular account.

————. *The Last Byzantine Renaissance.* Cambridge: Cambridge University Press, 1970.

*————. *The Sicilian Vespers: A History of the Mediterranean World in the Late Thirteenth Century.* Cambridge: Cambridge University Press, 1992 (1958).

Schevill, Ferdinand. *Medieval and Renaissance Florence: Volume II: The Coming of Humanism and the Age of the Medici.* New York: Harper, 1961 (1935).

*Setton, Kenneth. "The Byzantine Background to the Italian Renaissance." *Proceedings of the American Philosophical Society* 100, 1 (1956): 1–76.

Setton, Kenneth M., ed. *A History of the Crusades.* 5 vols. Madison: University of Wisconsin Press, 1969–85.

Ševčenko, Ihor. "Byzantium and the Slavs." *Harvard Ukrainian Studies* 8 (1984): 289–303.

————. "The Decline of Byzantium as Seen Through the Eyes of Its Intellectuals." *Dumbarton Oaks Papers* 15 (1961): 169–86.

————. *Ideology, Letters, and Culture in the Byzantine World.* London: Variorum, 1982. Collected articles of a leading Byzantinist.

————. "Russo-Byzantine Relations After the Eleventh Century." In *Proceedings of the XIIIth International Congress of Byzantine Studies,* 93–104. Edited by J. M. Hussey, D. Obolensky, and S. Runciman. Oxford: Oxford University Press, 1967.

————. "Three Paradoxes of the Cyrillo-Methodian Mission." *Slavic Review* 23 (1964): 220–36.

————. "Theodore Metochites, the Chora, and the Intellectual Trends of His Time." In Paul A. Underwood, ed., *The Kariye Djami, Volume 4: Studies in the Art of the Kariye Djami and Its Intellectual Background,* 19–55. Princeton: Princeton University Press, 1975.

Sinkewicz, R. E. "The Doctrine of the Knowledge of God in the Early Writings of Barlaam the Calabrian." *Medieval Studies* 44 (1982): 181–242.

Smith, Christine. *Architecture in the Culture of Early Humanism: Ethics, Aesthetics, and Eloquence, 1400–1470*. Oxford: Oxford University Press, 1992. Credits Chrysoloras with inspiring the ideal of the "Renaissance Man."

Stephens, John. *The Italian Renaissance: The Origins of Intellectual and Artistic Change Before the Reformation*. London: Longman, 1990.

Thomson, Ian. "Manuel Chrysoloras and the Early Italian Renaissance." *Greek, Roman and Byzantine Studies* 7 (1966): 63–82.

*Treadgold, Warren. *A History of the Byzantine State and Society*. Stanford: Stanford University Press, 1997. Now the standard textbook for Byzantine history (replacing George Ostrogorsky's *History of the Byzantine State*).

Turner, A. Richard. *Renaissance Florence: The Invention of a New Art*. New York: Abrams, 1997.

Turner, C. J. "The Career of George-Gennadius Scholarius." *Byzantion* 39 (1969): 420–55.

Ullman, Berthold L. *The Humanism of Coluccio Salutati*. Padua: Antenore, 1963.

Underwood, Paul A., ed. *The Kariye Djami, Volume 4: Studies in the Art of the Kariye Djami and Its Intellectual Background*. Princeton: Princeton University Press, 1975. Includes outstanding articles by John Meyendorff and Ihor Ševčenko.

Urvoy, Dominique. *Ibn Rushd (Averroës)*. London: Routledge, 1991.

Veyne, Paul, ed. *A History of Private Life I: From Pagan Rome to Byzantium*. Translated by Arthur Goldhammer. Cambridge, MA: Harvard University Press, 1987.

von Grunebaum, G. E. *Classical Islam: A History, 600 A.D.–1258 A.D.* Translated by Katherine Watson. Chicago: Aldine, 1970.

———. *Islam and Medieval Hellenism: Social and Cultural Perspectives*. London: Variorum, 1976. Collected studies.

Vryonis, Speros, Jr. *Byzantium: Its Internal History and Relations with the Muslim World: Collected Studies*. London: Variorum, 1971.

———. "Byzantium and Islam, Seven–Seventeenth Century." In *East*

European Quarterly 2, 3 (1968): 205–40. Reprinted with original pagination (Study IX) in *Byzantium: Its Internal History and Relations with the Muslim World: Collected Studies.* London: Variorum, 1971.

————. *The Decline of Medieval Hellenism in Asia Minor and the Process of Islamization from the Eleventh through the Fifteenth Century.* Berkeley: University of California Press, 1971.

Walzer, Richard. "The Arabic Transmission of Greek Thought to Medieval Europe." *Bulletin of the John Rylands Library* 29 (1945): 3–26.

————. *Greek into Arabic.* Cambridge, MA: Harvard University Press, 1962.

Ware, Timothy. *The Orthodox Church.* New edition. Harmondsworth: Penguin, 1993.

Watt, W. Montgomery. *Islamic Philosophy and Theology: An Extended Survey.* Edinburgh: Edinburgh University Press, 1985.

*Webster, Leslie, and Michelle Brown. *The Transformation of the Roman World, AD 400–900.* Berkeley: University of California Press, 1997.

Weinstein, Donald. *Savonarola and Florence: Prophecy and Patriotism in the Renaissance.* Princeton: Princeton University Press, 1970.

Weiss, Roberto. "Jacopo Angeli da Scarperia." In *Medioevo e Rinascimento: Studi in Onore de Bruno Nardi,* vol. 2. Florence: Sansoni, 1955.

*Whittow, Mark. *The Making of Byzantium, 600–1025.* Berkeley: University of California Press, 1996. Now the standard textbook on this period. Unusually insightful.

Wiet, Gaston. *Baghdad: Metropolis of the Abbasid Caliphate.* Norman: University of Oklahoma Press, 1971.

Wilcox, D. *The Development of Florentine Humanist Historiography in the Fifteenth Century.* Cambridge: Harvard University Press, 1969.

*Wilson, N. G. *From Byzantium to Italy: Greek Studies in the Italian Renaissance.* Baltimore: Johns Hopkins, 1992. Excellent, but not for the faint of heart.

*————. *Scholars of Byzantium.* Revised edition. London: Duckworth, 1996. Ditto.

Woodward, C. M. *George Gemistos Plethon: The Last of the Hellenes.* Oxford: Oxford University Press, 1986.

Woodward, William Harrison. *Studies in Education During the Age of the Renaissance, 1400–1600.* New York: Russell and Russell, 1965 (1906).

―――. *Vittorino da Feltre and Other Humanist Educators.* New York: Columbia University, 1964.

Yates, Frances A. *The Art of Memory.* Chicago: University of Chicago Press, 1974 (1966).

INDEX

About the Author

COLIN WELLS has studied with eminent Byzantinist Speros Vryonis Jr. at UCLA and holds an MA in Greats (Greek and Latin language and literature) from Oxford University. He has written numerous articles on world history and culture for over a decade. He lives in upstate New York.